Teaching against Violence
Reassessing the Toolbox

TITLES IN THE SERIES:

Title 1   is published by ATHENA2 and Women's Studies Centre, National University of Ireland, Galway;

Titles 2–8 are published by ATHENA3 Advanced Thematic Network in Women's Studies in Europe, University of Utrecht and Centre for Gender Studies, Stockholm University;

Title 9-10 are jointly published by ATGENDER, The European Association for Gender Research, Education and Documentation, Utrecht and Central European University Press, Budapest.

Title 11   is jointly published by ATGENDER, The European Association for Gender Research, Education and Documentation, Utrecht, Central European University Press, Budapest and DAPHNE III Programme of the European Union for the Project 'EMPoWER: Empowerment of Women - Environment Research'.

Edited by Ines Testoni, Angelika Groterath,
Maria Silvia Guglielmin, Michael Wieser

Teaching against Violence Reassessing the Toolbox

*Teaching with Gender. European Women's Studies in
International and Interdisciplinary Classrooms*

A book series by ATGENDER

ATGENDER. The European Association for Gender Research,
Education and Documentation
Utrecht
&
Central European University Press
Budapest–New York

Cover Illustration:
© *"Yes, it is possible!" by Ines Testoni*

Series editors: Nadezhda Aleksandrova, Sveva Magaraggia, Annika Olsson, Andrea Pető

Editorial board: Barbara Bagilhole, Gunilla Bjeren, Rosi Braidotti, Anna Cabó, Sara Goodman, Daniela Gronold, Aino-Maija Hiltunen, Nina Lykke, Linda Lund Pedersen, Elżbieta H. Oleksy, Anastasia-Sasa Lada, Susana Pavlou, Kirsi Saarikangas, Adelina Sánchez, Harriet Silius, Svetlana Slapsak, Berteke Waaldijk

Editorial assistant: Mónika Magyar

Joint publication by:
ATGENDER,
The European Association for Gender Research, Education and Documentation
P. O. Box 164, 3500 AD Utrecht, The Netherlands
Telephone: (+31 0) 30 253 6013
E-mail: info@atgender.eu, Website: http://www.atgender.eu

Central European University Press
An imprint of the Central European University Limited Liability Company
Nádor u. 11, H-1051 Budapest, Hungary
Telephone: (+36-1) 327-3138, Fax: (+36-1) 327-3183
E-mail: ceupress@ceu.hu, Website: http://www.ceupress.com
224 West 57th Street, New York NY 10019, USA
Telephone: (+1-212) 547-6932, Fax: (+1-646) 557-2416
E-mail: martin.greenwald@opensocietyfoundations.org

"This publication has been produced with the financial support of the DAPHNE III Programme of the European Union for the Project 'EMPoWER: Empowerment of Women - Environment Research'. The contents of this publication are the sole responsibility of the Authors of each contribute (Article/Chapter) and can in no way be taken to reflect the views of the European Commission"

It is realized with the scientific collaboration of the CIRSG (Centro Interdipartimentale di Ricerca Studi di Genere – Interidpartimental Centre of Gender Studies Research, University of Padova) and of the GDG (Gruppo Discriminazione di Genere – Gender Discrimination Group of AIP – Association Italian Psychology)

ISSN 2227-5010

ISBN 978-615-5225-93-2

Library of Congress Cataloging-in-Publication Data

A CIP catalog record for this book is available upon request

Printed in Hungary by Prime Rate Kft.

TABLE OF CONTENTS

The Activism of Black Feminist Theory in Confronting Violence Against Women: Interconnections, Politics and Practice

"Brothers for life": A campaign addressing gender based violence on (de/re) constructing masculinities in South Africa. "Yenza Kahle!" - Do the Right thing!

The effectiveness of the EMPoWER project and intervention: Psychodrama and the elaboration of domestic violence in Italy, Austria, Bulgaria, Portugal, Romania, and Albania

LIST OF TABLES

FOREWORD: GENDER EDUCATION AS A FIRST-LINE TOOL TO FIGHT VIOLENCE AGAINST WOMEN

Ines Testoni

Introduction

This volume is the result of an analysis carried out by various scholars working at the international level on the issue of Gender-Based Violence (GBV). It pays particular attention to domestic violence, as in this field feminism has tenaciously sought to change the condition of women and, as a result, many international policies have promoted a significant social transformation. Despite these positive steps, which have increased the self-determination of women, allowing them to improve their agency in every domain of private and public life, the problem still exists. Therefore we question, with pain and bewilderment, but also with determination to continue advancing, how it is possible—after the Declaration of Human Rights and the development of feminism—that violence against women is still so deeply rooted in every culture and even in Western countries. If we consider social policies as a fundamental factor that signals individual and social awareness and action, the political commitment against GBV that is now more than four decades long should have accomplished more.

In fact, political action against GBV began in 1979, when the United Nations (UN) drafted the Convention on the Elimination of all Forms of Discrimination against Women (CEDAW) and defined "discrimination against women" as any distinction, exclusion, or restriction made on the basis of sex that has the effect of impairing or nullifying the recognition, enjoyment, or exercise by women of human rights and fundamental freedoms in the political, economic, social, cultural, and civil dimensions. The application of the CEDAW agenda, in 1981, required that the ratifying states incorporate gender equality into their specific legislation, abolish all discriminatory references in their laws, and enact new specifications to fight such discrimination. Then in 1994 the UN classified GBV as any act resulting in physical, sexual, or mental harm or suffering to women, including threats of such acts, coercion, or arbitrary deprivation of liberty, whether in public or in private life. Furthermore, it emphasized that violence against women is a global health and development issue, entailing a host of policies aimed at changing public education and promoting action programs around the world.[1] This political ideology has been accepted, and it paved the way for the European Istanbul Convention, which since 2011 has been working to create a series of specific social measures and promote the "four Ps": prevention, protection, support of victims, and prosecution of offenders.

Despite the activation of the four-Ps social interventions, derived from forty years of CEDAW action and largely prepared in the agenda of the Fourth World Conference on Women, where the principles of the Third Wave of Feminism (TWF) were acknowledged as fundamental, the systematic lockout of women from social and political power persists. This results in the phenomenon of discrimination, so that in almost all areas of life, the status and the condition of women are usually the lowest and the poorest, affecting women's private and social life.[2] Furthermore, intimate partner violence seems to be a social evil that is still hard to remedy. In fact, the media attention given to the occurrence of intimate partner violence does not necessarily correspond to the actual number of incidents of violence, because even today there is a large gap between the actual incidents of violence and the number that is reported to the police. The real number is much higher. Even if we are astonished by the quantity of victims of such violence reported at last in the media, the fact still remains concealed, as until a few years ago GBV was culturally and morally accepted, and then the problem was simply left in the shadow of indifference and social collusion. Furthermore, the "black number" that defines the unreported acts of crime perpetrated against women remains a problem even in the areas where the culture of gender equality is widely promoted.

Part of the reason that GBV has not yet been resolved is that policies still need to become more encompassing in order to change the relationship between society and individuals. If we consider basic gender equality parameters, it appears that no country actually treats its women the same as its men, and there are also differences between Western and non-Western cultures with respect to this disparity.[3] The data provided by the Global Economic Forum seems to confirm that Western

---

[1] Daniela Gronold, Brigitte Hipfl, and Linda Lund Pedersen, *Teaching with the Third Wave: New Feminists' Explorations of Teaching and Institutional Contexts* (Utrecht: Teaching Series, ATHENA3, 2009).

[2] See http://www2.ohchr.org/english/bodies/cedaw/; http://www.coe.int/t/dghl/standardsetting/convention-violence/default_en.asp.

[3] See World Economic Forum, http://www.weforum.org/pdf/Global_Competitiveness_Reports/Reports/gender_gap.pdf; UNDP: http://hdr.undp.org/docs/network/hdr_net/GDI_GEM_UNDP_Gender_Score_Card.pdf.

countries are reducing the gap between women and men, but it is also true that the situation varies between the United States and Europe, and even more so within Europe. In general, the women in United States have more self-determination than their European counterparts, and women in Northern Europe are much less disadvantaged than those in the former Soviet republics and the Mediterranean.[4] It may be that in the United States and in Northern Europe, policies more effectively address individual-society relationships, and this has supported the transition from an ideological dimension to social practice. In many Western countries the revolutionary theory of TWF is widely known, but in some countries the discussion remains relegated to academic settings and thus is not able to develop in parallel with women's ability to enjoy measurable benefits. For example, Italy is a Western Mediterranean country where the academic debate about gender studies is very extensive, but at the same time the number of femicides is increasing faster than in any other European country: almost every second day a woman is murdered by her husband, boyfriend, or ex-lover. The Italian situation is so severe that, during the Twentieth Session of the UN Human Rights Council, on June 25, 2012, the special rapporteur Rashida Manjoo opened the session on "Violence against Women: Its Causes and Consequences" with an important remark denouncing the Italian situation and underscoring the separation between *de jure* and *de facto*: "Although the Italian legal framework largely provides for sufficient protection for violence against women, it is characterized by fragmentation, inadequate punishment of perpetrators and lack of effective redress for women victims of violence." In this regard, she stressed that a weak political will and a lack of funds available for programs in the area of women's rights "affects the responsibility of the Central Government to fulfill, with due diligence, its international and national obligations to effectively address violence against women."[5]

This UN report depicts the current situation in Italy, despite the fact that gender studies at the academic level has achieved increasing international success. Given the current situation, we can also state that in many other Western countries, the second and third waves of feminism have in theory opened up the horizons on female self-determination, subjectivity, agency, and the right to equality,

[4] See UN Women, http://www.endvawnow.org/en/articles/299-fast-facts-statistics-on-violence-against-women-and-girls-.html.

[5] See Wideplus, 2013: http://wideplusnetwork.wordpress.com/news/un-special-rapporteur-on-feminicide-and-violence-against-women-in-italy/.

but that this has not carried over into reality. However, it is important to high-light that the Italian situation is not the worst. For example, the women who live in Turkey, the country where the Istanbul Convention was stipulated, live in con-ditions that are certainly more dire. This country is still waiting to become part of the EU, and the debate over its membership has become a major controversy among the Council of Europe. The first reason for this interminable argument is the fact that Turkey does not seem to follow the 1993 Copenhagen criteria, which require member states to respect human rights in order to become eligi-ble, and the dreadful conditions for women are indexed in this aspect as non-respected. This problem has been recognized by the government, so the fact that Turkey has been blocked from joining the EU has facilitated a change in the women's empowerment. In fact, in 2001 Turkey reformed the Civil Code, result-ing in the legalization of divorce and in the reduction of discrimination against women. Nevertheless, despite this progress and despite the fact that on Interna-tional Women's Day on March 8, 2012, the parliament passed a new law address-ing the issue of violence against women, in this country, according to the data released by the Women's Rights Center of Istanbul Bar Association, 85 percent of registered divorce applications are due to violence (approximately 2,000 annu-ally), and approximately 300 women have applied for protection.[6] This means that European policies may promote the empowerment and the liberation of women but that this is not enough to change the concrete situation. The Italian and Turkish examples are useful to illustrate how policies created as a result of feminist and gender studies theories may change women's political situation, but the policies need to be followed up with another kind of intervention that can link the socio-cultural dimensions with the psychological and individual ones.

Many authors have already emphasized that more research is needed to identify the causes and the outcomes of the gap between *de jure* and *de facto* and to describe how the type of violence inflicted on women varies depending on the cultural context, particularly in the Western world, where policies to empower women are already in place. The literature on this topic is extensive; however, it is possible to highlight some key points that are useful in promoting change.[7] In

---

[6] See http://www.istanbulbarosu.org.tr/images/haberler/GENDER_PRESENTATION.pdf; UN Women, http://progress.unwomen.org/pdfs/EN-Report-Progress.pdf; and ACUNS, http://acuns.org/femicide-a-global-problem/

[7] See Nancy Felipe Russo and Angela Pirlott, "Gender-Based Violence: Concepts, Methods, and Findings," *Annals of the New York Academy of Sciences* 1087 (2006): 178–205.

our opinion, the most important among them is the relationship between policy and educational processes, because this may form the foundation for real empowerment, by overcoming female vulnerability through the activation of both individual and social dimensions. The difficulty is to define the intersections between the various areas of studies that are useful for improving the psychological and social awareness of female subjectivity and agency.

The "missing link" between de jure and de facto

Feminist action certainly influenced the egalitarian policies of the last century, but TWF seems to be facing a particular difficulty in that, after enabling changes to existing laws, it is not able to transform these laws into practice and coherent social behavior.

Indeed, TWF developed during a time of major social change in human history: the break-down of U.S.-USSR bipolarism and a consequent decline in Marxist ideologies, the progressive crisis of liberal capitalism, the development of digital-tech, "glocal" multiculturalism, "political correctness," and, last but not least, after the sexual revolution breakthroughs, the rise of gay pride and post/trans-genderism. TWF has taken on all of these issues, trying to overcome the remaining legacy of traditional patriarchal systems. Furthermore, the emergence of queer theory, cyber and cyborg feminism, transgender and queer-gender politics, cultural post-humanism, post-sexualism, and advanced biotechnology including contraception and assisted-reproductive technology (which is freeing women from the determinism of nature) has resulted in the rejection of a gender binary that classifies humanity into two different and irreducible forms—masculine and feminine.[8] These theories open up the possibility for contemporary society to be able to guarantee the right of self-determination, but in practice that does not actually occur. Indeed, discrimination against women is still a huge problem and seems to be viewed as less important than other priorities resulting from the recent rapid social changes. This situation gives the impression that TWF is unable to involve the most recent generations of young women and is

---

[8] Judith Butler, *Gender Trouble: Feminism and the Subversion of Identity* (New York: Routledge, 1990); Leslie Feinberg, *Trans Liberation: Beyond Pink or Blue* (Boston: Beacon Press, 1999); Donna J. Haraway, "A Cyborg Manifesto: Science, Technology, and Socialist-Feminism in the Late Twentieth Century," in *Simians, Cyborgs and Women: The Reinvention of Nature*, ed. Donna J. Haraway (New York: Routledge, 1991), 149–181; Sue V. Rosser, "Through the Lenses of Feminist Theory: Focus on Women and Information Technology," *Frontiers: A Journal of Women Studies* 26, no. 1 (2005): 1.

intrinsically powerless to indicate solutions for the serious inequality that women experience. Notwithstanding the considerable efforts by European policies to reduce this gap, nothing seems to diminish the persistent humiliation of women and their submission to traditional logic that keeps them strongly subordinate to men, thus making incompatible the dimensions of *de jure* and *de facto*.

To the extent that this situation results in part from a substantial lack of gender equality education, the book addresses this need by proposing two types of educational materials. The first one is inherent to the methodologies that can be used to discuss the themes analyzed in each chapter; the second one illustrates the results of some social and educational interventions aimed at promoting agency in women who are victims of domestic violence and at reducing the gap between women and men. Assuming the feminist intersectionalist suggestions, in whose perspective gender discussion implies the relationships among multiple dimensions and modalities of social interactions and subject formations,[9] both the kinds of education presented develop within the juncture between social thought and psycho-educational action, focusing on specific strategies aimed at changing the concrete situation and at measuring their efficaciousness in producing change. We think that the usefulness of this second aspect is related to its ability to translate every policy change into actual measurable action plans that highlight the methodologies utilized in reaching specific aims.

As the AtGender agenda illustrates, change is possible if women acquire the power to manage the ideologies taught in school and translate policy action into psychosocial and pedagogical practice, whose efficacy can be measured by showing the replicability of the adopted strategies. With this perspective, the volume fully adheres to the mission of the AtGender series Teaching with Gender, which is ultimately focused on this aim. The enhancement of women's awareness about their condition and the fundamental right to freedom is possible, especially thanks to educational activities that involve women themselves in producing a psychosocial outcome that is able to change the cultural frame on which policies are founded. Moreover, in each chapter the book underlines the importance of the replication/dissemination of concepts/actions promoting women's empowerment and dedicates a specific final part to the teaching-gender

---

[9] Leslie McCall, "The Complexity of Intersectionality," *Journal of Women in Culture and Society* 30, no. 3 (2005): 1771–1800. http://www.journals.uchicago.edu/doi/pdf/10.1086/426800.

discussion. Since the *fil rouge* of the entire work is the idea that educational processes provide the missing link between policies and psychosocial relationships in the fight against GBV, the educational dimension is therefore incorporated in the development of the entire volume, beginning with a discussion about policies and social thought, and finishing off with a description of activities carried out in light of gender consciousness-raising and overcoming discrimination.

Inscribed in the mission of Teaching with Gender, the volume, focused on the missing link between policy and the psychosocial dimension, collaborates in the construction of a possible bridge between the social and personal dimensions through educational operationalization. It also introduces the following novel concepts to feminist thought: the discussion of a new perspective in black feminist theory, the involvement of males in social education against GBV and the efficaciousness of active techniques of intervention, derived from psychodrama.

Innovative elements in the fight against gender-based and domestic violence

Many people (not only men but also women) do not understand sexism, or if they do, they think it is not a problem. Such a misunderstanding produces the disavowal of politics and practices promoting gender equality and reflects the reality that most people interiorize these themes from traditional (that is, "patriarchal") points of view, still dominant today, thus invalidating the relationship between egalitarian law and everyday life. Since this difficulty is particularly evident in Italy, the book begins by discussing the Italian legal context and comparing it to the European one. The issues are discussed by Alisa Del Re in her paper "About Legislation against Domestic Violence in the EU and Italy." As the author explains, according to studies released by the Council of Europe, between 12 and 15 percent of women in Europe have been victims of domestic violence after the age of sixteen. Despite the fact that domestic violence is recognized throughout Europe as the most salient type of violence against women and is treated as a violation of fundamental human rights, and despite the activities of the European regulatory framework and the international partnerships existing among EU member states, there are major differences in how domestic violence is addressed from the political and legislative point of view. The lack of comparable data on the actual size of the phenomenon also makes it difficult to manage the problem in an efficient way. Alisa

Del Re provides an analysis of European legislation on this issue and various other legislative interventions in individual states with particular reference to the Italian situation, focusing on the variability of the laws and actions, given that they deeply affect the dynamics of the creation of a European citizenship for women.

An example that illustrates from theory to social practice how to break free from a very serious condition of oppression is offered by feminists who have suffered from a double disadvantage, being both women and black. Black women are victims of two atrocious forms of dehumanization: racism and gender discrimination. Suryia Nayak, in her chapter "The Activism of Black Feminist Theory [BFT] in Confronting Violence against Women," introduces the interventions of BFT as a lens of critical analysis to deconstruct feminist discourses and practices about violence against women. This contribution uses conceptual tools developed within BFT both as the subject and method of enquiry. This paper argues that just as racism operating within the regime of visibility has nothing to do with the color of skin, sexual violence against women such as rape, pornography, sexual abuse, prostitution, forced marriage, and female genital mutilation has nothing to do with sex and the erotic. The author underlines that if the space and place we inhabit produces us, the ways in which the psychic life of power[10] operates will be specific to space and place in terms of gender, race, class, and sexuality. However, because "the master's tools will never dismantle the master's house," and in order not to use "epistemic violence" to think about violence against women, new forms of dialogue, communication, interaction, and collective practices need to be imagined, developed, and practiced. Nayak's suggestion is that BFT, born out of subjugated knowledge in the matrix of power, offers a "politics of location" that is pivotal to negotiating interdisciplinary, inter-subjective, psychic, emotional, political, and practical solutions to the problems of gender violence.

Another innovation in feminist educational strategies is discussed in the following chapter: the active involvement of males. Looking at the persistent dramatic female condition, the denial of necessary positive male involvement would be a grave underestimation of the problem and perhaps, on the other hand, even a radical understatement of the possibility of men's humanity. It is certainly important to assume this possibility, but it is also necessary to consider how female self-determination and agency can be reached by women without excluding men. The

---

[10] Judith Butler, *The Psychic Life of Power* (Stanford, CA: Stanford University Press, 1997).

risk derived from the exclusion of men from the promotion of peace and equality in a post-colonial culture is to indefinitely fight against the parallel development of backslash against female empowerment.

Indeed, the post-colonial feminist perspective has developed some of the most important contributions in the direction of human rights, promoting women's capacity to participate in the peace process, involving men in the advancement in peace, developing the security and stability of democratic policies that guarantee comprehensive rights to women, including the right to take part in the political process and the right to social and political equality. In this scenario, the policies promoted in the most Westernized part of Africa—South Africa—may be considered an important intersection in the area of overcoming traditional-colonial culture, between peacekeeping processes, human rights promotion, and the solution of gender-based discrimination and violence. This testimony is presented by Phoebe Kisubi Mbasalaki in the contribution "'Brothers for Life': A Campaign Addressing Gender-Based Violence (de/re) Constructing Masculinities in South Africa." South Africa has robust policies and programs of intervention in place to address violence against women, although the majority of these are more reactive than preventative, but limitations on financial and human resources frustrate these efforts, blocking their effective implementation. It is worth noting that initiatives to thwart violence against women recognize the need to interrogate hegemonic masculinities, and hence efforts such as the "Brothers for Life" campaign have developed. This campaign seeks to establish a male identity that is linked to healthy, nonviolent, and more gender-equitable behavior. The campaign's variety of media draw upon the concept of brotherhood to convey to men the importance of the decisions they make and how these decisions impact their future and that of their dependents. The paper discusses some of the efforts in place to address violence against women in South Africa, drawing on examples from the latest preventative measures, such as the "Brothers for Life" campaign—deconstructing these through a feminist lens.

Changing women's education: From educative punishment to empowerment

Violence against women may also be determined by the difficulties TWF has encountered in transforming legal changes made by feminists into viable social practices. In many gender-based discourses, this phenomenon is often called "backlash" to criticize the perceived political implications of almost any issue having to do with women, and especially to deplore many representations of women in popular culture and the effect of these representations. One of the most difficult factors to change is the role of women who assume an anti-feminist attitude because they do not know the history of women's condition and do not understand how they are discriminated against: often the "victim" is not aware of the extent that she is treated unjustly. This attitude is the result of centuries of patriarchal education that demanded that women be systematically subordinated. The strategy of using education to keep women subordinate has progressively become less of an issue thanks to an increase in women's awareness, which has determined what Cornelius Castoriadis called "reforming education and social systems," towards an "autonomous society" versus the "heteronomous society." The two concepts are opposite: in the second case, society is composed of members responding to an extra-social authority; in the first example, members are aware of creating their own institutions (laws, traditions, and behaviors), and explicitly self-centering (self-determining) in order to become increasingly capable of critical self- and social thought.[11] This idea symbolizes a milestone in psychological thought, because it is founded upon the essential construct of "individuation" and its basic implication: individuals who have gained the ability to manage their personal freedom are self-determined.

Today women can become more self-determined than in the past, partially because their education has changed, and it is not the same as the one that was taught to their predecessors. Until the declaration of fundamental human rights and universal suffrage, the "edification" of women was aimed at guaranteeing that their will would remain subordinated to hegemonic and patriarchal power. The maintenance of women in a state of adherence to male domination was created through systematic training, disabling them from individuation in the name of "heteronomous" volitions: God and deities, laws of nature, the necessity of history, and so on. The first symbolic representation responsible for limiting women's agency is "motherhood," which before the feminist revolution was primarily managed by religious value-oriented criteria. The topic of heteronomy implied by faith is widely considered in the human rights debate, because worldwide religions set norms for what is considered ethical in order to obey God or

---

[11] Cornelius Castoriadis, *Philosophy, Politics, Autonomy* (Oxford: Oxford University Press, 1991).

godheads. Many religions state that women must submit to the will of God that establishes the manner in which collective moral principles and policies must manage female fertility. The "holy" has become a leading actor in the international stage in opposing women's human right to control their own fertility. But reproductive autonomy is an indispensable condition for women's sociocultural equality with men and, therefore, a fundamental human right.

The following chapters consider important initiatives from places like Ireland, Portugal, and Italy, where religion has particularly influenced the cultural frame of mind by orienting gender-role differentiation and the subordination of women. This section of contributions begins with an emblematic chapter that discusses a specific aberration of the relationship between sacred Catholic motherhood and social violence against women. Auxiliadora Pérez-Vides, in her "Gender, Deviance, and Institutional Violence in Ireland's Magdalene Laundries," describes how the Magdalene institutes constituted spatial metaphors of the socially sanctioned, national, and religious manipulation of women's bodies in Ireland. Following this line of argument, the author examines Aisling Walsh's TV film *Sinners*[12] and Peter Mullan's highly acclaimed film *The Magdalene Sisters*.[13] Her analysis explores and denounces Ireland's atrocious treatment of deviant sexuality by portraying the context in which outcast women were forced to live and the bleak conditions of their childbirth and mothering experiences. Pérez-Vides argues that the type of gender violence that the Magdalene women had to endure at the hands of their families, nuns, priests, and lay professionals in these institutions illustrates a culturally sanctioned understanding of female bodily deviance as well as a strict system of corporeal expiation, by which they were separated not only from normative society, but also from the right to choose, the right to privacy, and other basic rights.

Archaic social models that have been more or less unconsciously internalized provide the justification for numerous intimate victim-perpetrator relationships, among which domestic violence is the most salient example. The following three chapters consider some specific aspects of the consequences of female subordination and the possibility of intervening in order to change the situation.

---

[12] *Sinners,* directed by Aisling Walsh (Parallel Productions/BBC Northern Ireland, 2002).

[13] *The Magdalene Sisters*, directed by Peter Mullan (PFP Production in association with Temple Films, 2002).

Marlene Matos, Anita Santos, and Rita Conde, in the chapter "Gender and Domestic Violence in Portugal," provide their contribution as evidence to establish the scientific and social relevance of the problem in Portugal. The authors discuss the views that have oriented public policies and technical interventions with victims, illustrating how these emphasize the impact of violence and its adverse consequences, usually portraying victims as "traumatized," "impotent," and "passive," while these same interventions pay little attention to the change processes. This is why the authors have conducted studies that identify the strategies women use in order to cope with domestic violence, recognizing the psychological processes involved in the construction of adaptive processes. Specifically, they have studied the contribution of psychological interventions with female victims (individuals and groups) and also analyzed the impact of prevention campaigns among juveniles in order to measure the impact of education. These studies may provide significant input for intervention efforts with victims, leading to intervention models that rely on strengthening and empowering women's resources. The psychosocial and cognitive intervention described in this contribution is particularly pertinent because it is the most widely used one for enabling female self-determination. It triggers the motivation to change by leveraging an understanding of the factors that determine abusive relationships.

Next to the psychosocial cognitive approach, some new strategies are increasingly used in this specific field of intervention. Among these, psychodrama and sociodrama seem particularly promising, because of their ability to meet the criteria of TWF, especially with regard to the "embodiment" factor. Following Simone de Beauvoir's claim that "one is not born, but, rather, becomes a woman," which has been appropriated and reinterpreted by the perspective of constituting acts, where Butler's performative account of gendered subjectivity shows how sex and gendered identification come to *appear* natural starting from socio-constructionist processes, nowadays it is clear that it is important to involve the entire body in the experience of learning processes aimed at empowering women.[14] Indeed, Butler's perspective has opened the philosophical concept of "acting" in the theatrical sense, and this is the reason for considering psychodrama and sociodrama—which are types of psychosocial and psychotherapeutic

---

[14] Judith Butler, *Gender Trouble: Feminism and the Subversion of Identity,* cit.

techniques ideated by Jacob Moreno.[15] These techniques are used with small or large groups and use guided dramatic action to elaborate problems or issues of an individual—and are elective techniques for female empowerment within the TWF perspective. Psychodrama utilizes experiential methods and group dynamics to bring insight and personal growth to participants, who may explore their worldview and internal theater through action rather than through talking and classical psychological methods. In this way, it provides a safe environment to express strong feelings, under the guidance of a group leader who may be a psychotherapist or a counselor.

This theoretical backdrop creates the basis for the discussion of Ines Testoni, Alessandra Armenti, Alice Bertoldo, and their collaborators in the chapter "The Effectiveness of the EMPoWER Project and Intervention." In this text, the final phase of EMPoWER, a Daphne longitudinal research-intervention project carried out between 2011 and 2013 and involving six countries—Italy, Austria, Albania, Bulgaria, Portugal, and Romania—is presented. The focus of this contribution is on gender-based violence, studied within the family context and within a specific type of mother-daughter relationship. There were 136 women victims of domestic violence who took part in the study, and the effects of two different psychosocial interventions—ecological counseling and psychodramatic action—were measured. The importance of this chapter lies in the fact that it makes use of the longitudinal method, which measures change at two different points in time: at the beginning (before the intervention) and at the end (after the intervention). This research design required the instruments to be defined, in addition to measuring their validity and utilization. The results from the research demonstrated a high validity; moreover, the different tests validated the hypothesized model before the intervention in a randomized sample, showing positive correlations between indices of spontaneity and psychological well-being and negative correlations with indices of depression in the treatment group. The research supports the idea that both interventions (psychodramatic and ecological) strengthen the empowerment of women who have been victims of violence; however, psychodramatic techniques seem to be more effective in Eastern European countries. The focus of EMPoWER, adopting the pro-woman

---

[15] Jacob L. Moreno, *Interpersonal Therapy, Group Therapy and the Function of the Unconscious* (New York: Beacon House, 1954).

line, was the mother-daughter relationship, because the principal hypothesis focused on the idea that the "traditional" perspective that subjugates women is decreasing at a slow rate, and this seems to be partly due to the type of domestic intergenerational moral education that is passed on from mother to daughter.

In the previous chapters, psychodrama was used both as a technique to educate women victims of violence in order to emancipate them from the traditional representation of females and as a psychotherapeutic technique for treating adolescent women victims of sexual abuse. But psychodrama may also be a useful strategy for "teaching with gender" in school and university settings. In this case, the adoption of psychodrama is aimed at improving young women's individual prevention strategies so that they can avoid being preyed on. In fact, believing in the possibility of providing a concrete teaching example following the TWF perspective, the following authors' last chapter illustrates how to apply the model discussed in the previous contribution, through a primary prevention project carried out with female university students. Vincenzo Calvo, Marta Codato, Ines Testoni, and Alice Bertoldo, in "'Overcoming Female Subordination': An Experimental Process of Empowerment," describe the results of an intervention carried out utilizing sociodrama and active techniques. The aim of the project was to manage the relationship with the mother and her possible backlash against the emancipation of her daughter. The psychodramatic activities were aimed at reflecting on the maternal role in the transmission of traditional values that keep women confined in intimate relationships. Attachment theory assumed some specific importance, also making it possible to measure any changes in the relationship with the mother.

This contribution ends the volume by discussing the results of the research, which demonstrate the efficacy of the intervention and the possibility of measuring change after only one intervention focused on feminist objectives.

ABOUT LEGISLATION AGAINST DOMESTIC VIOLENCE IN THE EU AND ITALY

Alisa Del Re

> Domestic violence (is) "all forms of physical, psychological or sexual violence, and is as much about people who have had or are proposed to have an intimate relationship, and about subjects within a family who have more or less enlarged parental or affective relationship."[1]

Femicide as the culmination of domestic violence

Historically, the process through which the modern state was born granted men the power within the family. Men's domination over women was later transferred into laws, norms, and social structures. In the European national states the path to acquisition of citizenship rights for women has been asymmetric compared to that of male citizens, and many patriarchal structures remained active until well after the beginning of the twentieth century. In many states, family law continued to define the man as the head of the household up until the 1970s, giving him the right to discipline his wife and children. Raping one's wife was not considered a crime in many European countries until the end of the twentieth century. In the early 1970s the feminist movement raised the issue of interpersonal and structural violence against women as a social problem and found that the institutions were not very interested in the elimination of such violence.

Although equality between men and women is established by laws and by constitutional charters, as well as non-discrimination policies of the EU and interventions by the UN, in practice many women are stuck in abusive relationships because they are not materially helped to get out of them.

---

[1] World Health Organization, *WHO Multi-Country Study on Women's Health and Domestic Violence against Women: Summary Report; Initial Results on Prevalence, Health Outcomes and Women's Responses* (Geneva: WHO, 2005), http://who.int/gender/violence/who_multicountry_study/sur.

Any action to combat violence against women cannot be effective unless the problem of structural inequality is tackled, particularly with regard to domestic violence, including femicide.

Today, women are more in control of their bodies than of their representations.[2] In the phantasmagoria of images, representations of female bodies and male power bolster the traditional models of discriminating relationships between the sexes, and this contradiction is a fundamental root of violent behavior.[3] Even at the level of representation, action must be public.

On the feminist side of the commitment, new terms to describe violence against women have been coined. "Gynocide" is the term suggested by Daniela Danna,[4] showing that male violence in the era of globalization may be linked both to a break in the traditional gender model (in which violence was deeply embedded in the system of roles and power and thus not so explicit) and to a greater participation of women in everyday life and work. "Femicide" is the term used by Barbara Spinelli,[5] borrowed from Mexican anthropologist Lagarde,[6] to indicate systemic and structural violence to which women are subjected in the asymmetric context of power and life, a violence that affects women's bodies daily, escalating as far as rape and murder. Tamar Pitch[7] notes the close relationship between sexism and racism in recurring opinions, political views, and legislative action (security laws), and she denounces the instrumental use of the concept of "violence." In the postcolonial West, women's bodies are once again hostage to male-oriented policies made by men, which have the goal of producing new national political-cultural boundaries in order to keep out the "others," above all,

---

[2] Cf. L. Zanardo (2010), *Il corpo delle donne*, Milano Feltrinelli.

[3] Eleni Varikas, "Una parola 'sovranamente eversiva' Da Claire Demar al gender mainstreaming," in *Donne Politica Utopia*, ed. Alisa Del Re (Padua: Il Poligrafo, 2011), 41–59.

[4] Daniela Danna, *Ginocidio. La violenza contro le donne nell'era globale* (Milan: Eleuthera, 2007).

[5] Barbara Spinelli, *Femminicidio. Dalla denuncia sociale al riconoscimento giuridico internazionale* (Milan: FrancoAngeli, 2008); Barbara Spinelli, "Perché si chiama femminicidio," *La 27esimaora*, May 1, 2012, http://27esimaora.corriere.it/articolo/perche–si–chiama–femminicidio–2/.

[6] Marcela Lagarde, "Antropología, feminismo y política: violencia feminicida y derechos humanos de las mujeres," in *Retos Teòricos y nuevas practicas*, eds. Margaret Bullen and Carmen Diez Mintegui (San Sebastián: Ankulegi, 2006), 217–218. Lagarde, a Mexican parliamentarian, adds, "There are conditions for femicide when the state [or its institutions] does not give sufficient guarantees to girls and women and does not create conditions that ensure the safety of their lives in the community, at home, at work or in public spaces. And this is even more so when the authorities do not exercise their functions effectively. When the state is the structural part of the problem because of its patriarchal nature and because it tends to keep this type of order, femicide is a state crime." Ibid., 217 (trans. Alisa Del Re).

[7] Tamar Pitch, *La società della prevenzione* (Rome: Carocci, 2008).

migrants. In a social context where the dominant discourses on gender construct categories of "man" and "woman" as exclusive and hierarchically ordered, the representation of violence is itself highly sexualized and inseparable from the notion of gender.

The international framework

Since World War II, many international measures against violence on women have been enacted: the Universal Declaration of Human Rights (December 10, 1948), the United Nations Convention on the Suppression of the Traffic of Persons and the Exploitation of Prostitution (December 2, 1949), and the International Covenant on Civil and Political Rights and on Economic, Social and Cultural Rights adopted by the General Assembly in 1966 (which took effect in 1976).

But the specific complaint of "domestic violence" came much, much later. Attention to gender policies at the international level was manifested in a slightly more effective sense starting from the 1970s. In 1975 the UN proclaimed the International Year of the Woman and began a series of world conferences, the first of which was held that year in Mexico City. In 1979 the UN General Assembly adopted the Convention on the Elimination of All Forms of Discrimination against Women (CEDAW), entreating the states to eliminate gender inequalities suffered by women in public and private life; in 1999 an optional protocol was added that guarantees women the opportunity to submit an individual report to the Committee.[8] In the year 2000, at the twenty-third special session of the General Assembly of the United Nations, known as "Beijing+5," governments reaffirmed their commitment to the Fourth World Conference on Women in 1995. Some of the main recommendations contained in the document recog-

---

[8] Also of note is that in 1993 the General Assembly adopted the Declaration on the Elimination of Violence against Women. The issue of violence, along with the status of women in armed conflict, is considered in detail in the Platform for Action adopted at the Fourth World Conference on Women in Beijing in 1995. Also important are the Declaration and Program of Action of Vienna of June 25, 1993, adopted by the World Conference on Human Rights (A/CONF. 157/23) and UN Resolution No. 54/134 of December 17, 1999, proclaiming November 25 the International Day for the Elimination of Violence against Women. Finally, other interesting UN interventions on this topic are Resolution 58/147 of February 19, 2004, by the General Assembly stating that violence against women is a violation of human rights, and that of December 18, 2002, entitled "Measures for the Elimination of Crimes against Women Committed in the Name of Honor" (A/RES/57/179), in addition to the United Nations General Assembly Rsolution of December 19, 2006, entitled "Intensification of Efforts for the Elimination of All Forms of Violence against Women" (A/RES/61/143).

nized that stronger laws were necessary against all forms of domestic violence and that people need laws, policies, and educational programs to eradicate harmful traditional practices, such as genital mutilation, early and forced marriages, and honor killings, and to eliminate the commercial exploitation and sex trafficking of women and girls, infanticide, and crimes and racial violence caused by the issue of a dowry. But it was not until the Resolution of December 22, 2003, entitled "Elimination of Domestic Violence Against Women,"[9] that this issue was addressed and the need to eliminate domestic violence clearly recognized.

However, all these interventions, from the international conferences to the resolutions, have not been able to create a strong mobilization at the intergovernmental level in order to seriously combat violence against women. Particularly in the case of Italy, the CEDAW Committee, in the recommendations to the Italian government, stated that there was "concern about the high number of women killed by partners and former partners (femicides), which may indicate a failure of state authorities to adequately protect women victims from their partners or former partners." This is the first time that the CEDAW speaks of femicide in relation to a non-Latin American country, underscoring the probable inadequacy of the actions taken to protect women from violence. The CEDAW Committee highlighted its concern that in Italy there persist "socio-cultural attitudes that condone domestic violence": perhaps this is the point we have to start from in order to fight femicide.

Delimiting the field of investigation to Europe, it is necessary to report the most significant interventions of the Council of Europe. In particular, the Program of the European Campaign to Combat Violence against Women, including domestic violence,[10] and the Council of Europe Convention on the Protection of Children against Sexual Exploitation and Sexual Abuse[11] should be noted. Also noteworthy is the work of the Ad Hoc Committee of the Council of Europe Convention on preventing and combating violence against women and domestic violence (CAHVIO), created in December 2008 to prepare a future Council of Europe Convention on this issue, and the conclusions of the EPSCO

---

[9] A/RES/58/147, February 19, 2004.

[10] European Union, *Rompere il silenzio. Campagna europea contro la violenza domestica* (Luxembourg: Ufficio delle pubblicazioni ufficiali delle Comunità europee, 2000), http://dirittiumani.donne.aidos.it/bibl_1_temi/g_indice_per_temi/violenza_contro_le_ donne/f1_campagna_eu_viol.pdf.

[11] Council of Europe, *Council of Europe Convention on the Protection of Children against Sexual Exploitation and Sexual Abuse STCE no. 201*, October 25, 2007, http://conventions.coe.int.

Council of Ministers of March 8, 2010, on violence (Employment, Social Policy, Health and Consumer Affairs). The most recent intervention concerns the Council of Europe Convention on preventing and combating violence against women and domestic violence.[12]

This important convention stated that the achievement of equality *de jure* and *de facto* between women and men is a key element in preventing violence against women and that violence against women is a manifestation of historically unequal power relations between men and women that have led to domination over and discrimination against women by men, depriving women of their full emancipation. Recognizing that the structural nature of violence against women is gender-based and that violence against women is one of the crucial social mechanisms by which women are kept subordinate to men, it points out that women and girls are often exposed to serious violence such as domestic violence, sexual harassment, rapes, forced marriages, and crimes committed in the name of "honor" or "passion." This is a serious violation of human rights of women and girls and the main obstacle to achieving equality between women and men. In Art. 30 of the convention, an innovative concept is expressed with respect to gender violence: the need for compensation for victims, assigned by the state if the damage is not covered by other sources.

The European Union

The European Union (EU) Charter of Fundamental Rights of 2000[13] contains the foundations of the idea of dignity of individuals and equality between sexes (chapters 1 and 3). But it is necessary to get to the March 10, 2005, resolution of the European Parliament (EP) in order to see member governments called upon to take effective measures for the eradication of violence against women. Art. 11 reports that a clear political commitment to address domestic violence is totally lacking.

The EP resolution of November 26, 2009, on the Elimination of Violence against Women is fundamental. It follows the written statement of the EP on

---

[12] Council of Europe, *Council of Europe Convention on Preventing and Combating Violence against Women and Domestic Violence*, April 12, 2011, http://www.coe.int/t/dghl/standardsetting/equality/03themes/violence–against–women/Conv_VAW_en.pdf.

[13] 2000/C364/01, December 12, 2000.

April 21, 2009,[14] on the campaign "Say NO to Violence against Women." In all interventions the lack of regular and comparable data on violence against women in the European Union is highlighted. Although some EU member states have carried out important investigations on the subject, the results are not comparable, or they are obsolete. With the resolution on the Stockholm Program (November 25, 2009), the European Parliament asked the Agency for Fundamental Rights to compile and publish "reliable and comparable statistics on all causes of discrimination (...) and that these different causes be treated equally, also including comparative data on violence against women in the European Union." These reliable and comparable data are essential to assess the magnitude of the phenomenon and to find appropriate solutions.[15] In 2011–2012 the European Union Agency for Fundamental Rights (FRA)[16] conducted a survey across the EU on violence against women. Previously, in 2010–2011, the FRA conducted a preliminary study on violence against women in six EU member states: Finland, Germany, Italy, Poland, Spain and Hungary. This study was designed to assist the FRA in the development of survey questions capable of producing comparable results on the experiences of violence towards women in the EU, such as experiences of physical, sexual, and psychological violence at "home" and at work, as well as in a new context: the social networks. The results of the survey, which are to be released in 2013, will help to fuel the ongoing debate on action at an EU level to combat violence against women, for example through a new law, the harmonization of existing laws, or programs to raise awareness among EU citizens. In each country the survey will provide information related to police work, operators of health and social care sectors and civil society organizations, helping to distribute resources efficiently and improve services. For example, estimates of the number of cases of violence, the needs of victims, and their perceptions of the quality of the aid received can lead to re-evaluations of the resources available from government agencies and private assistance to the victims. In September 2010, the European Commission, at the end of the Lisbon Road Map,[17] adopted

---

[14] Unione Europea, *Gazzetta ufficiale dell'Unione Europea* 285 (2010): 53.

[15] Not only are the European data not updated, but additional information concerning the suicide of women in cases of domestic violence is often absent. For example, in Italy, although research on suicide has recently been carried out by ISTAT, domestic violence as a motivating factor was not taken into account.

[16] See http//: www.fra.europa.eu.

[17] European Union, "Road Map for Equality between Women and Men 2005–2010," http://europa.eu/legislation_summaries/.

a new five-year strategy for the promotion of equality between men and women (2010–2015), which translates into action the principles defined by the Women's Charter approved in early 2010.[18] The strategy on gender equality adopted by the European Commission foresees a series of measures based on five priorities: the economy and the labor market, equal pay, equality in positions of responsibility, the fight against gender violence, and the promotion of equality outside the EU. As regards the fight against gender violence, measures to be taken are cooperation with all member states to combat violence against women, and especially to eradicate female genital mutilation in Europe and worldwide. It should be noted that domestic violence is not particularly noted except as being "exogenous" and "culturally alien" to Europe. Also noteworthy is Decision no. 779 of June 20, 2007, establishing the Daphne III Program (2008–2013), which develops and reinforces a range of programs begun in 1997 under Daphne I (ended in 2003) and continued with Daphne II between 2004 and 2008.

National laws in different European countries

Among the European nations only a few have specific laws on domestic violence (Poland, Bulgaria, Belgium, Ireland, France).[19] Even fewer states punish domestic violence more severely than other forms of gender violence (Poland, Cyprus).[20] Some states, however, have adopted specific legislation on violence against women that also includes—but is not limited to—domestic violence (Sweden, Spain, Austria). Regarding sexual violence, the elements that define "rape" vary from state to state for the prediction of the act of penetration or more gener-

---

[18] The Charter presents a series of commitments based on agreed principles of equality between women and men in order to promote "equality in the labor market and equal economic independence for women and men," in particular through the "Europe 2020" strategy stating "equal pay for equal work" or "work of equal value" to foster cooperation with member states in order to significantly reduce the wage gap between men and women over the next five years. The strategy also focuses on equality in decision-making through EU incentive measures; the dignity and integrity of women, particularly by ending violence against women through a comprehensive policy framework; and equality between men and women outside the EU, addressing the issue in external relations and international organizations.

[19] See: http://ec.europa.eu/public_opinion/archives/ebs/ebs_344_en.pdf.

[20] France: Law no. 399, April 4, 2006, on the prevention and the countering of violence between spouses and partners or against children; Bulgaria: Law no. 27 of March 29, 2005, on contrast to domestic violence and gender violence; Poland: Law no. 180 of July 29, 2005, on contrast to domestic violence and gender violence; Austria: Federal Law to combat and prevent gender-based violence (approved in 2004); Belgium: Law of November 24, 1997, on the prevention and combating of violence between spouses and cohabitants; Ireland: Law of 1996 on domestic violence and abuse between spouses.

21

ally of a *sexual intercourse* that occurred, for the different characteristics of the conduct of the agent, and for the presence or absence of the victim's consent. In addition, many states have no appropriate standards to combat sexual harassment. In those where the standards are present, they are often included in labor law or within specific laws on violence against women. One feature common to all European countries to those where the offense is prosecuted *ex officio*, as well as to those in which violence can be prosecuted only upon complaint, is that violence against women most often goes unpunished. The most important reason is that women do not often report domestic violence, since they are often challenged by those who tend to downplay family disagreements and would rather settle the conflict in the name of family unity. Another common factor is the problematic relationship between repression and protective measures, protection from domestic violence and immigration laws. Of particular note is the lack of harmonization between penal and civil measures, since they often offer the same protection of interests in different degrees, or are alternatives to each other. For the woman who has suffered violence and seeks protection, this makes the legal path more tortuous.

The president of Amnesty International Italy, Christine Weise, with an explicit reference to the recommendations of the CEDAW Committee, which oversees the UN Convention on the Elimination of All Forms of Discrimination against Women, stated that gender discrimination in Europe and domestic violence are closely linked to the phenomenon of femicide and that action against it should be a priority for governments. The lack of concrete action to combat violence is a serious violation of human rights. A report by Amnesty International stated that Italy "must overcome the representation of women as sexual objects and challenge stereotypes about the role of men and women in society and family." In Denmark, the report identifies a number of non-consensual sexual crimes and abuses "in which the victim is defenseless because of an illness or intoxication, are not punishable by law if the perpetrator and the victim are married." In Finland "services for victims of violence are inadequate," particularly for victims of domestic violence, since, given that the centers are funded by Child Protection Services, they hosted mainly women with children, placing "many vulnerable people at risk of further violence." In Norway, "women are not adequately protected against violence in the law and practice," because, "despite the fact that the number of rapes reported to police has increased, more than 80 percent of these cases are closed before getting to trial." In Portugal, domestic violence "is a serious cause of concern" (in 2011 alone, there were 14,508 reports of domestic violence).[21]

One of the most important laws (and considered among the best laws in Europe by the organization Choisir Cause des Femmes) is the Ley Orgánica de Medidas de Protección Integral contra la Violencia de Género,[22] the law against gender violence in Spain, promulgated on December 28, 2004. It increases the penalties for assault and abuse from two to five years, but it also provides greater protection and assistance for female victims of abuse and provides them the right to unemployment benefits (unprecedented in Europe) if the woman quits her job following a domestic violence situation. It then established the right to social assistance, which includes integrated support services, emergency, and recovery, including the service of advocacy at state expense. The law is based on the principle of "equality between men and women" because violence is the most striking manifestation of inequality that exists. Victim protection is pursued through measures that address prevention, the punishment of the aggressor, and the measures of total care for victims. There is also a State Observatory for Gender Violence. In short, the law is a set of standards that aims not only to punish the aggressor with stiff penalties but also to protect and support victims in their daily lives.

The Italian situation

When the CEDAW Committee asked Italy on July 14, 2011, to provide data on femicides, the Italian government was not able to provide a timely response, simply because these data have never been collected. In July 2011 many women and associations (including the National Network of Anti-Violence Centers) gathered at the Italian platform "30 Years of CEDAW: Work in Progress" in order to provide the necessary information and draft what was known as the "Shadow Report" on the implementation of CEDAW in Italy. As for violence, the basic idea was that it was up to the institutions to take the necessary steps to prevent

---

[21] Amnesty International, "Annual Report 2011," http://www.rapportoannuale.amnesty.it/.

[22] Gobierno de España, Ministerio de la Presidencia, Agencia Estatal, "Ley Orgánica 1/2004, de 28 de diciembre, de Medidas de Protección Integral contra la Violencia de Género." *Boletín Oficial del Estado* 313 (2004): 42166. http://www.boe.es/buscar/doc.php?id=BOE-A-2004-21760.

femicide through cultural actions and adequate protection for those women who choose to exit all forms of violence (from trafficking to domestic violence).[23]

One chapter in the Shadow Report captured the inconsistencies in policies and enforcement of existing laws on male violence against women in our country. Only in 1996, with Law no. 66 on Sexual Violence, did Italy move violence from the title "crime against morality" to "crime against the person and against individual freedom." With Law no. 154/2001, measures against violence in family relationships were established, and finally with Law no. 38/2009 urgent measures concerning public security and, to combat sexual violence, terms of persecution (stalking) were activated. The lack of reliable data and serious surveys has led to the creation of a National Observatory on Domestic Violence (ONVD), founded in October 2006 in collaboration with the University of Verona and ISPESL (National Epidemiological Observatory on Living Environments), established in 2002 for purposes of study, research, and promotion aimed at improving safety in the living environment.[24] Complete investigations were undertaken without using the method of sample selections. This methodological choice allowed the building of a network that begins to quantify (and qualify) the "dark" side of the phenomenon and facilitate its emergence.

The analysis of the events outlined a critical framework: a reflection on it and on the existing legislative framework indicated the need to change paths. The activity of the ONVD involves many hands—academics and criminologists, emergency unit personnel, general practitioners, family planning clinics and regional personnel, agents of the state police, the carabinieri corps, police and judicial magistrates. All participants contribute with their specific skills to the identification of different forms of abuse and violence, and at the same time they give an indication of the actions to undertake.

In almost all the regions of Italy there are local anti-violence laws, the contents of which are very different, ranging from "Rules for the Protection and

---

[23] Daniela Danna, *Stato di famiglia. Le donne maltrattate di fronte alle istituzioni* (Rome: Ediesse, 2009).

[24] ISPESL's interest in the issue of domestic violence is due to the fact that this act, involving "weak" social players and acts of violence that are concealed and that occur in the domestic environment, is strongly connected to the protection of the health and safety of the people in the living space. For this reason, ISPESL, in collaboration with the Department of Medicine and Public Health, the University of Verona, the Verona Public Prosecutor, the Verona Hospital and the Prevention Department of Health Services No. 1 of Trieste, conducted a preliminary study [the National Centre on epidemiological conditions of health and safety in the living environment], published in December 2005 under the title "Domestic Violence: An Oxymoron to Understand and Unravel."

Enhancement of the Family"[25] to the regional law of the Piedmont Region[26] on "Establishment of a Solidarity Fund for Legal Aid to Women Victims of Violence and Abuse" and the "Regional Plan for the Prevention of Violence against Women and Support for Victims" of July 8, 2008, also of the Piedmont Region. In recent years, many regions have established standards for the activation of anti-violence centers and shelters. The laws are often uneven and ineffective; the regulations are contradictory, and some of them need to be modified. For instance, Art. 1 of the *Testo Unico* (Comprehensive Law) for Public Safety, states: "through its officers, and at the request of the parties, (the law) provides for the amicable settlement of private disputes." Such a definition lends itself to controversial interpretations, and certainly leads to a behavior that is contrary to the right of women to access judicial protection for self-preservation, exposing all parties to known and unknown risks. Given the law provision, one is almost obliged to avoid presenting a complaint.[27]

For this reason, many victims actually report violence only after many occurrences. According to the latest ISTAT data, in Italy one out of three women has been the victim of male aggression during her life. There are 6,743,000 women who have suffered physical and sexual violence (in 2011 there were 128 killed, ten more than the year before). Whether it is domestic violence, sexual abuse, rape, stalking, trafficking, forced prostitution, or infibulation, there is no doubt that this phenomenon originates in the unequal and discriminatory position of women in society and (then) within the family.

Local initiatives: Anti-violence centers, women's shelters, women's hotlines

Created in the mid-1980s, local initiatives in Italy have, with great determination, developed a method to work effectively to support and promote the rights of women and their empowerment.[28] Until now these have been the only structures to address the issue of male violence against women on a public level, not as

---

[25] LR no. 10, Sicily, July 31, 2003.

[26] LR, March 17, 2008.

[27] ONVD has so far published numerous territorial investigations, particularly focused in the Veneto, and manuals to ensure that operators can detect domestic violence. See http://www.onvd.org.

[28] Gabriele Codini, *La vittimologia e le vittime fragili. La situazione in Europa e i servizi di supporto* (Milan: FrancoAngeli, 2010).

one of the many problems of women in our country, but as a paradigm of male-female relationships and the power that is used against women. They also created networks of multidisciplinary support, initiating processes of change, prevention, protection, and social inclusion. The women who work in anti-violence centers and women's shelters are concerned with violence against women, both within and outside the family (physical, psychological, sexual, economic, stalking, trafficking), and with children who witness these types of violence in any form it is expressed. They manage the telephone reception and give information to walk-ins. They host women, adolescents, and children who have suffered violence, and they carry out activities designed to prevent and combat it. They support projects of individual women facing temporary hardship and difficulties as a result of ongoing or past violence, or violence suffered as a minor. They welcome women alone or with children, respecting cultural differences and the experiences of each one, in the awareness of the significance and impact of belonging to different ethnic groups, cultures, religions, social classes, and sexual orientations. They guarantee anonymity and secrecy to the women they host, and they undertake actions that affect these women only with their consent. These centers are often funded by local authorities, but they are staffed primarily by volunteers.

Conclusions

The interest in intervention against gender violence emerged at an international level as a result of the gradual awareness of the use of rape as a weapon of war. The UN interventions, the several conventions that have taken place over time, although signed by many governments, have not had sufficient compulsive power so far, and every intervention is paralyzed by a succession of recommendations, causing it to remain a "dead letter." According to the EU, the actions of the Commission and the Parliament have not been translated into coherent and consistent national policy. They pointed out the existence of a social problem that is imposed without a viable solution for all member states. The Council of Europe has proved to be much more attentive to the problem, but in this case, the application of the directives has occurred unevenly.

Men's violence against women—at home, at work, on the streets, in schools—is a crime which every year is enumerated, shown, and disclosed, although the data certainly underestimate the problem, and in many cases the statistics are not reliable. For over thirty years solutions have been given to governments in order to combat the leading cause of premature death for women, which is also an obstacle to the realization of human rights. Feminist movements have found partial but effective solutions at regional levels—from the *case delle donne* (women's shelters) to the anti-violence centers, often supported by local institutions.

The repetition of the offenses with the same or other victims and the spread of ownership behavior in men, despite the strong political reinterpretation of femicide by the women's movement, show that the inadequacy of the rules invalidates any cultural change.[29] According to some studies of the Council of Europe, 12–15 percent of women above the age of sixteen have suffered domestic violence.[30] Domestic violence, the most common and widespread form of gender violence, knows no geographical, cultural, ethnic, or class boundaries. It is now formally recognized as violence at every institutional level, as are all types of violence against women, and treated as a violation of fundamental human rights recognized and guaranteed by both the ECHR (European Convention on Human Rights and Fundamental Freedoms) and the Charter of Fundamental Rights. It is also subject to rules such as the Convention on Preventing and Combating Violence against Women and Domestic Violence of the Council of Europe (April 2011), as well as to the Directive of the European Parliament and Council on European Protection of November 15, 2011.

Despite the European regulatory framework and international partnerships among member countries of the EU, there are major differences in how domestic violence is addressed in law and policy. Furthermore, we still lack comparable data on the actual size of the phenomenon. Domestic violence remains a fundamental problem not yet solved, linked to the concern for victims' compensation, as indicated by the Council of Europe, and for any damage that may have repercussions on the entire lives of the victims and on future generations.

Implications for teaching

This text can be used to deepen understanding of important issues concerning the legislation against domestic violence in Italy and in other European countries

---

[29] Lea Melandri, "Violenza contro le donne: le firme non bastano," *Gli altri online,* May 10, 2012, http://www.glialtrionline.it/2012/05/10/lappello–di–snoq–contro–la–violenza–sulle–donneattente–le–firme–non–bastano/.

[30] AUSL Rimini: http://www.ausl.rn.it/doceboCms/page/89/dafne-dati-epidemiologici.html.

from a historical and transnational perspective. In particular, it provides a useful analysis that compares Italian legislative actions to combat domestic violence with those implemented in other European countries. The framework within which the regulation of sexual and domestic violence is discussed in this essay highlights the complexity of the legislative "spaces" that make up both penal and civil procedures that are based on different ideological backgrounds that thwart rather than facilitate women's legal efforts. Another important aspect concerns the lack of clear legal definitions of domestic/sexual violence and rape, which are particularly problematic when combined with issues relating to immigration laws or race and citizenship.

We stress the importance of taking actions that dismantle the structural inequality that sustains violence against women in all areas of private and institutional life.

As this paper highlights, the points mentioned above need to be discussed further, and various perspectives need to be integrated. This is the reason why the text is an important tool, as it can be included in course materials ranging from international relations, European policies, women's studies, and gender studies, to migration, law, politics, and social and cultural studies.

Questions

Given the complexity of the topic, it is important to proceed by clarifying different aspects that concern the legislation to protect women against violence.

Different paths can be taken in order to reflect on and discuss issues concerning violence against women in EU member states:

1. The text points out many problematics concerning the gap between existing European policies and single-country legislation. In which way does the broader European level affect the internal management of social policies in each country with respect to domestic violence?
2. How has the definition of domestic and sexual violence and rape been adopted by the EU to build coherent policies at the European level and consequently in each individual country?
3. Do EU policies on domestic and sexual violence reflect a post-colonial perspective? What aspects need to be improved?

4. The urgent need to create a legislative framework that protects women from male violence reflects the more intimate asymmetrical power imbalance that constitutes the relationship between men and women. Can you link the private sphere (such as the domestic/working/class/race aspect) to aspects concerning the implementation of EU policies at an international level?

Assignments

1. Analyze the historical development of European policies that protect women from violence. There are various ways to approach this:
- Describe the current policy situation in one individual European country (you can also compare two different countries), trying to analyze the country's particular history and cultural background (for example, post-socialist countries have developed a profoundly different legal framework from other European countries).
2. Immigration policies and violence against women: why are these issues so problematic? Chose a country case study and describe the weak and strong points of VAW legislation.

REFERENCES

Amnesty International. "Rapporto annuale 2011." http://www.rapportoannuale.amnesty.it/.

Codini, Gabriele. *La vittimologia e le vittime fragili. La situazione in Europa e i servizi di supporto.* Milan: FrancoAngeli, 2010.

Council of Europe. *Council of Europe Convention on Preventing and Combating Violence against Women and Domestic Violence.* April 12, 2011. http://www.coe.int/t/dghl/standardsetting/equality/03themes/violence–against–women/Conv_VAW_en.pdf.

Council of Europe. *Council of Europe Convention on the Protection of Children against Sexual Exploitation and Sexual Abuse STCE no.* 201. October 25, 2007. http://conventions.coe.int.

Danna, Daniela. *Ginocidio. La violenza contro le donne nell'era globale.* Milan: Eleuthera, 2007.

Danna, Daniela. *Stato di famiglia. Le donne maltrattate di fronte alle istituzioni.* Rome: Ediesse, 2009.

European Union. "Road Map. Tabella di marcia per la parità fra le donne e gli uomini 2005–2010." http://europa.eu/legislation_summaries.

European Union. *Gazzetta ufficiale dell'Unione Europea* 285 (2010): 53.

European Union. *Rompere il silenzio. Campagna europea contro la violenza domestica.* Luxembourg: Ufficio delle pubblicazioni ufficiali delle Comunità europee, 2000. http://dirittiumani. donne.aidos.it/bibl_1_temi/g_indice_per_temi/violenza_contro_le_ donne/f1_campagna_eu_ viol.pdf.

Gobierno de España, Ministerio de la Presidencia, Agencia Estatal. "Ley Orgánica 1/2004, de 28 de diciembre, de Medidas de Protección Integral contra la Violencia de Género." *Boletín Oficial del Estado* 313 (2004), 42166–42197. http://www.boe.es/buscar/doc.php?id=BOE-A-2004-21760.

Halimi, Gisèle. *La Clause de l'Européenne la plus favorisée. Des Femmes, Choisir la cause des femmes.* Paris: Des femmes Antoinette Fouque, 2008.

Lagarde, Marcela. "Antropología, feminismo y política: violencia feminicida y derechos humanos de las mujeres." In *Retos Teòricos y nuevas practicas*, eds. Margaret Bullen and Carmen Diez Mintegui, 217–218. San Sebastián: Ankulegi, 2006.

Lagarde, Marcela. "Por la vida y la libertad de las mujeres fin al feminicidio." In *Resistencia y alternativas de la mujeres frente al modelo globalizador*, eds. Leonor Concha Aida and Gabriella Labelle, 114–126. México City: Red Nacional de Género y Economia, 2005.

Melandri, Lea. "Violenza contro le donne: le firme non bastano." *Gli altri online,* May 10, 2012. http://www.glialtrionline.it/2012/05/10/lappello-di-snoq-contro-la-violenza-sulle-donneattente-le-firme-non-bastano.

Pitch, Tamar. *La società della prevenzione*. Rome: Carocci, 2008.

Spinelli, Barbara. "Perché si chiama femminicidio." *La 27esimaora,* May 1, 2012. http://27esimaora.corriere.it/articolo/perche-si-chiama-femminicidio-2/ (accessed October 10, 2012).

Spinelli, Barbara. *Femminicidio. Dalla denuncia sociale al riconoscimento giuridico internazionale.* Milan: FrancoAngeli, 2008.

Varikas, Eleni. "Una parola 'sovranamente eversiva.' Da Claire Demar al gender mainstreaming." In *Donne Politica Utopia*, ed. Alisa Del Re, 41–59. Padua: Il Poligrafo, 2011.

World Health Organization. *WHO Multi-Country Study on Women's Health and Domestic Violence against Women: Summary Report; Initial Results on Prevalence, Health Outcomes and Women's Responses.* Geneva: WHO, 2005. http://who.int/gender/violence/who_multicountry_study/sur.

THE ACTIVISM OF BLACK FEMINIST THEORY IN CONFRONTING VIOLENCE AGAINST WOMEN: INTERCONNECTIONS, POLITICS, AND PRACTICE

Suryia Nayak

In the previous chapter of this volume, Alisa Del Re calls the acts and conse-quences of violence against women "femicide." She is right to do so, because violence against women is a matter of life and death that "knows no geographi-cal, cultural, ethnic, or class boundaries."[1] An understanding of femicide that includes the persistent attack on women's human rights enables analysis of the "living death" that many survivors of sexual violence experience. As a matter of the life and death of women and their human rights, it is crucial that connections between teaching, critical analysis, and interventions to confront femicide are continually reviewed and articulated loud and clear.

This paper uses Audre Lorde's essay "Uses of the Erotic: The Erotic as Power"[2] as an analytical framework to explore an account of gender violation experienced by Patricia Hill Collins. The intention is to demonstrate that the activism of Black feminist theory in general, and the activism of Lorde's scholar-ship in particular, are effective tools for confronting and teaching about femicide. Drawing on bell hooks's idea of "Teaching to Transgress,"[3] this paper uses the activism of Black feminist "[t]heory as liberatory practice."[4] In the context of this paper, reference is made to gender violence, but the focus is on violence against Black women, with specific reference to the function and production of the objectification of Black women. The use of the activism of Black feminist theory to examine the complex intersection of multiple complex vectors of oppression in the sexual denigration of Black women is quite deliberate. The point I am making here is that any hope of meaningful alliances across difference to combat

---

[1] Alisa Del Re, "Review of the Legislation against Domestic Violence in Europe and Italy."

[2] Audre Lorde, "Uses of the Erotic: The Erotic as Power" (paper delivered at the Fourth Berkshire Conference on the History of Women, Mount Holyoke College, MA, August 25, 1978). Published as a pamphlet by Out and Out Books, 1978; reprinted in Audre Lorde, *Sister Outsider* (Trumansburg, NY: Crossing Press Feminist Series, 1984).

[3] bell hooks, "Teaching to Transgress: Education as the Practice of Freedom" (New York: Routlege, 1994).

[4] Ibid., 59.

gender violence will fail if Black feminist interventions, wisdom, and experience continues to be marginalized. Furthermore, it will fail if any element in that alliance replicates the unequal power relations at work in gender violence through hegemonic thinking and positioning in that alliance, thereby replicating the very problem it seeks to address.[5]

The activism of Black feminist theory

This paper uses the term "the activism of Black feminist theory" to insist on the mutually constitutive relationship between theory and activism that emphasizes the "...links between Black feminism as a social justice project and Black feminist thought as its intellectual centre."[6] It is a direct challenge to the binaries of activism or theory, and experience or scholarship, that questions what counts as theory and who counts as theorist.[7] Indeed, examination of the constituent elements of the activism of Black feminist theory demonstrates that it emerges out of the dialectical and the dialogical. It emerges out of the dialectical because it is formed out of the suppression of Black women's voice, thinking, and scholarship in order to articulate that suppression with the objective of confronting that suppression.[8] It emerges out of the dialogical because of the interconnections with the activism of social justice. The dialogical relationship between experience, practice, and scholarship produces the methodology of the activism of Black feminist theory, where the *how to do* and the *doing* of the project intersect. Carole Boyce Davies asserts that "Black feminist criticisms, then, perhaps more than many of the other feminisms, can be a praxis where the theoretical positions

---

[5] Norma Alarcón, "The Theoretical Subject(s) of This Bridge Called My Back and Anglo-American Feminism." In Gloria Anzaldúa, ed., *Making Face, Making Soul/Haciendo Caras: Creative and Critical Perspectives by Women of Color* (San Francisco: Aunt Lute Books, 1990): 356–369; Valerie Amos and Pratibha Parmar, "Challenging Imperial Feminism," *Feminist Review* 17 (1984): 3–19; Avtar Brah, *Cartographies of Diaspora: Contesting Identities* (Abingdon: Routledge, 1996); Avtar Brah and Ann Phoenix, "Ain't I A Woman? Revisiting Intersectionality," *Journal of International Women's Studies* 5, no. 3 (May 1, 2004): 75–87; Barbara Christian, "The Race for Theory" (1987), in J. James and T.D. Sharpley-Whiting, eds., *The Black Feminist Reader* (Oxford: Blackwell Publishers, 2000) 11–23; The Combahee River Collective, "A Black Feminist Statement" (1977), in *The Black Feminist Reader*, eds. J. James and T.D. Sharpley-Whiting (Oxford: Blackwell Publishers, 2000): 261–270.

[6] Patricia Hill Collins, *Black Feminist Thought: Knowledge, Consciousness, and The Politics of Empowerment* (London: Routledge, 2000), xi.

[7] Barbara Christian (1987), "The Race for Theory," in J. James and T.D. Sharpley-Whiting, eds., *The Black Feminist Reader* (Oxford: Blackwell Publishers, 2000), 11–23.

[8] Hill Collins, *Black Feminist Thought*, 3-4.

and the criticism interact with the lived experience."[9] The work of Audre Lorde continues to be instrumental in this process and is evidence of the translation and relevance of her work to current feminist practice and experience.

The tools we use, why and how we use them, what we leave out and what we include and the connections we make between tools reflect power relations.[10] Hill Collins makes this point clearly in relation to the positioning of Black feminist theory, stating that "[t]he shadow obscuring this complex Black women's intellectual tradition is neither accidental nor benign."[11] I want to make a deliberate intervention of using the "intellectual tradition" of the activism of Black feminist theory in general and the "intellectual tradition" of Audre Lorde in particular to interrogate aspects of the pernicious crime of femicide. AnaLouise Keating comments, "Like Allen's embodied mythic thinking and Anzaldua's mestiza consciousness, Lorde's 'erotic' indicates a nondual transformational epistemology that combines visionary language with cultural critique. Just as Allen's embodied mythic thinking enables her to synthesize spiritual, political, and material issues, Lorde's theory of the erotic enables her to unite alternate ways of thinking with material change."[12] Keating also refers to Lorde's approach as a "transformational epistemology" using performative "threshold locations" to "move beyond the existing frameworks by exposing the hidden, masculine, Eurocentric biases that structure binary thinking."[13] Within the context of this paper, the notion of "threshold locations" concerns the interconnections of Black feminisms to confront the function and production of disconnection at work within this racist, homophobic patriarchy.

Objectify myself: Objectify her

Writing about the sexual politics of Black womanhood with particular reference to violence against Black women, the Black feminist scholar Patricia Hill Collins

---

[9] Carole Boyce Davies, *Black Women, Writing and Identity: Migrations of the Subject* (London: Routledge, 1994), 55; Amina Mama, *Beyond the Masks: Race, Gender and Subjectivity* (London: Routledge, 1995).

[10] *Chandra Talpade* Mohanty (1984), "Under Western Eyes: Feminist Scholarship and Colonial Discourses." In C.T. Mohanty, *Feminism without Borders: Decolonizing Theory, Practicing Solidarity* (Durham: Duke University Press, 2003): 17–42.

[11] Hill Collins, *Black Feminist Thought*, 3.

[12] AnaLouise Keating, *Women Reading Women Writing: Self-Invention in Paula Gunn Allen, Gloria Anzaldua and Audre Lorde* (Philadelphia: Temple University Press, 1996), 49.

[13] Ibid., 6–7.

comments, "I was invited to objectify myself in order to develop the objectivity that would allow me to participate in her objectification."[14] The context in which this comment was made refers to three separate occasions where Hill Collins was part of the audience in which three different academic scholars (a white feminist, a white male, and a black male) used Sarah Baartman's image.[15] Hill Collins states the issues clearly: "I saw the reactions of young Black women who saw images of Sarah Baartman for the first time.... They saw and felt the connections among the women exhibited on the auction block, the voyeuristic treatment of Sarah Baartman, the depiction of Black women in pornography, and their own daily experiences of being under sexual surveillance."[16] When Hill Collins questioned the "prominent White scholar"[17] about his pornographic use of the presentation slides, "He defended his 'right' to use public domain material any way he saw fit, even if it routinely offended Black women and contributed to their continued objectification."[18] The "prominent Black male scholar" who made no mention of Sarah Bartmann's gender "[d]espite the fact that we stared at a half-naked Black woman"[19] responded to Hill Collins by stating, "I'm concerned about race here, not gender!"[20] These encounters encompass the complexity of the politics and practice of entering into a dialogue across difference, where issues of race,

---

[14] Hill Collins, *Black Feminist Thought*, 142.

[15] The African slave woman Saartjie "Sarah" Baartman (also spelled Bartmann) (1790s–1815) was exhibited across nineteenth-century Europe as a living specimen of an anthropological freak. Displayed as the "Hottentot Venus," Baartman was forced to stand naked before the crowds, and her image swept through British and European culture as a representation of sexual perversion. Baartman was the object of medical and scientific research that produced ideas about Black women's sexuality and representations of Black women's supposedly insatiable sexual appetite. These representations continue to reproduce contemporary objectifications of Black women's bodies and sexuality used to justify the position and function of Black women in society. After Baartman died in 1815, her vagina and brain were displayed in the Musee de l'Homme in Paris until 1985. It was not until 2002 that her skeleton and body parts were returned to Cape Town, where she now rests in Eastern Cape, the place of her birth. Suzan-Lori Parks, *Venus* (Dramatists Play Service, 1998), Sadiah Qureshi, "Displaying Sara Baartman, the 'Hottentot Venus,'" *History of Science* 42 (2004): 233; Crais Clifton and Pamela Scully, *Sara Baartman and the Hottentot Venus: A Ghost Story and a Biography* (Princeton: Princeton University Press, 2008); Deborah Willis, ed., *Black Venus 2010: They Called Her "Hottentot"* (Philadelphia: Temple University Press, 2010).

[16] Hill Collins, *Black Feminist Thought*, 142–143.

[17] Ibid.

[18] Ibid.

[19] Ibid.

[20] Ibid.

gender, and sexual violence intersect.[21] In particular, Hill Collins highlights how the mechanisms of objectification work across temporal and spatial contexts, including subjectivity and inter-subjectivity to regulate, constitute, and construct power relations that shape gender violence.[22]

Interconnections: Relations of proximity

This paper uses the interventions of the activism of Black feminist theory in relation to interconnections, intersectionality, binary positions, and representation as a tool of critical analysis to deconstruct discourses and practices that legitimize violence against women. Furthermore, this paper uses conceptual tools developed within the activism of Black feminist theory both as the subject and method of inquiry. It will become evident that both the subject under analysis and the method used to examine the subject under analysis mirror and constitute each other. The ways in which women are physically, emotionally, and sexually violated and survive these experiences need to be understood in relation to racism and those other weights of oppression that press us down. The daily reality of living with the effects of racism and sexism, combined with other pressures such as poverty, disability, and homophobia, is exhausting. Using the activism of Black feminist theory as an analytical lens to scrutinize the specificity of Black women's needs (which are all too frequently ignored or bolted onto general service provision, policy, and teaching) performs two actions. First, it asserts the importance of Black women's thinking, which is also too frequently ignored or bolted on to a general analysis of sexual violence. Second, it asserts the specificity of Black women's experience of violation within racism. For example, the Black feminist concept of intersectionality conceptualizes interlocking and mutually

---

[21] Kathy Davis, "Intersectionality as Buzzword: A Sociology of Science Perspective on What Makes a Feminist Theory Successful," *Feminist Theory* 9, no. 1 (April 2008): 67–85. Helma Lutz, Maria Teresa Herrera Vivar, and Linda *Supik*, eds., *Framing Intersectionality: Debates on a Multi-Faceted Concept in Gender Studies* (Farnham: Ashgate, 2011) Leslie McCall, "The Complexity of Intersectionality," *Signs: Journal of Women in Culture and Society* 30, no. 3 (Spring 2005): 1771–1800. Ann Phoenix and *Pamela* Pattynama, eds., "Special Issue on 'Intersectionality.'" *European Journal of Women's Studies* 13, no. 3 (August 2006): 187–192. Yvette Taylor, Sally Hines, and Mark E. Casey, eds. *Theorizing Intersectionality and Sexuality* (Basingstoke: Palgrave Macmillan, 2010).

[22] Sara Suleri (1992), "Woman Skin Deep: Feminism and the Postcolonial Condition." In B. Ashcroft, G. Griffiths, and H. Tiffin, eds., *The Post-Colonial Studies Reader*, 2nd ed. (London: Routledge, 2006): 250–255.

reinforcing vectors[23] that could refer to public, private, gender, silence, body, and family. Referring specifically to sexual violence against Black women, Hill Collins argues for an analysis of sexual violence in the context of all systems of oppression because "This conceptualization views sexuality as conceptual glue that binds intersecting oppressions together. Stated differently, intersecting oppressions share certain core features. Manipulating and regulating the sexualities of diverse groups constitutes one such shared feature."[24]

The challenge of Crenshaw's theory of intersectionality is the challenge presented in the aphorism, "the personal is the political." Intersectionality goes beyond merely combining inadequate and oppressive socioeconomic, political, and legal structures, and inadequate feminist theories and practices. In regard to this point, Hill Collins offers a useful distinction between intersectionality and her own concept of the matrix of domination: "...I use and distinguish between both terms in examining how oppression affects Black women. Intersectionality refers to particular forms of intersecting oppressions, for example, intersections of race and gender, or of sexuality and nation. Intersectional paradigms remind us that oppression cannot be reduced to one fundamental type, and that oppressions work together in producing injustice. In contrast, the matrix of domination refers to how these intersecting oppressions are actually organized."[25] However, even though there is an intersection of issues, elements, and mechanisms that legitimizes violence against women, the politics and practice of confronting violence against women is not interconnected. Indeed, binary positions, fragmentation, and splitting, which work to silence survivors of gender violence, become replicated within the politics and practice of challenging violence against women. This lack of connection is exacerbated in the politics, discourse, and representation of sexual violence against Black women. Crenshaw explains that "[a]lthough racism and sexism readily intersect in the lives of real people, they seldom do in feminist and antiracist practices. And so, when the practices expound identity as woman or person of color as an either/or proposition, they relegate the identity of women of color to a location that resists telling Political, practical, and policy

---

[23] Kimberlé Crenshaw, *Demarginalizing the Intersection of Race and Sex: A Black Feminist Critique of Antidiscrimination Doctrine, Feminist Theory, and Antiracist Politics* (Chicago: University of Chicago Legal Forum, 1989); Jennifer Nash, "Re-Thinking Intersectionality," *Feminist Review* 89 (2008): 1.

[24] Hill Collins, *Black Feminist Thought*.

[25] Ibid., 18.

solutions to tackle violence against women need to be founded on the interdependency of difference.[26] In other words, the concept and practice of interconnection is central to understanding and working to confront gender violence. Hill Collins explains that "[f]or Black women, ceding control over self-definitions of Black women's sexualities upholds multiple oppressions. This is because all systems of oppression rely on harnessing the power of the erotic."[27] This paper argues that the activism of Black feminist theory born out of intersecting subjugated knowledge in the matrix of power [28] offers a "politics of location"[29] that is pivotal to negotiating interdisciplinary, inter-subjective, psychic, emotional, political, and practical solutions to the problems of gender violence. This paper asserts that a feminist critical analysis of "...relations of proximity [that] highlight the facts of connection or dis/connection"[30] is central to finding creating new meanings, solutions, and tools to confront violence against women.

Lorde and Hill Collins's encounter

I return to the experience of Patricia Hill Collins quoted at the beginning of this paper: because she identifies the propositions at work in the dynamics of her experience as precisely what is at work in the subjugation of women through sexual violation. Patricia Hill Collins describes a particular encounter that brings her into a particular proximity to another Black woman, namely Sarah Baartman. I want to offer

---

[26] Audre Lorde, "Age, Race, Class and Sex: Women Redefining Difference" (delivered at the Copeland Colloquium, Amherst College, MA, April 1980) (reprinted in Audre Lorde, *Sister Outsider*, Trumansburg, NY: Crossing Press Feminist Series, 1984); Gloria Anzaldua, "La conciencia de la mestiza," reprinted in *Writing on the Body*, eds. Katie Conboy, Nadia Medina, and Sarah Stanbury (New York: Columbia University Press, 1997); Judith Butler, *Precarious Life: The Powers of Mourning and Violence* (London and New York: Verso, 2004); Erica Burman, "From Difference to Intersectionality: Challenges and Resources." *European Journal of Psychotherapy, Counselling and Health* 6, no. 4 (December 2004): 293–308; Andrea Krizsan, Hege Skjeie, and Judith Squires, eds., *Institutionalizing Intersectionality: The Changing Nature of European Equality Regimes* (Basingstoke: Palgrave Macmillan, 2012); Dagmar Schiek and Anna Lawson, eds., *European Union Non-Discrimination Law and Intersectionality: Investigating the Triangle of Racial, Gender and Disability Discrimination* (Farnham: Ashgate Publishing, 2011); Nira Yuval-Davis, "Intersectionality and Feminist Politics," *European Journal of Women's Studies* 13, no. 3 (2006): 193–209.

[27] Hill Collins, *Black Feminist Thought*, 128.

[28] Ibid.

[29] Carole Boyce Davies, *Black Women, Writing and Identity*, 153; Caren Kaplan, "The Politics of Location as Transnational Feminist Practice," in *Scattered Hegemonies, Postmodernity and Transnational Practice*, eds. Inderpal Grewal and Caren Kaplan (Minneapolis: University of Minnesota Press, 1994).

[30] Elspeth Probyn, "The Spatial Imperative of Subjectivity," in *Handbook of Cultural Geography*, eds. Kay Anderson, Mona Domosh, Steve Pile, and Nigel Thrift (London: Sage, 2003), 290–299; Sara Ahmed, *Strange Encounters: Embodied Others in Post-Coloniality* (London: Routledge, 2000).

an encounter of Hill Collins's experience through a particular proximity to Audre Lorde via her 1978 paper "Uses of the Erotic: The Erotic as Power." The rationale for using this framework of analysis is, first, that Lorde's paper provides a feminist analysis of the intersection of objectification, the politics of location, and disconnection as key props in the foundation of patriarchal constructions of the erotic. The point here is that these are the same props used in patriarchal constructions of the cause and sanctioning of gender violence. Second, the juxtaposition of Patricia Hill Collins and Audre Lorde offers an encounter between two Black women that is in stark contrast to the one Patricia Hill Collins was invited to participate in with Sarah Baartman. In other words, the analysis and the tools used here offer a connection that does not trade on objectification and thus demonstrate an alternative non-objectifying connection. Non-objectifying connections offered, developed, and lived through the activism of Black feminist theory stand in defiance of the connections that trade on objectification described by Patricia Hill Collins that are present in too many accounts by survivors of gender violence and were not addressed in analyses and interventions designed to confront gender violence. Third, in the spirit of reassessing the tool box available to teach about and confront sexual violence against Black women, I want to demonstrate that Black feminist tools developed in the 1970s[31] work alongside tools developed in 2000 (Hill Collins includes her experience in the second, revised 2000 edition of her 1990 publication *Black Feminist Thought*), and actually the juxtaposition of the activism of Black feminist thinking across space and time is a tool that should be reassessed and used more often.

Productions of distortion

"I was invited to objectify myself in order to develop the objectivity that would allow me to participate in her objectification."[32] Here Hill Collins presents a sequence involving three main propositions contingent upon the first proposition:

- I objectify myself—I distort myself
- I develop objectivity—distorted thinking
- I participate in her objectification—distortion of her

---

[31] Lorde wrote her paper in 1978.

[32] Hill Collins, *Black Feminist Thought*, 142.

Examination of the sequence reveals that Hill Collins has to distort herself and her thinking as a condition for the distortion of Sarah Baartman. Hill Collins is invited to subject herself to the same process of objectification that Sarah Baartman is subjected to and, as will become evident, the invitation is a crucial aspect of the process. Furthermore, the distortion of Baartman into an object is the distortion of Hill Collins into an object and, ultimately, the distortion of all Black women into objects. What is performed here is the construction of the objectification of the Black woman produced through a repetitive chain of distortions. What is demonstrated here is the function of the construction of the distortion.

The point is not the fact of the distortion. Indeed, to rest on this alone would be a distraction and diversion from the crux of the matter—namely, the production of the construction of distortion and what this production functions to do. Nor is this to imply that there could be no distortion. Furthermore, the inquiry into the function and production of the construction would do well to include questions of who and what is foreclosed, and who and what is privileged, in the construction. Butler explains that "construction is neither a subject nor its act, but a process of reiteration by which both 'subjects' and 'acts' come to appear at all. There is no power that acts, but only a reiterated acting that is power in its persistence and instability."[33] In "Uses of the Erotic: The Erotic as Power," Lorde repeatedly refers to distortion as a mechanism of the "reiterated acting that is power." Lorde's use of the rhetorical device of repetition performatively re-inscribes the relationship between distortion and reiteration as demonstrated in the following excerpts: "In order to perpetuate itself, every oppression must corrupt or distort those various sources of power within the culture of the oppressed that can provide energy for change"[34] and "...that we cannot grow beyond whatever distortions we may find within ourselves keeps us docile and loyal and obedient, externally defined, and leads us to accept many facets of our oppression as women"[35] and also "...this misnaming of the need and the deed give rise to that distortion which results in pornography and obscenity..."[36] In other words, distortion functions as a mechanism to sustain and extend oppression. However, the rigor of the analysis and its translation into effective feminist

---

[33] Judith Butler, *Bodies That Matter: On the Discursive Limits of "Sex"* (New York: Routledge, 1993), 9.

[34] Audre Lorde, "Uses of the Erotic: The Erotic as Power," 53.

[35] Ibid., 58.

[36] Ibid., 59.

interventions lie in being suspicious of anything that claims to have escaped distortion.

Setting up the polarities of the "distorted" and the "not distorted" may function as a political tactic of the "*strategic* use of positivist essentialism"[37] (emphasis original). However, failure of the tactic lies in the transformation of the essentialist from a strategy to a claim of representation. This point is made by Spivak in her explanation of two meanings of the word "representation": "Treading in your shoes, wearing your shoes, that's *Vertretung*. Representation in that sense: political representation. *Darstellung-Dar*, there, same cognate. *Stellen*, is to place, so "placing there." *Representing*: proxy and portrait.... Now, the thing to remember is that in the act of representing politically, you actually represent yourself and your constituency in the portrait sense, as well"[38] (italics and emphasis original).

Applying Spivak's two meanings of "representation" to the issue of distortion, it would seem that distortion by proxy or "treading in the shoes of" Baartman would enable a discourse and analysis of the pornographic objectification of her body, while holding on to the temporal and spatial instability of "treading in" the shoes of indeterminate perspectives. For example, the body of Baartman is not in fact distorted. The distortion is a product of, and produces, the reiterated acts of the abuse of power. The body of Baartman is "treading in the shoes of distortion," and any analysis of the "representation" of her body in the shoes of distortion must be from a position of "treading in the shoes of" "conventions of representational realism."[39] However, a "placing there" of distortion, so that Baartman is represented as distorted, and the portrait of a distorted Baartman, functions to produce a fixed, concrete, essentialist identification of Baartman as the personification of distortion. Spivak's point, however, is not a reductionist proxy/portrait binary. Spivak contends that although it is important to understand the difference between essentialist and anti-essentialist positions, it is not possible to deconstruct "the treading in the shoes of" without simultaneously deconstructing the essentialist position that these are the true authentic shoes,

---

[37] Gayatri Chakravorty Spivak, *In Other Worlds: Essays in Cultural Politics* (London: Methuen, 2006), 281.

[38] Gayatri Chakravorty Spivak, *The Post-Colonial Critic: Interviews, Strategies, Dialogues*, ed. Sarah Harasym (New York: Routledge, 1990), 108.

[39] Sue Wilkinson and Celia Kitzinger, eds., *Representing the Other: A Feminism and Psychology Reader* (London: Sage, 1996), 15.

my shoes, and the only shoes. This would be tantamount to claiming that if the shoe fits, then the true subject of the shoe has been located. Landry and MacLean summarize the predicament succinctly: "[t]he critique of essentialism is predicated upon essentialism."[40]

The totalizing effect of distortion

The construction of distortion is effective because it serves to mask, disavow, and censor the existence, space, and energy for the disruption and destabilization of oppression. Perhaps this is why Butler states that "[w]hat I would propose in place of these conceptions of construction is a return to the notion of matter not as a site or surface, but as *a process of materialisation that stabilizes over time to produce the effect of boundary, fixity, and surface we call matter.*" (emphasis original)[41]

The temporal and spatial, fixed (in both senses of the word—immobile and contrived) matter of Black women's bodies produces fixed, degrading, obscene, shameful objectifications that legitimize sexual violence. Sianne Ngai explains that "...disgust is never ambivalent about its object. More specifically, it is never prone to producing the confusions between subject and object... disgust strengthens and polices this boundary."[42] The totalizing disgust of the obscene Black woman functions to fix "...its object as 'intolerable,' disgust undeniably has been and will continue to be instrumentalized in oppressive and violent ways."[43] Incorporating the process of stabilization imprisons women within the "*boundary, fixity*" (emphasis original)[44] of docility, obedience, and loyalty with no apparent alternative position. The repetitive action of performativity[45] continues as "*boundary, fixity*" becomes translated into women's compliance with sexual violence.

Patricia Williams's analysis demonstrates something of how the "*boundary, fixity*" works with specific reference to objectification: "A habit of think-

---

[40] Donna Landry and Gerald MacLean, eds., *The Spivak Reader: Selected Works of Gayatri Chakravorty Spivak* (New York: Routledge, 1996), 7.

[41] Judith Butler, *Bodies That Matter: On the Discursive Limits of "Sex"* (New York: Routledge, 1993), 9.

[42] Sianne Ngai, *Ugly Feelings* (Cambridge: Harvard University Press, 2005), 335.

[43] Ibid., 340.

[44] Judith Butler, *Bodies That Matter*, 9.

[45] Judith Butler (1999), "Preface." In J. Butler, *Gender Trouble: Feminism and the Subversion of Identity*. 3rd ed. (New York: Routledge, 2006) (originally published in 1990 by Routledge).

ing that permits the imagination of the voyeur to indulge in auto-sensation that obliterates the subjectivity of the observed. A habit of thinking that allows that self-generated sensation to substitute for interaction with a whole other human being, to substitute for listening or conversing or caring... the object is pacified, a malleable 'thing' upon which to project."[46] Here, Williams's use of "a habit of thinking" resonates with Butler's "reiterated acting that is power," and Williams's reference to the "auto-sensation that obliterates the subjectivity of the observed" resonates with Lorde's rejection of "...using another's feelings as we would use a kleenex."[47] Objectification is a mechanism that forges "false and treacherous connections"[48] through a process of disconnection based on distortion. This is illustrated in the disconnection of sensation from feeling, and the disconnection of "self-generated sensation" from "interaction with a other whole human being."[49] In accordance with Williams's analysis, Lorde concludes that "Pornography emphasizes sensation without feeling."[50] Lorde is clear that "The erotic cannot be felt secondhand."[51] Hill Collins explains, "Contemporary pornography consists of a series of icons or representations that focus the viewer's attention on the relationship between the portrayed individual and the general qualities ascribed to that class of individuals."[52] These intersecting distortions become an incorporated norm that "...qualifies a body for life within the domain of cultural intelligibility."[53] However, the terms of viability are simultaneously the terms for lack of viability. Lack of viability of Black women as human beings "within the domain of cultural intelligibility" is well-documented by Black feminists.[54]

---

[46] Patricia Williams, *The Rooster's Egg: On the Persistence of Prejudice* (Cambridge, MA: Harvard University Press, 1995), 123.

[47] Audre Lorde, "Uses of the Erotic: The Erotic as Power," 58.

[48] Audre Lorde (1980), "Age, Race, Class, and Sex: Women Redefining Difference." In Audre Lorde, *Sister Outsider: Essays and Speeches* (Trumansburg, NY: The Crossing Press, 1984), 115.

[49] Patricia Williams, *The Rooster's Egg: On the Persistence of Prejudice*, 123.

[50] Audre Lorde, "Uses of the Erotic: The Erotic as Power," 54.

[51] Ibid., 59.

[52] Ibid., 136.

[53] Judith Butler, *Bodies That Matter*, 2.

[54] Angela Davis, "Rape, Racism and the Capitalist Setting," *Black Scholar* 9, no. 7 (1978): 24–30; Angela Davis, *Women, Race and Class* (New York: Vintage Books, 1981); bell hooks, *Ain't I A Woman: Black Women and Feminism* (London: Pluto Press, 1982); Alice Walker, *You Can't Keep a Good Woman Down: Stories* (New York: Harcourt Brace Jovanovich, 1981); Alice Walker, *The Color Purple* (New York: Washington Square Press, 1982).

The invitation

> "...I was invited to objectify myself in order to develop the objectivity that would allow me to participate in her objectification."[55]

Other components of the sentence above open up further lines of inquiry, and it is worth dwelling upon these because the issues raised are the issues that Lorde is concerned with. They are issues that are fundamental to our understanding of the mechanisms used in sexual violence against women and the development of emancipatory interventions to confront this pernicious problem. Hill Collins uses words that simultaneously invoke her subjectivity and position her subjectivity in relation to Baartman. The uses of "I," "me," "myself," and "her" identify and locate the subjectivity of Hill Collins and Baartman as the conduit for the process of objectification. This stands in contrast to the invitation, which has no pronoun. Hill Collins states, "I was invited." Here, the lack of a pronoun, the use of the passive voice and an unnamed, unidentified inviter leave the "invited" unfixed. In other words, the initiator of the invitation is left open. Alistair Pennycook explains that pronouns "...are in fact very complex and political words, always raising difficult issues of who is being represented. There is, therefore, never an unproblematic 'we' or 'you' or 'they' or 'I' or 'he/she.'"[56] In the context of the situation in which Hill Collins was "invited to objectify myself in order to develop the objectivity that would allow me to participate in her objectification," the invitation could be epistemology, social constructions, social sanctions, and/or representations.

The questions that could be, and indeed, frequently are asked by women survivors of sexual violence are: does invitation imply choice? Does the choice invoked in the invitation designate responsibility? Survivors of gender violence are left feeling: if I am invited and accepted the invitation, then I am responsible for the consequences of the invitation. The invitation locates shame and blame with the survivor of sexual violence and not with the originator of the invitation, nor with the invitation itself. The invitation situates responsibility in the subjec-

---

[55] Hill Collins, *Black Feminist Thought*, 142.

[56] Alistair Pennycook, "The Politics of Pronouns," *ELT Journal* 48, no. 2 (April 1994): 173.

tivity of the survivor of sexual violence. This keeps the process of objectification alive so that self-blame becomes self-objectification, which in turn becomes a significant block to the self-connection that is so vital to the recovery process.

Objectification causes emotional, psychological, and physical fragmentation because the self becomes too contemptible to be in proximity with. This condition of self-abhorrence, self-blame, and overwhelming shame creates disintegration and prevents a sense of self-connection that is crucial to the recovery process. However, I would argue—and here is where I would question Lorde's proposal—that the challenge for feminist thinking and interventions is to hold on to a rigorous analytical framework in order to track the maneuvers of distortion. For example, the notion that distortion resides and functions only in disconnection would foreclose analysis of the location and function of distortion within self-connection.

Lorde argues that the process of disconnection functions to distort and suppress the erotic in order to prevent women from using the erotic as a source of power, revelation, and transformation: "[t]he erotic has often been misnamed by men and used against women. It has been made into the confused, the trivial, the psychotic, the plasticized sensation. For this reason, we have often turned away from the exploration and consideration of the erotic as a source of power and information, confusing it with its opposite, the pornographic."[57]

Close scrutiny of the language used by Lorde and Hill Collins indicates that this process of distortion is a construction; Hill Collins says, "in order to develop" and Lorde says, "[i]t has been made into." In other words, there is a deliberate manipulation occurring that these two, and many other Black feminists, seek to identify, expose, and challenge. Furthermore, the words "develop" and "made into" open up the possibility of a different "develop" and a different "made into," leaving room for social change, emancipatory interventions, imagination, and activism. Further close scrutiny of the words used by Hill Collins indicates further elements that intersect to produce a powerful package of distortion, objectification, and regulation. Her use of the word "objectivity" invokes the idea of an obtainable position of impartiality and neutrality, conjuring up the notion of a truth contingent upon fairness. The word "objectivity" functions

---

[57] Audre Lorde, "Uses of the Erotic: The Erotic as Power," 54.

to resist questioning, because to question that which has a claim of objectivity would be to question fairness, impartiality, and neutrality.

The psychological and emotional impact of this sequence is interrogated by "The Duluth Model: Social Change to End Violence against Women, Domestic Abuse Intervention Programs (DAIP)"[58] and articulated within the Duluth "Power and Control Wheel." The Duluth program discusses how the claim to "objectivity" is used by those who abuse power over women through sexual and domestic violation in order to distort perception. The consequence of distorted perception is self-doubt and a lack of trust in cognitive functioning. This results in confusion, fear, dependency, and deep internal disconnection. Lorde describes the process in the following way: "[a]s women, we have come to distrust that power which rises from our deepest and nonrational knowledge. We have been warned against it all our lives by the male world, which values this depth of feeling enough to keep women around in order to exercise it in the service of men, but which fears this same depth too much to examine the possibilities of it within themselves. So women are maintained at a distant/inferior position to be psychically milked, much the same way ants maintain colonies of aphids to provide a life-giving substance for their masters."[59] The unequal power relation that Lorde refers to is picked up in Hill Collins's use of the word "allow." Connotations of the word "allow" invoke a power dynamic between the "allowed" and that which, or who, "allows." This power dynamic conjures up the conditions upon which being "allowed" depends and gives rise to the notion of a border and criteria for crossing the border. To "allow" is not the same as to enable or to empower. Interestingly, Hill Collins places the passive "allow" with the active "participate" in which she is invited to be active. This implies more than a reductionist regime of visibility. In other words, "allow me to participate in her objectification" involves more than Hill Collins's looking at Baartman.

Just as racism operating within the regime of visibility has nothing and everything to do with the color of skin,[60] sexual violence against women, such as rape, pornography, sexual abuse, prostitution, forced marriage, and female genital mutilation, has nothing and everything to do with sex and the erotic.

---

[58] "The Duluth Model," http://www.theduluthmodel.org/.

[59] Audre Lorde, "Uses of the Erotic: The Erotic as Power," 53–54.

[60] Kalpana Seshadri-Crooks, *Desiring Whiteness: A Lacanian Analysis of Race* (London: Routledge, 2000).

In other words, "[t]he parallels between distortions of deep human feelings in racial oppression and of the distortions of the erotic in sexual oppression are striking."[61] Participation brings to mind all of the implications of Butler's theory of performativity and the repetitive re-inscribing of identity categories, subjectivity, and positioning. Hill Collins's use of the word "participation" invokes the ways in which racism and sexism intersect through mechanisms of representation as a tool of oppression. The role and meaning of "participation" are significant components of the self-blame, self-hatred, and self-disconnection that survivors of sexual violation grapple with, and have to confront in the process of recovery.

Disconnection and connection

Any intervention or analysis, whether packaged in the form of teaching, policy, activism, or scholarship in response to a problem, needs to have a detailed understanding of the mechanics of that problem—namely, how and why it works. Lorde argues that racist, homophobic, and patriarchal formulations of the erotic function to suppress detailed critical analysis, stating, "...we have often turned away from the exploration and consideration of the erotic as a source of power and information, confusing it with its opposite, the pornographic."[62] Here, Lorde's point is that the erotic is the source of critical inquiry, so that suppression of the erotic is, by definition, the suppression of detailed critical analysis.

The trick of the distortion of the erotic is that "confusing it with its opposite, the pornographic," means that the source of critical analysis to enable women to be "less willing to accept powerlessness, or those other supplied states of being... such as resignation, despair, self-effacement, depression, self-denial"[63] is where it is least expected. In other words, who would look to the pornographic as "our most profoundly creative source"?[64] Who would think of "the pornographic, the abused, and the absurd"[65] and "the trivial, the psychotic, the plasticized sensation"[66] as "a

---

[61] Hill Collins, *Black Feminist Thought*, 171.

[62] Audre Lorde, "Uses of the Erotic: The Erotic as Power," 54.

[63] Ibid., 58.

[64] Ibid., 59.

[65] Ibid.

[66] Ibid., 54.

well of replenishing and provocative force"[67] to women? In a racist, homophobic patriarchy, such juxtapositions would appear to be non-rational and chaotic. However, uncovering the mechanisms by which "We have been taught to suspect this resource, vilified, abused, and devalued within western society"[68] is precisely the task of breaking silence about sexual violence against women.

Indeed, a significant part of the journey of recovery for women survivors of sexual violence is being able to trust that "uses of the erotic" that wield "power *over*" can be displaced by "uses of the erotic" in a form of "power *to*." It should be noted that the notions of "power *over*" and "power *to*" that I am using here pick up on particular discourses of power that are used within some feminist activist contexts, primarily with specific reference to confronting sexual violence.[69]

Moving from generality to specificity

I propose that Lorde's feminist use of the erotic provides a rigorous framework for enabling "the transformation of silence into language and action"[70] that is vital for survivors of sexual violence. Lorde states that "...the erotic is not a question only of what we do; it is a question of how acutely and fully we can feel in the doing."[71] Furthermore, Lorde proposes: "Our erotic knowledge empowers us, becomes a lens through which we scrutinize all aspects of our existence, forcing us to evaluate those aspects honestly in terms of their relative meaning within our lives... not to settle for the convenient, the shoddy, the conventionally expected, nor the merely safe."[72] The therapeutic potential of feminist consciousness-rais-

---

[67] Ibid.

[68] Ibid., 53.

[69] Amy Allen, "Foucault on Power: A Theory for Feminists." In S.J. Hekman, ed., *Feminist Interpretations of Michel Foucault* (University Park, PA: Pennsylvania State University Press, 1996), 265–282; Amy Allen, "Rethinking Power," *Hypatia* 13, no. 1 (1998): 21–40; Amy Allen, *The Power of Feminist Theory: Domination, Resistance, Solidarity* (Boulder, CO: Westview Press, 1999); Amy Allen, *The Politics of Our Selves: Power, Autonomy, and Gender in Contemporary Critical Theory* (New York: Columbia University Press, 2008); A. Allen, "Power and the Politics of Difference: Oppression, Empowerment, and Transnational Justice," *Hypatia* 23, no. 3 (2008): 156–172; Jean Bethke Elshtain, "Feminist Discourse and Its Contents: Language, Power, and Meaning," *Signs: Journal of Women in Culture and Society* 7, no. 3 (Spring 1982): 603–621; Janice Yoder and Arnold Kahn, "Toward a Feminist Understanding of Women and Power," *Psychology of Women Quarterly* 16, no. 4 (December 1992): 381–388.

[70] Audre Lorde (1977), "The Transformation of Silence into Language and Action." In A. Lorde, *Sister Outsider: Essays and Speeches* (Trumansburg, NY: The Crossing Press, 1984), 40.

[71] Audre Lorde, "Uses of the Erotic: The Erotic as Power." 54.

[72] Ibid., 57.

ing and teaching about violence against women works in direct relation to "how acutely and fully" we collectively and honestly scrutinize the discourse, behaviors, and impact of sexual violence. For example, in relation to gender violence, this could represent moving from the "general" to the "specific." Too often, therapeutic and political interventions in relation to women's experiences of sexual violence fail to get close to the specificity of those experiences. Lorde argues that "[t]he erotic is a measure,"[73] and application of this in terms of moving from the general to the specific is vital for a number of reasons:

First, staying with the "general" is used to silence the "specific," creating a barrier to survivors speaking out about the particular acts and processes they have endured, and continue to endure. Generalities skim over the specificities of the horrors of sexual violation.

Second, overt and subtle resistance to interrogating the specific mechanisms used in the control and regulation of women subjected to gender violence reaffirms the survivor's sense of shame, blame, and disconnection. The logic becomes that the unnameable must remain unnameable because it is so abhorrent.

Third, resistance to naming the specific acts and processes used in gender violence confirms to the survivor that the experience needs to remain hidden and silenced in order not to contaminate others.

Finally, resting within the "psychic retreat"[74] of generalities is to be complicit with, and to maintain distance from, the destructive consequences of disconnection. The disconnection "...puts woman in the position of experiencing herself only fragmentarily..."[75] and maintains her isolation from others.

"Uses of the Erotic": Fear and proximity

Both Ahmed[76] and Lorde explore the ways in which fear operates in relation to two specific axes: those of "proximity" and "anticipation." The logic is that, because we fear the anticipated, we keep a distance; we do not get too near to

---

[73] Ibid., 54.

[74] John Steiner, *Psychic Retreats: Pathological Organizations in Psychotic, Neurotic and Borderline Patients* (London: Routledge, 1993), 1.

[75] Luce Irigaray (1977), *This Sex Which Is Not One*, reprinted in Katie Conboy, Nadia Medina, and Sarah Stanbury, eds., *Writing on the Body: Female Embodiment and Feminist Theory* (New York: Columbia University Press, 1997), 254.

[76] Sara Ahmed, *The Cultural Politics of Emotion* (London: Routledge, 2004).

the unknown. In turn, this regulates movement. It follows, therefore, that if the anticipated is to be kept at a distance to prevent close proximity, then this will influence, inform, and affect movement, position, and situation. Productions of the distortion of the erotic keep women at a distance from each other and from their own/collective creativity. Subsequently, productions of distortion function to make the notion and/or experience of difference suspect. Ahmed explains it in the following way, "Fear's relation to the object has an important temporal dimension: we fear an object that approaches us.... Fear involves an *anticipation* of hurt or injury. Fear projects us from the present into a future.... So the object that we fear is not simply before us, or in front of us, but impresses upon us in the present, as an anticipated pain in the future"[77] (emphasis original). The point is that fear gains legitimacy through terror, anxiety, and a phobia of the anticipated, of that which is unknown, unfamiliar, and different. Proximity is key; no one wants to get too close to that which they are fearful of. This restricts movement, limits, regulates (becomes self-regulating of) position, and maintains a fixity. This is not in keeping with the notion of a shifting, decentered, unanchored epistemology and subjectivity. This is not in keeping with the qualities, experience, knowledge, and power necessary to lessen the threat of difference, to stretch out and build bridges with others.

This delimited, fixed, distant position influences the vantage point for vision and looking. Donna Haraway also asks some important questions in relation to vision and looking: "How to see? Where to see from? What limits to vision? What to see for? Whom to see with? Who gets to have more than one point of view? Who gets blinded? Who wears blinders? Who interprets the visual field? What other sensory powers do we wish to cultivate besides vision?"[78] Interrogation of these questions requires close proximity to the concepts, positions, and elements that have been kept at a distance. Implicit in the questions posed by Haraway is that some are allowed or enabled to see and some are not; some have their vision restricted and some do not. Butler comments, "This kind of questioning often engenders vertigo and terror over the possibility of losing social sanctions, of leaving a solid social station and place. That this terror is so well known gives the most credence to the notion that gender identity rests on

---

[77] Ibid., 65.

[78] Donna Haraway (1988), *The Persistence of Vision*, reprinted in Katie Conboy, Nadia Medina, and Sarah Stanbury, eds., *Writing on the Body: Female Embodiment and Feminist Theory* (New York: Columbia University Press, 1997), 289.

the unstable bedrock of human invention."[79] Similarly, Ahmed concludes, "So the question of what is fearsome as well as who should be afraid is bound up with the politics of mobility, whereby the mobility of some bodies involves or even requires the restriction of the mobility of others."[80]

"Uses of the Erotic": The spatial politics of fear

In relation to the specific ways in which fear regulates movement and orchestrates a particular relationship between the body, the psyche, and the world, both Lorde and Ahmed refer to the capacity for "being open" or "openness." Lorde states, "[a]nother important way in which the erotic connection functions is the *open* and fearless underlying of my capacity for joy. In the way my body stretches to music and *opens* into response, hearkening to its deepest rhythms, so every level upon which I sense also *opens* to the erotically satisfying experience..."[81] (emphasis added). Notice that Lorde puts together "open and fearless" in her description of how the erotic functions. Conversely, Ahmed explains how fear operates precisely not to open up: "...openness itself is read as a site of potential danger, and as demanding evasive action. Emotions may involve *readings of such openness*, as spaces where bodies and worlds meet and leak into each other. Fear involves reading such openings as dangerous; the openness of the body to the world involves a sense of danger, which is *anticipated as a future pain or injury....* Fear involves shrinking the body; *it restricts the body's mobility precisely insofar as it seems to prepare the body for flight*"[82] (emphasis original). Here, Ahmed makes the link between reading openness and shrinking containment that results in a "spatial politics of fear."[83] Ahmed uses this link to develop a feminist analysis of how women are restricted within social spaces. Taking up the constituent elements of fear, including the representation of women's bodies, the demand for retreat as the body recoils and shrinks, and the subsequent shrinking of social space, Ahmed concludes, "Vulnerability is not an inherent characteristic of

---

[79] Judith Butler (1987), "Variations on Sex and Gender: Beauvoir, Wittig, Foucault," in *The Judith Butler Reader*, ed. Sara Salih with Judith Butler (Oxford: Blackwell Publishing, 2004), 27.

[80] Sara Ahmed, *The Cultural Politics of Emotion* (London: Routledge, 2004), 70.

[81] Audre Lorde, "Uses of the Erotic: The Erotic as Power," 56.

[82] Ahmed, *The Cultural Politics of Emotion*, 69.

[83] Ibid.

women's bodies; rather, it is an effect that works to secure femininity as a delimitation of movement in the public, and over-inhabitance in the private."[84] Similarly, Lorde speaks about how particular spaces, including the private, are delimited because "...the erotic is so feared, and so often relegated to the bedroom alone..."[85] The restriction of women's access to certain spaces legitimates an artificial separation between public and private, and between legitimate and illegitimate mobility, producing a binary that Lorde's reclamation of the erotic seeks to challenge.

In relation to the binary between public and private spaces, and how this particular binary constitutes subjectivity and manages differences, Grosz[86] pushes the analysis further. Speaking about lesbianism specifically and discourses about the erotic, desire, and women's sexuality in general, Grosz talks about the "... split between what one is and what one does that produces the very possibility of a notion like 'the closet,' a distinction between private and public that refuses integration."[87] The split between public and private serves as a key element preserving "regimes of sexuality."[88] This "codification and control of sexuality"[89] functions to legitimize sexual violence against women exemplified in continuing legal and policy battles in relation to rape, immigration, and the physical, emotional, and material implications of domestic abuse. It is clear from the wealth of feminist scholarship in this area that the binary of public/private operates to control and constrain what is heard/unheard, seen/unseen, in relation to women's voices, evidence, and representations.[90] Throughout her paper, Lorde shifts between, and outlines, the inextricable links between physical and social spaces, and mobility and psychic spaces. Gloria Anzaldúa comments, "Borders are set up to define the places that are safe and unsafe, to distinguish *us* from *them*. A border is a divid-

---

[84] Ibid., 70.

[85] Audre Lorde, "Uses of the Erotic: The Erotic as Power," 57.

[86] Elizabeth Grosz, *Space, Time and Perversion* (London: Routledge, 1995).

[87] Ibid., 225.

[88] Ibid., 217.

[89] Ibid., 221.

[90] Erica Burman, "Engendering Culture in Psychology," *Theory and Psychology* 15, no. 4 (2005): 527–548; Mark Cowling and Paul Reynolds, eds. *Making Sense of Sexual Consent* (Aldershot: Ashgate Publishing, 2004); Miranda Horvath and Jennifer Brown, eds. *Rape: Challenging Contemporary Thinking* (Cullompton: Willan Publishing, 2009); Selma James, *Sex, Race and Class: The Perspective of Winning; A Selection of Writings, 1952–2011* (Oakland: PM Press, 2012); Nadia Siddiqui, Ismail Sajida, and Meg Allen, *Safe to Return? Pakistani Women, Domestic Violence and Access to Refugee Protection; A Report of a Trans-National Research Project Conducted in the UK and Pakistan* (Manchester: South Manchester Law Centre in partnership with Manchester Metropolitan University, 2008); Ingrid Palmary, Erica Burman, Khatidja Chantler, Peace Kiguwa, eds., *Gender and Migration: Feminist Interventions* (Zed Books, 2010).

ing line, a narrow strip along a steep edge. A borderland is a vague and undeter-mined place created by the emotional residue of an unnatural boundary. It is in a constant state of transition. The prohibited and forbidden are its inhabitants" (emphasis original).[91] In contrast to the spatial politics of fear, Lorde provides a feminist analysis of the ways in which intersubjective connections could bridge differences, cross dichotomous borders, and transgress boundaries prescribed by a patriarchal epistemology of the erotic. Lorde's treatise on the erotic can be read as a treatise outlining the erotic as a force for interdependency, for connection, and for a mutual sharing, with the potential for transformational emancipatory change. In her concluding remarks of her address, Lorde states: "This deep participation has often been the forerunner for joint concerted actions not possible before."[92] Here, Lorde is not just giving voice to a vision yet to be realized, but, rather, she is indicating that "the erotic as power" as feminist praxis already exists "more within the realm of the 'elsewhere' of diasporic imaginings than the precisely locatable."[93]

"Uses of the Erotic": Bridge of connection

Teaching about the issue of sexual violence against women requires detailed deconstruction of the constituent components of the mechanisms used within this violation. The component of disconnection is central both in terms of the process of the abuse of power and in relation to the trauma experienced as a result of that abuse. Lorde presents a detailed reassessment of the erotic, expos-ing techniques such as fear, proximity, anticipation, mobility, and vision used by patriarchy to distort the erotic as a force of connection to one of disconnection. Furthermore, Lorde demonstrates that the sum of these is greater than the indi-vidual parts to create an effective strategy of appropriation that places a woman "in the position of experiencing herself only fragmentarily, in the little-struc-tured margins of a dominant ideology, as waste, or excess, what is left of a mirror invested by the (masculine) 'subject' to reflect himself, to copy himself."[94]

---

[91] Gloria Anzaldúa, *Borderlands/La Frontera: The New Mestiza* (3rd ed.) (San Francisco: Aunt Lute Books, 2007), 25.

[92] Audre Lorde, "Uses of the Erotic: The Erotic as Power," 59.

[93] Carole Boyce Davies, *Black Women, Writing and Identity*, 88.

[94] Luce Irigaray (1977), *This Sex Which is Not One*, reprinted in Katie Conboy, Nadia Medina, and Sarah Stanbury, eds., *Writing on the Body: Female Embodiment and Feminist Theory* (New York: Columbia University Press, 1997), 254.

Examination of disconnection under the analytical lens of Lorde's work indicates that the component of disconnection is not an arbitrary or random consequence of the experience of gender violence. Lorde emphasizes a Black feminist "uses of the erotic" that is primarily a force for connection that enables "unbearable rationality" and prioritizes "the importance of intersubjective bonds,"[95] which recognizes multiple, decentered, shifting subjectivity. Thus the erotic functions as a necessary bridge enabling deep self-connection and connection with others in the situation where "The contingent, self-incoherent subject is dependent upon the recognition of the other," which means that "we are from the start, ethically implicated in the lives of others."[96] Lorde explains, "For the bridge which connects them is formed by the erotic—the sensual—those physical, emotional, and psychic expressions of what is deepest and strongest and richest within each of us, being shared: the passions of love, in its deepest meanings."[97] Thus it is possible to re-read Lorde's vision of the "uses of the erotic" as part of a wider tradition of Black feminist discourses on connection and difference that both preceded and anticipated Kimberlé Crenshaw's seminal work[98] on, and current debates about, intersectionality. This point is demonstrated in Lorde's claim that the erotic "... forms a bridge between the sharers which can be the basis for understanding much of what is not shared between them, and lessens the threat of their difference."[99] Here I want to make a link between Lorde's metaphor of "bridge," Hill Collins's experience of objectification, and the necessity for intersectional approaches to feminist thinking and interventions to confront sexual violence against women.[100]

Conclusion

Hill Collins identifies three sequential elements in her experience and process of gender violation, namely: "to objectify," or disconnection from self; "objectivity,"

---

[95] Judith Butler, "Giving an Account of Myself" (Spinoza Lecture 32.2 21–41 2002 in *Diacritics*) (reprinted in *The Judith Butler Reader*, ed. Sara Salih with Judith Butler, Oxford: Blackwell Publishing, 2004).

[96] Ibid.

[97] Audre Lorde, "Uses of the Erotic: The Erotic as Power," 56.

[98] Kimberlé Crenshaw, *Demarginalizing the Intersection of Race and Sex: A Black Feminist Critique of Antidiscrimination Doctrine, Feminist Theory, and Antiracist Politics* (Chicago: University of Chicago Legal Forum, 1989).

[99] Audre Lorde, "Uses of the Erotic: The Erotic as Power," 56.

[100] L.L. Lockhart and F.S. Danis, eds., *Domestic Violence: Intersectionality and Culturally Competent Practice* (New York: Columbia University Press, 2010).

or disconnection from mobility of position; and "objectification," or disconnection from other women. The point is that connection necessitates close deconstruction of and resistance to the mechanisms of disconnection. Lorde offers a vivid, sensual description of the intimacy involved in a proximity of connection: "During World War II, we bought sealed plastic packets of white, uncolored margarine, with a tiny, intense pellet of yellow coloring perched like a topaz just inside the clear skin of the bag. We would leave the margarine out for a while to soften, and then we would pinch the little pellet to break it inside the bag, releasing the rich yellowness into the soft pale mass of margarine. Then taking it carefully between our fingers, we would knead it gently back and forth, over and over, until the color had spread throughout the whole pound bag of margarine, thoroughly coloring it. I find the erotic such a kernel within myself. When released from its intense and constrained pellet, it flows through and colors my life with a kind of energy that heightens and sensitizes and strengthens all my experience."[101]

Application of the essence of this description to teaching, policy, intervention, activism, and scholarship raises questions concerning who or what is allowed to influence or color strategies, service provision, campaigns, law, and therapeutic work. A key question is, how is the issue of connection and disconnection considered in encounters with survivors of gender violence, in teaching and learning about sexual violence, among providers of services and between different organizations, different discourses, disciplines, and ideological positions? I contend that the activism of Black feminist theory is essential in addressing the complexities of this mission that is a matter of life and death for women.

Implications for teaching

This paper investigates the constitutive "Uses of the Erotic" with specific reference to:

- The problematic of the guises and function of "distortion";
- The mutually contingent, constitutive relationships between fear and proximity, and disconnection and connection;

---

[101] Audre Lorde, "Uses of the Erotic," 57.

- How Lorde identifies and proposes an alternative radical reworking of the erotic as the basis for harnessing the power for transformation;
- 'Uses of the Erotic: The Erotic as Power" as a tool for intervention and thinking in relation to violence against women.

I demonstrate that the strategies of a close re-reading of the construction of Lorde's text, tracing the lines of her inquiry, exploration of her claims, and textual analysis of her literary techniques, demonstrate how she builds a theory of reclamation as a mode of political resistance. For example, her title, "Uses of the Erotic: The Erotic as Power," refuses any fixed, decided position of possession, or right or wrong. The title itself is an indeterminate space without protagonist, without moral judgment, and without a decided "uses of." Left open, the unknown, unspecified demarcations of "uses of" leaves space for the signification of the erotic to be altered. The uncertainty invoked in the title stands in defiance of the fixed positions of the male-fashioned erotic that she is contesting. However, the audience is left in no doubt that there is an inextricable relationship between the erotic and power.

Questions

1. What are the "uses of the erotic" a production of, and what do the "uses of the erotic" produce?
2. How can Audre Lorde's Black feminist "Uses of the Erotic: The Erotic as Power" function as "...a lens through which we scrutinize all aspects of our existence, forcing us to evaluate those aspects honestly in terms of their relative meaning within our lives"?[102]

Assignments

1. With specific reference to violence against women, provide a critical analysis of how Audre Lorde's "Uses of the Erotic: The Erotic as Power" provides "a new critical social theory that provides us with the grammar

---

[102] Audre Lorde, "Uses of the Erotic: The Erotic as Power," 57.

and vocabulary to describe and define difference and the complex nature of oppression."[103]

2. "Representation is never merely descriptive: it serves also a constitutive and regulatory function which is obscured in (but never absent from) accounts relying upon conventions of representational realism."[104] Thinking about the implications of this quote, provide a critical analysis of the function and production of exhibiting the African slave woman Sarah Baartman as the anthropological freak called "Hottentot Venus."

3. Placing Lorde alongside Foucault, provide a critical analytical exploration of how the construction of the erotic is "...one of the prime effects of power that certain bodies, certain gestures, certain discourses, certain desires, come to be identified and constituted as individuals."[105]

4. With specific reference to "Uses of the Erotic: The Erotic as Power," provide a critical analysis of the inevitable tensions in proposing the interdependency of difference and non-hierarchical alliances, while advocating for recognition of the specificity of the lives of Black women.

REFERENCES

Ahmed, Sara. *Strange Encounters: Embodied Others in Post-Coloniality*. London: Routledge, 2000.

Ahmed, Sara. *The Cultural Politics of Emotion*. London: Routledge, 2004.

Alarcón, Norma. "The Theoretical Subject(s) of This Bridge Called My Back and Anglo-American Feminism." In *Making Face, Making Soul/Haciendo Caras: Creative and Critical Perspectives by Women of Color*, ed. G. Anzaldúa, 356–369. San Francisco: Aunt Lute Books, 1990.

Allen, Amy. "Foucault on Power: A Theory for Feminists." In *Feminist Interpretations of Michel Foucault*, ed. S.J. Hekman, 265–282. University Park, PA: Pennsylvania State University Press, 1996.

Allen, Amy. "Rethinking Power." *Hypatia* 13, no. 1 (1998): 21–40.

---

[103] R.P. Byrd, "Introduction: Create Your Own Fire; Audre Lorde and the Tradition of Black Radical Thought." In *I Am Your Sister: Collected and Unpublished Writings of Audre Lorde*, eds. R.P. Byrd, J. Betsch Cole, and B. Guy-Sheftall (Oxford: Oxford University Press, 2009), 21.

[104] Sue Wilkinson and Celia Kitzinger, eds., *Representing the Other: A Feminism and Psychology Reader* (London: Sage, 1996), 15.

[105] M. Foucault, "Two Lectures," in *Power/Knowledge: Selected Interviews and Other Writings, 1972–1977, by Michel Foucault*, ed. C. Gordon (Brighton: Harvester, 1980), 98.

Allen, Amy. *The Power of Feminist Theory: Domination, Resistance, Solidarity*. Boulder: Westview Press, 1999.

Allen, Amy. "Power and the Politics of Difference: Oppression, Empowerment, and Transnational Justice." *Hypatia* 23, no. 3 (2008): 156–172.

Allen, Amy. *The Politics of Our Selves: Power, Autonomy, and Gender in Contemporary Critical Theory*. New York: Columbia University Press, 2008.

Amos, Valerie, and Pratibha Parmar, "Challenging Imperial Feminism." *Feminist Review* 17 (1984): 3–19.

Anzaldúa, Gloria. *Borderlands/La Frontera: The New Mestiza*, 3rd ed. San Francisco: Aunt Lute Books, 2007.

Boyce Davies, Carole. *Black Women, Writing and Identity: Migrations of the Subject*. London: Routledge, 1994.

Brah, Avtar. *Cartographies of Diaspora: Contesting Identities*. Abingdon: Routledge, 1996.

Brah, Avtar, and Ann Phoenix. "Ain't I A Woman? Revisiting Intersectionality." *Journal of International Women's Studies* 5, no. 3 (May 1, 2004): 75–87.

Burman, Erica. "From Difference to Intersectionality: Challenges and Resources." *European Journal of Psychotherapy, Counselling and Health* 6, no. 4 (December 2004): 293–308.

Burman, Erica. "Engendering Culture in Psychology." *Theory and Psychology* 15, no. 4 (2005): 527–548.

Butler, Judith. (1999) "Preface." In J. Butler, *Gender Trouble: Feminism and the Subversion of Identity*, 3rd ed. New York: Routledge, 2006. (Originally published in 1990 by Routledge.)

Butler, Judith. *Bodies That Matter: On the Discursive Limits of "Sex."* New York: Routledge, 1993.

Butler, Judith. "Giving an Account of Myself" (Spinoza Lecture 2002 in *Diacritics* 32.2, 21–41). Reprinted in *The Judith Butler Reader*, ed. Sara Salih with Judith Butler. Oxford: Blackwell Publishing, 2004.

Butler, Judith. *Precarious Life: The Powers of Mourning and Violence*. London and New York: Verso, 2004.

Byrd, R.P. "Introduction: Create Your Own Fire; Audre Lorde and the Tradition of Black Radical Thought." In *I Am Your Sister: Collected and Unpublished Writings of Audre Lorde*, eds. R.P. Byrd, J. Betsch Cole, and B. Guy-Sheftall, 3–36. Oxford: Oxford University Press, 2009.

Christian, Barbara. (1987) "The Race for Theory." In *The Black Feminist Reader*, eds. J. James and T.D. Sharpley-Whiting. Oxford: Blackwell Publishers, 2000, 11–23.

Clifton, Crais, and Pamela Scully. *Sara Baartman and the Hottentot Venus: A Ghost Story and a Biography*. Princeton: Princeton University Press, 2008.

Cowling, Mark, and Paul Reynolds, eds. *Making Sense of Sexual Consent*. Aldershot: Ashgate Publishing, 2004.

Crenshaw, Kimberlé. "Mapping the Margins: Intersectionality, Identity Politics, and Violence Against Women of Color." *Stanford Law Review* 43, no. 6 (1991): 1241–1299.

Crenshaw, Kimberlé. *Demarginalizing the Intersection of Race and Sex: A Black Feminist Critique of Antidiscrimination Doctrine, Feminist Theory, and Antiracist Politics.* Chicago: University of Chicago Legal Forum, 1989.

Davis, Angela. "Rape, Racism and the Capitalist Setting." *Black Scholar* 9, no. 7 (1978): 24–30.

Davis, Angela. *Women, Race and Class.* New York: Vintage Books, 1981.

Davis, Kathy. "Intersectionality as Buzzword: A Sociology of Science Perspective on What Makes a Feminist Theory Successful." *Feminist Theory* 9, no. 1 (April 2008): 67–85.

Elshtain, Jean Bethke. "Feminist Discourse and Its Contents: Language, Power, and Meaning." *Signs: Journal of Women in Culture and Society* 7, no. 3 (Spring 1982): 603–621.

Foucault, M. "Two Lectures." In C. Gordon, ed. *Power/Knowledge: Selected Interviews and Other Writings, 1972–1977, by Michel Foucault*, 80–105. Brighton: Harvester, 1980.

Grosz, Elizabeth. *Space, Time and Perversion.* London: Routledge, 1995.

Haraway, Donna (1988). "The Persistence of Vision." In *Writing on the Body: Female Embodiment and Feminist Theory*, eds. Katie Conboy, Nadia Medina, and Sarah Stanbury, 283–295. New York: Columbia University Press, 1997.

Helma Lutz, Maria Teresa Herrera Vivar, and Linda Supik, eds. *Framing Intersectionality: Debates on a Multi-Faceted Concept in Gender Studies.* Farnham: Ashgate, 2011.

Hill Collins, Patricia. *Black Feminist Thought: Knowledge, Consciousness, and the Politics of Empowerment.* London: Routledge, 1990 (2nd ed., 2000).

hooks, bell. *Ain't I A Woman: Black Women and Feminism.* London: Pluto Press, 1982.

Horvath, Miranda, and Jennifer Brown, eds. *Rape: Challenging Contemporary Thinking.* Cullompton: Willan Publishing, 2009.

Irigaray, Luce. "This Sex Which Is Not One" (1977). Reprinted in *Writing on the Body: Female Embodiment and Feminist Theory.* New York: Columbia University Press, 1997.

James, Selma. *Sex, Race and Class: The Perspective of Winning; A Selection of Writings, 1952–2011.* Oakland: PM Press, 2012.

Kaplan, Caren. "The Politics of Location as Transnational Feminist Practice." In *Scattered Hegemonies, Postmodernity and Transnational Practice*, eds. Inderpal Grewal and Caren Kaplan. Minneapolis: University of Minnesota Press, 1994.

Keating, AnaLouise. *Women Reading Women Writing: Self-Invention in Paula Gunn Allen, Gloria Anzaldua and Audre Lorde.* Philadelphia: Temple University Press, 1996.

Krizsan, Andrea, Hege Skjeie, and Judith Squires, eds. *Institutionalizing Intersectionality: The Changing Nature of European Equality Regimes.* Basingstoke: Palgrave Macmillan, 2012.

Landry, Donna, and Gerald MacLean, eds. *The Spivak Reader: Selected Works of Gayatri Chakravorty Spivak*. New York: Routledge, 1996.

Lockhart, L.L., and F.S. Danis, eds. *Domestic Violence: Intersectionality and Culturally Competent Practice*. New York: Columbia University Press, 2010.

Lorde, Audre. "Age, Race, Class and Sex: Women Redefining Difference." Delivered at the Copeland Colloquium, Amherst College, MA, April 1980 (reprinted in Audre Lorde. *Sister Outsider*. Trumansburg, NY: Crossing Press Feminist Series, 1984).

Lorde, Audre. "Uses of the Erotic: The Erotic as Power." Paper delivered at the Fourth Berkshire Conference on the History of Women, Mount Holyoke College, MA, August 25, 1978. (Published as a pamphlet by Out and Out Books; reprinted in Audre Lorde. *Sister Outsider*. Trumansburg, NY: Crossing Press Feminist Series, 1984.)

Lorde, Audre (1977). "The Transformation of Silence into Language and Action." In Audre Lorde. *Sister Outsider*. Trumansburg, NY: Crossing Press Feminist Series, 1984.

Mama, Amina. *Beyond the Masks: Race, Gender and Subjectivity*. London: Routledge, 1995.

Lori Parks, Suzan. *Venus*. Dramatists Play Service, 1998.

 McCall, Leslie. "The Complexity of Intersectionality." *Signs: Journal of Women in Culture and Society* 30, no. 3 (Spring 2005): 1771–1800.

Mohanty, Chandra Talpade (1984). "Under Western Eyes: Feminist Scholarship and Colonial Discourses." In C.T. Mohanty, *Feminism without Borders: Decolonizing Theory, Practicing Solidarity*, 17–42. Durham: Duke University Press, 2003.

Nash, Jennifer. "Re-Thinking Intersectionality." *Feminist Review* 89 (2008): 1–15.

Ngai, Sianne. *Ugly Feelings*. Cambridge: Harvard University Press, 2005.

Palmary, Ingrid, Erica Burman, Khatidja Chantler, and Peace Kiguwa, eds. *Gender and Migration: Feminist Interventions*. Zed Books, 2010.

Pennycook, Alistair. "The Politics of Pronouns." *ELT Journal* 48(2) (April 1994): 173–178.

Phoenix, Ann, and Pamela Pattynama, eds. "Special Issue on 'Intersectionality.'" *European Journal of Women's Studies*, 13, no. 3 (August 2006): 187–192.

Probyn, Elspeth, "The Spatial Imperative of Subjectivity," in *Handbook of Cultural Geography*, eds. Kay Anderson, Mona Domosh, Steve Pile, and Nigel Thrift, 290–299. London: Sage, 2003.

Qureshi, Sadiah. "Displaying Sara Baartman, the 'Hottentot Venus.'" *History of Science* 42 (2004): 233–257.

Schiek, Dagmar, and Anna Lawson, eds. *European Union Non-Discrimination Law and Intersectionality: Investigating the Triangle of Racial, Gender and Disability Discrimination*. Farnham: Ashgate Publishing, 2011.

Seshadri-Crooks, Kalpana. *Desiring Whiteness: A Lacanian Analysis of Race*. London: Routledge, 2000.

Siddiqui, Nadia, Ismail Sajida, and Meg Allen, *Safe to Return? Pakistani Women, Domestic Violence and Access to Refugee Protection; A Report of a Trans-National Research Project Conducted in the UK and Pakistan.* Manchester: South Manchester Law Centre in partnership with Manchester Metropolitan University, 2008.

Spivak, Gayatri Chakravorty. *The Post-Colonial Critic: Interviews, Strategies, Dialogues*, ed. Sarah Harasym. New York: Routledge, 1990.

Spivak, Gayatri Chakravorty. *In Other Worlds: Essays in Cultural Politics.* London: Methuen, 2006.

Steiner, John. *Psychic Retreats: Pathological Organizations in Psychotic, Neurotic and Borderline Patients.* London: Routledge, 1993.

Suleri, Sara. (1992) "Woman Skin Deep: Feminism and the Postcolonial Condition." In *The Post-Colonial Studies Reader*, eds. B. Ashcroft, G. Griffiths, and H. Tiffin, 2nd ed., 250–255. London: Routledge, 2006.

Taylor, Yvette, Sally Hines, and Mark E. Casey, eds. *Theorizing Intersectionality and Sexuality.* Basingstoke: Palgrave Macmillan, 2010.

The Duluth Model. http://www.theduluthmodel.org/ (accessed September 28, 2012). Domestic Abuse Intervention Programs (DAIP). Home of the Duluth Model: Social Change to End Violence against Women (1980) *Home Page.* [Online] [accessed September 28, 2012] http://www.theduluthmodel.org/.

Wilkinson, Sue, and Celia Kitzinger, eds. *Representing the Other: A Feminism and Psychology Reader.* London: Sage, 1996.

Willis, Deborah, ed. *Black Venus: They Called Her "Hottentot."* Philadelphia, PA: Temple University Press, 2010.

Yoder, Janice, and Arnold Kahn. "Toward a Feminist Understanding of Women and Power." *Psychology of Women Quarterly* 16, no. 4 (December 1992): 381–388.

Yuval-Davis, Nira. "Intersectionality and Feminist Politics." *European Journal of Women's Studies* 13, no. 3 (2006): 193–209.

"BROTHERS FOR LIFE": A CAMPAIGN ADDRESSING GENDER-BASED VIOLENCE ON (DE/RE) CONSTRUCTING MASCULINITIES IN SOUTH AFRICA. *"YENZA KAHLE!" DO THE RIGHT THING!* [1]

Phoebe Kisubi Mbasalaki

> *"A man*
> *Who respects his woman*
> *And never*
> *Lifts a hand to her.*
> *Respect and protect your partner.*
> *Take an active stand in protecting women and*
> *children and do whatever it takes to shield them*
> *from physical and mental harm."* [2]

Introduction

Black feminist theory has been articulated in the preceding chapter as a powerful and effective tool in confronting gender violence. The Brothers for Life campaign can be seen in the same light as an emerging tool on the African continent. This campaign marks a paradigm shift in the interventions that address violence against women and girls (VAW) in Africa, mostly because it unravels men and masculinities. It was launched in South Africa in 2009, and it seems to be expanding to other parts of Sub-Saharan Africa, such as Tanzania, Zambia, and Zimbabwe. Some in development circles have even referred to it as a radical approach, in the sense that it steps away from the oppressor/oppressed conceptualization of gender relations that has dominated the gender and development field as it disentangles masculinities, their construction, and how they sometimes operate to marginalize women as well as oppress some men. This shift

---

[1] This is the slogan of the Brothers for Life campaign. *Yenza Kahle* is a Xhosa phrase meaning "do the right thing." Xhosa is one of eleven official languages spoken in South Africa.

[2] Brothers for Life, "Poster Campaigning against Violence against Women," http://www.brothersforlife.org/ (accessed December 10, 2012).

falls within the "African feminism" parameters and is arguably situated within the African Third Wave of Feminism (TWF), where there has been a conscious decision not to alienate African men. Furthermore, men and masculinity studies are consciously taking into account African masculinities, albeit within the HIV discourse. Despite this evident shift and references to the radicalism of this campaign, one may ask: does this campaign step away from the dominant institution of patriarchy, or is it really informed by some aspects of standpoint theory[3] located within a realm of private patriarchy?[4] What kind of masculinities, then, does such a campaign promote? Could what is being promoted be a new form of hegemonic masculinity?[5] This paper will unravel the campaign through gendered prisms, drawing on the aforementioned concepts.

As articulated in the opening chapter, violence against women and girls[6] is a pervasive human rights issue with public health consequences. Around the world, at least one in every three women has been beaten, coerced into sex, or otherwise abused.[7] Violence against women, whether committed with boots, fists, or weapons, is rooted in perverse discrimination which denies women equality to men. Although no society is violence-free, South Africa has an alarming level of violence against women and girls. In fact, some[8] argue that violence levels are increasing rather than diminishing despite intervention measures, a disturbing state of affairs. Interventions do however have inadequate funds and resources to meet the demand. Data on sexual offenses collected for the UN study[9] on women and security in Africa shows a national rate of 66,079 recorded cases in 2003–2004, rising to 70,514 cases for 2008–2009, with a slight drop to 66,196 for the

---

[3] Sandra Harding, ed., *The Feminist Standpoint Theory Reader: Intellectual and Political Controversies* (New York and London: Routledge, 2004).

[4] Sylvia Walby, *Gender Transformations* (London and New York: Routledge, 1997).

[5] Jeff Hearn, "From Hegemonic Masculinity to the Hegemony of Men," *Feminist Theory* 5, no. 1 (2004): 49.

[6] The Declaration on the Elimination of Violence against Women, adopted by the United Nations General Assembly in 1993, defines violence against women as "any act of gender-based violence that results in, or is likely to result in, physical, sexual or psychological harm or suffering to women, including threats of such acts, coercion or arbitrary deprivation of liberty, whether occurring in public or private life."

[7] Lori Heise, Mary Ellsberg, and Megan Gottemoeller, "Ending Violence against Women," *Population Reports* no. 11 (1999), http://www.isis.cl/jspui/handle/123456789/35904.

[8] Marie-France Desjardins and Phoebe Kisubi Mbasalaki, *Gender and Small Arms in Africa: A Contribution to Enhanced Security* (New York, London, and Geneva: UNDP, IANSA, and UNIDIR, 2012).

[9] Ibid.

reporting period of 2010–2011.[10] Although the peak is recorded for the 2008–2009 reporting period, the latest data from 2010–2011 indicates a slightly higher rate than that of 2003–2004. As many argue, the increase in reported cases could be attributed to increased reporting mechanisms and a robust database as a result of the countless campaigns visible in all media outlets on sexual and gender-based violence. Coupled with this, the increase could also be due to some other reasons that have yet to be fully explored.

South Africa is a unique country in the Sub-Saharan context; among other things, it is the largest energy producer and consumer on the African continent.[11] Although its citizens only relatively recently emerged from five decades of apartheid, this country has made significant progress in the eighteen years since democratization. Commonly referred to as an "emerging" economy, it is experiencing an economic boom. South Africa has a recognizable economic presence in the global arena and thus is a member of the G20 as well as the "trendy" BRICS.[12] However, this economic boom does not appear to be trickling down to ordinary people, indicating that the ills of apartheid will take a long time to redress. This has to be understood within the general backdrop of South Africa's sharp race and class cleavages, albeit softening in some respects in the post-apartheid era. South Africa has a mixed economy with a high rate of poverty and low gross domestic product (GDP) per capita, with women bearing the brunt of this in addition to violence and the disproportionate impact of HIV. As the most general backdrop to this paper, I argue that the contemporary position of women in South Africa needs to be understood in the context of the ways colonialism, capitalism, and apartheid have organized social relations and fractured society along racial, class, gendered, and sexualized lines. The current positioning of South African women is marked by the residual effects of the three aforementioned general conditions, which are still visible through high levels of unemployment, under-resourced schools, poor living conditions with substandard sanitation, and high levels of interpersonal and sexual violence.

---

[10] Ibid., 65.

[11] CNBC Explains, "BRICS: CNBC Explains," http://www.cnbc.com/id/44006382/BRICS.

[12] "BRICS" stands for Brazil, Russia, India, China, and South Africa. When South Africa joined the association in 2010, the "BRIC" countries were renamed BRICS. The BRICS countries have come to be seen as a symbol of the shift in global economic power away from the developed G8.

The knowledge production and portrayal of South African women, espe-cially within the HIV and development discourse, greatly reflects Foucault's notion of power/knowledge: early on in the epidemic, women were represented as docile victims, diseased and abused. Indeed female bodies have borne the textual imprints[13] of the HIV epidemic as well as violence in South Africa. None-theless, it should not escape our minds that women played a major role in the struggle against apartheid, which was quintessential to the Foucaultian notion of "power and resistance." And as such, Badden et al.[14] state that one of the emergent subjectivities for women to apartheid was the formation of political organizations, both independently and alongside men. The heart of the apartheid struggle in the 1970s and 1980s was in South African townships,[15] and town-ship women played a significant role. Hasim[16] notes how opposition politics in 1980s South Africa was dominated by organizations whose major objective was to mobilize women for the national liberation struggle rather than for women's liberation. Although the global wave in the 1970s and 1980s was liberation from sexism and women's empowerment, within the South African context, eradicat-ing racism took precedence over obliteration of sexism as the struggle against apartheid peaked. In fact, Hasim argues in her insightful article that the mobili-zation of the struggle process had the effect of reinforcing rather than challenging patriarchal relations of domination, as is visible in the post-apartheid "hangover effects," some of which fuel women's current subordination in South African society, which is rife with gender-based violence (GBV). Berger[17] quotes Albie Sachs, who bluntly declared: "It is a sad fact that one of the few profoundly non-racial institutions in South Africa is Patriarchy."[18] The patriarchal institution and practices have changed over time, but the status quo of women's subordination in South Africa endures.

---

[13] Michel Foucault, *The History of Sexuality*, vol. 1, *An Introduction* (Penguin Books, 1978).

[14] Sally Badden, Shireen Haseem, and Sheila Meintjes, *Country Gender Profile: South Africa* (Brighton: Institute of De-velopment Studies, University of Sussex, 2000).

[15] Townships are communities in South Africa on the outskirts of big cities where the apartheid government prescribed and restricted the residence of Africans and other people of color. In post-apartheid South Africa, many of these still suffer from hangover effects of apartheid and thus have meager socioeconomic opportunities.

[16] Shireen Hasim, "Gender, Social Location and Feminist Politics in South Africa," *Transformation* 15 (1991): 65.

[17] Iris Berger, *Threads of Solidarity: Women in South African Industry 1900–1980* (Bloomington, IN, and London: Indi-ana University Press and James Currey, 1992).

[18] Albie Sachs, *Sexism and the Law* (1986), 15 (cited in Iris Berger, *Threads of Solidarity*).

An intervention like Brothers for Life that directly addresses masculinities, and to a certain extent patriarchy, is long overdue. With one in every four South African men admitting to having raped a woman,[19] a campaign like this that mobilizes men from all over the country to start working together and build a stronger and healthier society is crucial. Until very recently, efforts to engage men in reducing gender inequality have been on a small scale with limited sustainability, and yet many men are willing to participate. Indeed, men can play a vital role in improving their own health as well as that of their families and the community at large. This campaign is therefore based on the theory of "positive normativity" and as such, calls on positive aspects of masculine behavioral repertoire -—a proactive approach rather than a reactive one. With the unqualified backing of the deputy president of South Africa, Kgalema Motlanthe, the Brothers for Life campaign has notable governmental and local support. Arguably, this campaign may fit well within the TWF as well as the post-2015 Millennium Development Goals (MDG) agenda. Indeed, such an approach to addressing violence against women did not come out of a vacuum; it is strongly situated within the policy framework of the South African Department of Health's National Strategic Plan, as well as others such as the South Africa Domestic Violence Act.

"Talking" policies

With democratization in 1994, South Africa set out to develop and implement a plethora of legislation, much of which redressed the ills of apartheid as well as wrongs affecting women and children. As a result, South Africa is now renowned for having one of the world's most progressive constitutions, which provides for the establishment of one sovereign state, a common South African citizenship, and a democratic system of governance committed to achieving equality between women and men and people of all races by providing for the prohibition of racial, gender, and all other forms of discrimination.[20] Furthermore, the 1990s were a radical time on the African continent, building on the impetus from the 1980's emergent "women in development." This period was rife with

---

[19] Kristin Palitza, *Mobilising Men All over the Country to Join in and Support Each Other: A Brother for Life* (Sonke Gender Justice Network, Johns Hopkins Health and Education in South Africa, 2011).

[20] Government of the Republic of South Africa and UNDP, *Millennium Development Goals: Country Report 2010* (Pretoria: Government of South Africa and UNDP, 2010)

momentum—women's issues were picked up by the various governments as a direct result of the wave of activism in support of women's empowerment following the 1995 Beijing conference.[21] One of the direct outcomes of this was the establishment of ministries of gender/women affairs. It is during this period, coupled with the democratization process, that some policies in South Africa were developed and implemented to redress the ills affecting women. In addition, South Africa subscribes to a number of international and regional gender-related protocols, such as the Convention to Eliminate All Forms of Discrimination against Women (CEDAW), the Beijing Platform for Action, and the SADC[22] Protocol on Gender and Development, to mention but a few. All these, together with women's activism and South Africa's progressive constitution, contributed to and shaped the currently "engendered" policy framework. The Domestic Violence Act,[23] which was enacted to "afford survivors of violence maximum protection from domestic abuse,"[24] was a direct result of the aforementioned. This Act is particularly radical because it makes reference to and acknowledges same-sex relationships. It is worth noting that in relation to domestic violence policy enactment and implementation, South Africa is quantum leaps ahead of the rest of Sub-Saharan Africa. While a number of African countries have only recently tabled or ratified a domestic violence policy, in South Africa such a policy has been in place, at this writing, for fourteen years. In fact, as a direct result of the Domestic Violence Act, South Africa has a rigorous and well-established data collection system, which is crucial for evidence-based planning and intervention.

The Employment Equity Act,[25] another momentous policy, curtails discrimination in employment, occupation, and income within the open labor market. Last but not least is the Promotion of Equality and Prevention of Unfair Discrimination Act,[26] which was passed to ensure that women enjoy equal rights and freedoms in addressing the wrongs of the past. Indeed, this momentous policy framework has worked towards addressing violence against women; the

---

[21] This was a momentous conference on women and development issues, organized by the Commission on the Status of Women. The resulting document—the Beijing Platform for Action—was adopted and has been ratified by a number of countries globally.

[22] SADC stands for Southern African Development Community, one of the African regional economic communities.

[23] Domestic Violence Act, December 2, 1998.

[24] South African Government Information, http://www.info.gov.za/events/national/16days_didyouknow.html.

[25] Employment Equity Act, October 19, 1998.

[26] Promotion of Equality and Prevention of Unfair Discrimination Act, February 2, 2000.

Brothers for Life campaign is a direct result of this. The impact of all these policies has yet to be measured; however, VAW remains unabated in South Africa.

The Brothers for Life campaign

Increasingly, the development world's efforts to address social ills such as gender-based violence, HIV, and alcohol abuse, as well as health in general, acknowledge the links between all these issues. This shift in approach is gaining momentum and the buzz word in development circles is "intersectionality."

This differs somewhat from the intersectionality theory - which disentangles all axes of difference and their enactment of power such as race, class, gender, sexuality, religion, ethnicity as coalesce - because it rather looks at drivers of certain behaviours in relation to GBV, HIV and alcohol use, and how these reinforce each other. As a result, current interventions attempt to address these in an "all-encompassing" approach has seen some level of success over the last five years or so. Launched in 2009, the Brothers for Life campaign is one such all-encompassing initiative. It has a plethora of recognizable local and international funders, including Johns Hopkins Health and Education in South Africa (JHHESA), Sonke Gender Justice Network, USAID, the South African National Council (SANAC), the South African Department of Health, PEPFAR,[27] UNICEF, UNAIDS, Oxfam, and more than 100 civil society partners.[28] Anyone in development/humanitarian circles would certainly appreciate this kind of patronage—these are some big names. Alongside this barrage of international funders, there is noteworthy local patronage, such as the unsolicited backing of the deputy president, as well as financial support—a recent UNAIDS report notes that only 12 percent of HIV expenditure is from international sources.[29] This indeed increases the level of local ownership of interventions, not only within the HIV discourse but with such a campaign as well.[30] However, government funding to combat VAW leaves much to be desired. Organizations working within this

---

[27] PEPFAR stands for the President's Emergency Plan for AIDS Relief, a U.S. government initiative to help save the lives of those suffering from HIV/AIDS around the world, with a strong emphasis on prevention.

[28] Johns Hopkins Health Education in South Africa, "Working with Men," http://jhhesa.org/working-men.html

[29] Michel Sidibé, *UNAIDS Special Report: How Africa Turned AIDS around; Celebrating 50 Years of African Unity* (Geneva: UNAIDS, 2013).

[30] Sonke Gender Justice Network—one of the key stakeholders in Brothers for Life—is also leading another campaign appealing to the government of South Africa to increase its budget for activities addressing violence against women.

field—such as Sonke Gender Justice Network—are picking up as a campaign and calling on the government of South Africa to increase the budget for VAW-related programs and activities.

The Brothers for Life campaign has also gone to great lengths to secure endorsements from sports and TV personalities, both local and international. One can read this as a parading of celebrities, reflecting the global trend of worshipping stars. Whether these stars partake in this campaign out of genuine conviction or are just ticking a box of participation in a charity cause is uncertain. The campaign managed to involve renowned football clubs and stars such as Manchester United and FC Barcelona,[31] all of whom participated in the campaign just before the 2010 World Cup, which was hosted by South Africa. The barrage of local stars includes South African football stars,[32] South African rugby captain John Smit, South African cricket captain Graeme Smith, and the Bulls rugby player Tiger Mangweni. Among the local stars are also TV celebrities, notably Patrick Shai, a renowned actor who speaks honestly and courageously about his past as a violent husband and father in a TV ad.[33] It is a gripping and moving clip.[34]

Prior to the start of this campaign, research was carried out by key stakeholders in October 2008 and February 2009, including a literature review and qualitative research to understand men as an audience as well as behavioral drivers of HIV, the findings of which informed the campaign messages. Brothers for Life is therefore a national men's campaign targeting men aged 30 and over with messages and education on HIV prevention, healthy living, and healthy relationships. To prevent HIV, for instance, this campaign calls for male medical circumcision, condom use, HIV testing, discouragement of multiple concurrent partnerships, male involvement in prevention of mother-to-child transmission (PMTCT), and discouraging alcohol abuse. It also tackles manhood and resolutely campaigns against GBV. This campaign is not a standalone but works alongside other prevention campaigns within the realm of HIV and VAW. It is

---

[31] International participants in this campaign have included Ryan Giggs (Manchester United), Patrice Evra (Manchester United), Mame Biram Diouf (Manchester United), Lionel Messi (FC Barcelona), Yaya Toure (FC Barcelona), Thierry Henri (FC Barcelona), and Seydou Keita (FC Barcelona).

[32] Among them are Matthew Booth, Teko Modise, and Benni McCarthy.

[33] Brothers for Life, "The Patrick Shai Story," http://www.brothersforlife.org/sites/default/files/patrick_shai.pdf.

[34] Brothers for Life, "Resources," http://www.brothersforlife.org/resources.html.

so far the first initiative of its kind to address men on a national scale. It targets the older generation, focusing on men who are aged 30 and over and hence most likely to either be in a relationship or married with children—part of a family. This age group has commonly been neglected, as previous campaigns focused mostly on young people. Yet this generation of men has a high incidence of HIV, among other things. According to the Sonke Gender Justice Network, a key partner in the Brothers for Life campaign, "the campaign identity is based on the aim of creating a movement of good men that will ignite and spread throughout South Africa." The campaign consists of four main components—awareness-raising through South African mass media, community mobilization through local organizations that work with men, advocacy for more and better services for men, and a fact-packed men's health toolkit to help men and boys take action.[35]

The Brothers for Life campaign draws on the "spirit of brotherhood" that strongly exists among men by encouraging men to positively influence each other. The notion of "brotherhood" is rooted within the African culture, where "brothers" do not necessarily have to be blood brothers but a group of men who know each other and are connected by a communal bond. Thus brothers are expected to look out for each other—to "have each other's back," so to speak, as well as keep each other's behavior in check. The "brotherhood" notion is especially strong in South Africa, given the history of apartheid, in which African men had to forge close relationships to fight the ruthless colonial masters. At the time they commonly called themselves "comrades," a term still regular use in today's South Africa. Indeed, these terms carry with them heavy responsibilities, such as "protector," "provider," friend, and colleague, with some of these being informed by patriarchy. One could argue that the brotherhood notion draws on the positive aspects of manhood, such as being a good father and a caring lover, although the flip side of the coin in certain respect is masculine dominance. Women are assigned a passive and sometimes invisible role, are relegated to the "behind the scenes." This reinforces certain notions, such as "it's a man's world," a world ruled by the brothers, with only an afterthought given to the sisters. The patriarchal aspect is evident in this campaign, given its pronounced male dominance. Thus it reflects Walby's[36] notion of "private patriarchy," which involves the concept of

---

[35] Kristin Palitza, *Mobilising Men All over the Country to Join in and Support Each Other: A Brother for Life* (Sonke Gender Justice Network, Johns Hopkins Health and Education in South Africa, 2011).

[36] Walby, *Gender Transformations*.

exclusion, that is, excluding women from the public arena. Although the campaign discussed here presents a slight contrast to Walby's notion, which focuses on the domestic realm, the exclusionary aspect accurately describes the Brothers for Life campaign. In fact, one can argue that this campaign draws on some aspects of Harding's[37] notion of "standpoint theory" in the sense that it upholds the power structures of dominant social groups (such as patriarchy), thereby contributing to "distorted and partial accounts of nature's regularities and underlying causal tendencies."[38] And perhaps as a consequence, male dominance, rather than progress towards gender equality, is likely to remain the status quo.

Then again, perhaps such a male social space is necessary for interrogating masculinities and working towards new kinds of South African masculinities that promote progressive social change. The brotherhood sold by these campaigns reflects the new South Africa, the "rainbow" nation, where men of all color participate—a "color-blind" campaign so to speak. The new South Africa is also evident in black South Africans' embrace of sports that were promoted as white-only during the apartheid era (other than soccer), such as rugby and cricket, and hence the appearance of sporting stars from all fields. It shows a united front of men from the heterogeneous ethnicities represented in contemporary South Africa. This also emphasises the fact that violence against women is not just a "black" problem but affects all ethnicities within this diverse society. The line of stars from diverse ethnic backgrounds embracing one another as brothers stands in stark contrast with the ethos of the apartheid regime, which institutionalized segregation. It is a testimony to what was cultivated during the reconciliation and transition process initiated by the Nelson Mandela government in the mid-1990s.

Those who call this campaign radical argue that it is a new and different way to cover men's health issues in the media; it proposes breaking away from stereotypes and instead treating men as complex individuals whose behavior is informed not only by their own notions of what it means to be a man but also by their communities, their families, their culture and, at times, the media.[39] The approach is indeed novel, making use of the media to reach men on a massive

---

[37] Harding, *Feminist Standpoint Theory Reader: Intellectual Political Controversies.*

[38] Ibid., 26.

[39] Melissa Meyer and Helen Struthers, *(Un)Covering Men: Rewriting Masculinity and Health in South Africa* (Auckland Park, South Africa: Jacana Media, 2012).

level to address intersecting issues such as sexual health, VAW, relationships, and men's health. To a certain extent, it does break away from the stereotype of the South African black man, especially the "township man" who was and is commonly represented as violent.[40] This stereotype is a direct result of the apartheid system, which was extremely violent and also failed to provide Africans and other ethnicities proper education and employment. Indeed, during the apartheid era, the township boy or young man was associated with gangs commonly known as "Tsotsis," who had a clear identity and their own language, called *tsotsitaal* (Tsotsi language), which was a mixture of Afrikaans[41] and English. Initially, Tsotsis manipulated the white-controlled system through their wits, style of dress, and behavior. But as conditions in the townships worsened, they turned to robbery and violent crime.[42] What grew alongside this was a stereotype in which a Tsotsi became synonymous with a black man, especially in South African townships.

The digital age calls for digital interventions such as the Brothers for Life campaign that smartly makes use of this. Accessibility to digital media on the African continent is on the rise; South Africa has a significant pool of users—by no means the entire population, but a large enough percentage to make possible a national campaign. The campaign makes use of traditional means such as posters, billboards, cars/buses, radio, and TV, but it also taps into the new era of mobile phones and online social networks. It also utilizes interpersonal communication and advocacy as its community education and mobilization strategies. For instance, there is a designated hotline for phone calls and texts, as well as an online social media presence. Men sign up and become members of the Brothers for Life group; this is how they support each other as well as keep each other in check. In addition to male-friendly health services, there are also periodic men-only community dialogue meetings where men's health, HIV, and VAW issues are interrogated in a male-only space.

The Brothers for Life campaign has certainly sparked dialogue concerning what manhood stands for in South Africa. At this writing, it has won up to six

---

[40] Another representation that commonly follows the Foucaultian power/knowledge notion.

[41] Afrikaans is spoken natively in South Africa. It originated from the Dutch settlers, commonly known as the Boers, in the eighteenth century.

[42] Myfundi.co.za, "The History of Townships in South Africa," http://myfundi.co.za/e/The_history_of_townships_in_South_Africa.

prestigious awards, both regionally and internationally, for its efforts. Notably is the story of South African actor Patrick Shai, who regretfully shares about being an abusive husband and father as well as calls on men to change in a video clip ad aired on national TV. The Johns Hopkins Health and Education South Africa website points out that qualitative research with audiences indicated that the aforementioned ad featuring Patrick Shai had an enormous emotional appeal on the views and attitudes of consumers, with many reflecting on their own behavior, experiences, and history in relation to GBV. And as such, the campaign promoted the uptake of services through the use of the stop-GBV helpline number, during which time the call rate by men to the helpline increased by 13 percent.[43]

Undeniably, some good things, such as the aforementioned increase in helpline calls, have come from this campaign so far. It is a novel approach that is very visible and has brought men on board to address gender inequality and power dimensions. It is an all-encompassing approach that is not being implemented as a new program but rather builds on and collaborates with already existing community initiatives, thus increasing its sustainability. However, this campaign does not step away completely from patriarchy. In fact, one could argue that it promotes a new kind of hegemonic masculinity—one that maintains unequal relations between men and women, with factors such as race, class, age, sexuality, religion, and environment impacting on the feasibility of attaining that masculine ideal.[44] The invisibility and passivity of women in these campaigns does border on reinforcing masculine dominance and female subjugation. However, could South Africa be ready for a completely radical approach that steps away from the unfamiliar, that is, completely stepping outside of patriarchy? Perhaps what is warranted is an approach that is not too extreme, but one that puts forth women as dominant and active agents in the process, as opposed to their current passive role. This approach would interrogate the socioeconomic, cultural, political, religious, and psychosocial norms that reproduce masculine dominance at the expense of women. It would that tie and center VAW to "men's issues" rather than continue the predominant reference to it as a "women's issue."

[43] Brothers for Life, "Brothers for Life Receives the Highest Global Advertising Accolade," http://jhhesa.org/news/brothers-life-receives-highest-global-advertising-accolade.html.

[44] Hearn, "From Hegemonic Masculinity to the Hegemony of Men"; Robert Morrell, *Changing Men in South Africa: Global Masculinities* (Durban: University of Natal Press, 2001).

Implications for teaching

This article highlights men's involvement in the fight against VAW as a long-overdue and positive step. Men are indeed willing to participate in the fight, and as the Brothers for Life campaign shows, they are taking responsibility for the well-being of their families and community at large. This campaign highlights a concerted effort from policies, governance, funders, men, and the community at large working towards the eradication of VAW and HIV—epidemics that have devastated South Africa. This is a proactive rather than reactive approach, arguably uncharted waters in the VAW discourse on the African continent, but firmly situated within the contemporary human rights era, although it has not completely stepped away from the patriarchal institution.

Questions

Given the socioeconomic, political, cultural, psychological, and interpersonal factors that facilitate and fuel violence against women and girls in any given context (such as in your country), interventions need to take all these aspects into account in order to be effective and efficient.

1. Now that you have a glimpse of how the Brothers for Life campaign works, do you think there are risks to promoting masculinities like this campaign does in this era? Why or why not?
2. Is there any context in which no patriarchy or patriarchal traits influence a society? And is there no hegemonic masculinity where there is no patriarchy?
3. How would you conduct a campaign like Brothers for Life differently in order to eradicate violence against women, given the complex and inextricably linked factors involved? How would you make women visible in such a campaign?

Assignment questions

1. If you were entrusted with a significant budget (say, 10 million euros) from your president and given five years, how would you forge a part-

nership with men in your country to make them ambassadors in fighting against gender-based violence? Develop a program and activities you would engage in over the five-year period, as well as mechanisms you would use to measure whether your program/activities are producing results.

2. If you were part of the post-2015 Millennium Development Goals panel, articulate how you would ensure that the issue of violence against women would not be left off the goals agenda this time around.

3. Noting that violence exists along a continuum and drawing parallels with the South African context, watch Spike Lee's 1989 film *Do the Right Thing*. Within the framework of intersectional theory, analyze the contextual "drivers" that promote violence, especially among men, and outline how you would advise governments to effectively address them.

REFERENCES

Badden, Sally, Haseem Shireen, and Meintjes Sheila. *Country Gender Profile: South Africa*. Brighton: Institute of Development Studies, University of Sussex, 2000.

Berger, Iris. *Threads of Solidarity: Women in South African Industry, 1900–1980*. Bloomington, IN, and London: Indiana University Press, 1992.

Brothers for Life. "Brothers for Life Receives the Highest Global Advertising Accolade." http://jhhesa.org/news/brothers-life-receives-highest-global-advertising-accolade.html (accessed December 17, 2012).

Brothers for Life. "Resources." http://www.brothersforlife.org/resources.html (accessed December 10, 2012).

Brothers for Life. "Poster Campaigning against Violence against Women." http://www.brothersforlife.org/ (accessed December 10, 2012).

Brothers for Life. "The Patrick Shai Story." http://www.brothersforlife.org/sites/default/files/patrick_shai.pdf (accessed December 10, 2012).

CNBC Explains. "BRICS: CNBC Explains." http://www.cnbc.com/id/44006382/BRICS (accessed December 7, 2012).

Desjardins, Marie-France, and Phoebe Kisubi Mbasalaki. *Gender and Small Arms in Africa: A Contribution to Enhanced Security*. New York, London, and Geneva: UNDP, IANSA, and UNIDIR, 2012.

Foucault, Michel. *The History of Sexuality*, vol. 1, *An Introduction*. Penguin Books, 1978.

Government of the Republic of South Africa and UNDP. *Millennium Development Goals: Country Report 2010*. Pretoria: Government of South Africa and UNDP, 2010.

Harding, Sandra, ed. *The Feminist Standpoint Theory Reader: Intellectual and Political Controversies*. New York and London: Routledge, 2004.

Hasim, Shireen. "Gender, Social Location and Feminist Politics in South Africa." *Transformation* 15 (1991): 65–82.

Hearn, Jeff. "From Hegemonic Masculinity to the Hegemony of Men." *Feminist Theory* 5, no. 1 (2004): 49–72.

Johns Hopkins Health Education in South Africa. "Working with Men," http://jhhesa.org/working-men.html.

Lori, Heise, Mary Ellsberg, and Gottemoeller Megan. "Ending Violence against Women." *Population Reports* no. 11 (1999). http://www.isis.cl/jspui/handle/123456789/35904.

Meyer, Melissa, and Helen Struthers. *(Un)Covering Men: Rewriting Masculinity and Health in South Africa*. Auckland Park, South Africa: Jacana Media, 2012.

Morrell, Robert. *Changing Men in South Africa: Global Masculinities*. Durban: University of Natal Press, 2001.

Myfundi.co.za. "The History of Townships in South Africa." http://myfundi.co.za/e/The_history_of_townships_in_South_Africa (accessed December 17, 2012).

Palitza, Kristin. *Mobilising Men All over the Country to Join in and Support Each Other: A Brother for Life*. Sonke Gender Justice Network, Johns Hopkins Health and Education in South Africa, 2011.

Sidibé, Michel. *UNAIDS Special Report: How Africa Turned AIDS around; Celebrating 50 Years of African Unity*. Geneva: UNAIDS, 2013.

South African Government Information. http://www.info.gov.za/events/national/16days_didyouknow.html (accessed December 7, 2012).

UNIFEM. *Violence against Women: Facts and Figures*. New York: UNIFEM, 2007.

Walby, Sylvia. *Gender Transformations*. London and New York: Routledge, 1997.

GENDER, DEVIANCE AND INSTITUTIONAL VIOLENCE IN IRELAND'S MAGDALENE LAUNDRIES: AN ANALYSIS OF TWO FILMIC REPRESENTATIONS OF ABUSE[1]

Auxiliadora Pérez-Vides

Introduction

This chapter inaugurates a section of the book devoted to the analysis of the transition from the application of repressive strategies upon women in terms of violence to more constructive means of female identity and empowerment in several contexts. In the case of Ireland, the interconnection of female deviance and violence has taken an interesting expression that is worthy of note. Traditionally rooted in conservative and Catholic discourses as a result of its decolonization from the British Empire, Irish society throughout the past century was characterized by the restriction of women's rights and the obliteration of female corporeality. The repression of what Cheryl Herr has termed "the erotics of Irishness"[2] was undertaken by means of a number of political, legal, and social measures aimed at the endorsement of national identity. For Herr, "the identity-obsession marks a social repression of the body on a grand scale. [...] The loss occurs on both individual and collective levels. Ireland has literally eroded, in the sphere of representations that constitute social identity, a comfortable sense of the body."[3] On this account, not only were sexual practices that deviated from the norm rejected and hidden from the public ethos, but women involved in them were also ostracized and treated as social outcasts. The epitome of this process of subjugation can be found in the institutionalization of unmarried mothers and other kinds of "wayward women" in the Magdalene laundries—named in a clear reference to the biblical character of the repentant prostitute. As part of what James M.

---

[1] The author wishes to acknowledge the funding provided by the Spanish Ministry of Economy and Competitiveness for the writing of this chapter (Research Project FEM2010–18142).

[2] Cheryl Herr, "The Erotics of Irishness," *Critical Inquiry* 17, no. 1 (1990): 1–34.

[3] Ibid., 6.

Smith calls "the nation's architecture of containment,"[4] the female body was used as a labor force for the economic benefit of the Church and also as the object of regular physical abuse, under the pretext of the inmates' need for rectification. This residential network was derived from the Victorian rescue work and refuges for "fallen women" and prostitutes, and it operated widely on the isle from the 1922 foundation of the Irish Free State until the late twentieth century. The laundries were mostly run by religious congregations as a result of, first, the state's transfer of responsibility to the Catholic Church, and second, a latent idiosyncrasy of social complicity. For reasons that included illegitimate pregnancies, "dissolute behavior," or having been sexually violated, these women were sent there by their own relatives and confined, usually for life, in an attempt to secure family respectability and avoid social stigmatization. In exchange, they were forced into a residential existence that consisted of prayer, silence, twelve-hour laundry work, and very little recreation. To use Maria Luddy's words, "life within these institutions was restricted and restrictive."[5] In the case of unmarried mothers, confinement also invariably meant their brutal separation from their illegitimate babies, who were sent to orphanages or handed over to foster families.

Despite the prominence of this system, it was shrouded in a nationwide conspiracy of silence; to a large part of Ireland's population, it remained unknown. However, in the last two decades a substantial body of critical accounts and adult-survivor memoirs have brought to light the terror regime that was regularly inflicted upon the Magdalenes, both physically and psychologically. By and large, these accounts problematize the mutual benefit of church and state in setting up this network and raise general awareness about the two-faced religiosity within the laundries. Likewise, they appeal to ideological negotiations of the past by readdressing their internal policies from victim-oriented perspectives, so that the experiences behind the official version can be exorcised.[6] Particularly gripping has

---

[4] As James M. Smith explained, apart from the Magdalene laundries, this network consisted of "mother and baby homes, county homes, industrial and reformatory schools and insane asylums." James M. Smith, *Ireland's Magdalen Laundries and the Nation's Architecture of Containment* (Notre Dame, IN: University of Notre Dame Press, 2007), 42. In all of them, violence was commonly used as a form of expiation, illustrating the entrenched intersection between moral rectification and corporeal resilience in Ireland.

[5] Maria Luddy, "Magdalen Asylums: 1765–1922," in *The Field Day Anthology of Irish Writing*. Vol. 5, *Irish Women's Writing and Traditions*, ed. Angela Bourke et al. (Cork: Cork University Press, 2002), 736.

[6] Among many others: June Goulding, *The Light in the Window* (Dublin: Poolbeg, 1998); Kathy O'Beirne, *Kathy's Story: A Childhood Hell inside the Magdalen Laundries* (Edinburgh: Mainstream Publishing, 2005); Sam Jordison, "Irish Gulags for Women: the Catholic Church's Magdalene Asylums," in *Everything You Know about God is Wrong*, ed. Russ

been the representation of this issue through powerful media like the visual arts and literature, as they acutely depict the many faults of the Irish system of gender-coding and consequently destabilize the foundations of the island's cultural order.[7] In this sense, these productions become an appropriate tool to discuss the perpetuation of violence on the island and the different mechanisms created in order to problematize its many social agents, so that their hindering effects upon female gender identity are eradicated. On a wider canvas, these productions attempt to unveil for national and international audiences the suppressive articulations of femininity and maternity on the isle, further calling for a renewed ethical order in which individual women's rights prevail over the national imagination.

Portraying gender polarities

In this essay I contend that as spatial artifacts of the nationalist and religious manipulation of femininity in Ireland, the Magdalene laundries constituted a form of residential restraint of ostracized women that was in itself an assault on women's right to gain control of their corporeality. In turn, within the laundries the Magdalenes' bodies became the archives whereby anxieties of cultural degradation were expiated. Remarkably, this purge was performed by the religious figures with rather violent methods of corporeal castigation and emotional coercion. Following this line of argument, I will examine Peter Mullan's highly acclaimed film *The Magdalene Sisters*[8] and Aisling Walsh's TV film *Sinners*.[9] It is my aim to explore how they denounce Ireland's atrocious treatment of female deviant sexuality by portraying the violence inflicted upon Magdalenes by the agents of hegemonic power, as well as the punitive incarceration context in which these outcast women were forced to live. My analysis of this specific strand of gender violence in Ireland engages with two different expressions: intrafamily abuse and punishment, and institutional cruelty and victimization. In this light,

---

Kick (New York: The Disinformation Company, 2007), 188–196. These books shed some light on the hidden elements of this residential system, displacing (il)legitimate interpretations of their social role.

[7] Although their analysis falls out of the scope of this essay, worthy of note are Patricia Burke Brogan, *Eclipsed* (Galway: Salmon Publishing, 1994), *Stained Glass at Samhain* (Sevenoaks, Kent: Salmon Publishing, 2003); Marita Conlon-McKenna, *The Magdalen* (London: Bantam Books, 1999), and the installations "The Secrets of the Magdalene Laundries" (2000) by Diane Fenster and "Call Me by Name" (2004) by Gerard Mannix Flynn.

[8] *The Magdalene Sisters*, directed by Peter Mullan (PFP Production in association with Temple Films, 2002).

[9] *Sinners,* directed by Aisling Walsh (Parallel Productions/BBC Northern Ireland, 2002).

I find particularly engaging Ariel Glucklich's postulates in her study *Sacred Pain: Hurting the Body for the Sake of the Soul*, where she states that:

> pain discourse reflects the way cultures "construct" the individual as a self and as a member of the community. It is not possible for individuals or cultures to talk about pain without simultaneously expressing social relations of power and the ideologies that contain them. This situates pain in a specific time and place.[10]

Thus I argue that both films suggest that the family and the clergy executed a type of domination that illustrates a culturally sanctioned condemnation of female bodily deviance as well as atrocious practices of expiation, by which these women were not only separated from the normative society but also forced continuously to bear the burden of their alleged fall. To this aim, a multi-layered form of appropriation was implemented, as the right to choose, to privacy, and other basic rights were consistently denied to the Magdalenes, exacerbating the effects of physical violence.

Taken together, *The Magdalene Sisters* and *Sinners* offer a comprehensive outlook on the pretexts on which women were consigned to the Magdalene laundries and the kind of reality that they lived there. Although both films are set in the 1960s, they are composite stories of several girls, setting forth the plight of the over 30,000 women who were incarcerated in the laundries over the period of their existence.[11] This is particularly true for *The Magdalene Sisters*, whose script was written by Mullan and which was inspired by Steve Humphries's documentary *Sex in a Cold Climate*,[12] gathering the testimonies of four women who survived the Magdalene laundries system between the 1940s and the 1960s. Whether films and other artistic fictionalizations represent these historical facts truthfully has been the subject of some critical attention.[13] Although that discus-

---

[10] Ariel Glucklich, *Sacred Pain: Hurting the Body for the Sake of the Soul* (Oxford: Oxford University Press, 2003), 14.

[11] The exact number is not clear, as the official record of inmates has not been submitted by the religious orders to date. For Smith, this is one reason "why Ireland's Magdalene laundries exist in the public mind at the level of story rather than history." Smith, *Ireland's Magdalen Laundries,* 138.

[12] *Sex in a Cold Climate*, directed by Steve Humphries (Testimony Films for Channel Four, 1998).

[13] Fintan O'Toole, "Attitudes That Led to Abuse Entrenched in System," *Irish Times*, May 15, 1999; Paula Murphy, "'Wayward Girls and Fallen Women': Negotiating Fact and Fiction in the Magdalen Laundries," in *Single Motherhood in Twentieth-Century Ireland: Cultural, Historical, and Social Essays*, eds. Cinta Ramblado-Minero and Auxiliadora Pérez-Vides (Lewiston, NY: Edwin Mellen Press, 2006), 139–153.

sion falls out of the scope of my analysis, it seems fair to note that in my opinion, they stand out as pioneering projections of Ireland's submerged socio-cultural milieu, adding extraordinarily to what Rosa González underscores as filmic undertakings of "a therapeutic re-visioning of traumatic episodes of the past."[14] What these productions clearly indicate is that in recent years Ireland has had to come to terms with the abuse of authority by its religious and spiritual guides and, more uncomfortably, with its collective participation in such a system through a rigorous silence about it. About the disturbing revelations of this disclosure, Fintan O'Toole observes that "what we see when we turn over the rock of secrecy and indifference is not some kind of exotic horror. It is our own State, our own culture, our own ideological assumptions. And it is not dead."[15]

In the two films, such wide-ranging involvement and accountability are rendered visible, laying similar emphasis on the shift from family hegemony to institutional restraint that was experienced by young deviant women. At the outset, the directors equally highlight the initial vulnerability and puzzlement that the girls endured before their confinement. Thus they are portrayed as victims rather than agents in the alleged sexual transgression that motivates their detention. A very powerful scene opens Mullan's film, depicting the wedding banquet during which Margaret, one of the protagonists, is raped by her cousin, Kevin. The guests' sentimental and festive feelings while a priest sings a traditional Irish ballad contrast with the first form of intrafamily violence that Margaret suffers.[16] Tricked by Kevin into a back room, she is physically and sexually assaulted by him, despite her earnest protests: "Behave yourself. You're my cousin. What would your father say?" Although the violation happens off-screen, it is revealed by showing Margaret's numbness after the abuse. Apart from locating her story, many of the common circumstances, people, and attitudes that deter-

---

[14] In a similar vein, a recent wave of documentaries, memoirs, films, and scholarly studies has delved into the bleak experiences and the brutality experienced by boys and girls inside Irish industrial schools and orphanages, which were generally managed by Catholic orders. Together with the Magdalene laundries and other Church-related scandals, these episodes have been brought out for public discussion, painfully shattering Ireland's self-indulging image. See Mary Raftery and Eoin O'Sullivan, *Suffer the Little Children: The Inside Story of Ireland's Industrial Schools* (Dublin: New Island Books, 1999); *Song for a Raggy Boy*, directed by Aisling Walsh (Subotica Entertainment, 2003); Kathleen O'Malley, *Childhood Interrupted: Growing up under the Cruel Regime of the Sisters of Mercy* (London: Virago Press, 2005).

[15] Fintan O'Toole, "The Sisters of No Mercy," *Observer*, February 15, 2003.

[16] In a powerful and thought-provoking combination of folkloric and religious imagery, the chosen ballad is "The Well below the Valley," whose lyrics speak of the devastating effects of incest upon a young woman. Similarly, the *bodhran* used by the priest is decorated with an image of Christ being sent by Pontius Pilate for public judgment.

81

mined young women's committal to the laundries are sharply represented here by Mullan. Namely, the camera soon progresses to concentrate on the victim's bewilderment and the immediate consequences of reporting what has just happened to her.[17] While the songs continue, and after she tells a close female friend about the events, her discursive capacity fades away. The music completely drowns out the discussion of the episode among the male relatives, who from then on take up the leading role in interpreting the incident. By contrast, Margaret's voice remains totally unheard throughout the last part of the scene. This hypermasculine handling of violence is further materialized by the immediate intervention of the priest and sadly sanctioned by her mother's silenced complicity and her father's repudiation of her. Most importantly, the question of the young man's culpability never enters the discussion. Indeed, this fact accounts for the patriarchal appropriation of the female body as well as the homogenization of women's experiences and the demonization of female sexuality. According to Pat Brereton's interpretation of this manipulation, "Can we presume the rapist defends himself, claiming 'she was asking for it'?"[18]

It is precisely this double standard that Walsh also criticizes in her film through Rose (who is also called Theresa; the nuns, as they often did to Magdalene women, gave her a new name in her new institutional life).[19] She is an orphan country girl signed in by her aunt after being impregnated by her brother, Eamon. The director critiques this form of gender-biased punishment through Theresa's words to her brother in one of his rare visits during her two-year confinement: "They stole my beautiful baby. And I am supposed to be grateful? They took my life away. I know what we did was wrong, I accept that. But it was both of us. Tell me: why was your life worth protecting more than mine?" In doing so, Walsh denounces how male authority figures perpetuated the criminalization of the female subject yet did not hold men accountable. Hence she underscores the ideological immediacy between sexual indecency and female condemnation. The effects of this conceptual partiality have been extensively commented on by

---

[17] Indeed, one of the protagonists of *Sex in a Cold Climate* remarks: "The biggest sin in Ireland—well, apart from having a baby before you have been married—was to talk." Thus expressiveness and punishment become entwined in the violent background of both the Magdalenes and the girls incarcerated in the laundries. Reporting was as bad as the abuse itself, and rather frequently, it set in motion the Magdalene machinery. Similarly, other Magdalene survivors have mentioned their inability to fully express the pain they were made to suffer, which testifies to its extreme cruelty.

[18] Pat Brereton, "Religion and Irish Cinema: A Case Study," *An Irish Quarterly Review* 97 (2008): 325.

[19] Maria Luddy, "Magdalen Asylums: 1765–1922," 736.

Ailbhe Smyth, who maintains that the abstraction of the female experience leads to dehumanization, which acquires a very dramatic dimension when it comes to sexual violence: "Mass rape devastates each woman separately and individually; policies of collective control are lived as acts of individual annihilation, in geno-cidal/gynocidal wars. But each woman bears the mark, and the hurt, in her body, in her head, in her soul, in her sense of herself."[20]

Intra-institutional terror

A reading of the two filmic texts in terms of their portrayal of gender violence allows for several interpretations of the atrocities committed against these women inside the laundries. Both directors convey how, as the guarantors of the dissemi-nation of the Catholic doctrine and moral codes, the nuns and the clerical figures imposed their system of beliefs over the inmates not only by physical maltreat-ment but also through psychological harassment. The commodification of the deviant female body as a profitable labor force figures as the primary expression of violence, given the physical conditions in which the women are forced to work. As the stories unfold, the two films make clear that the women's suffocating working conditions inside the laundries as well as their exploitation for the Church's eco-nomic benefit were forms of psychic violence. What most appalls the audience, though, is that any misbehavior was brutally reproved. Transgressions of the rules of silence and servitude were immediately punished by cruel methods of physical violence and psychological intimidation. As Frances Finnegan puts it:

Control was maintained [...] by means of discipline, silence, surveillance and work. Since those entering the Homes were already disposed to penance, feelings of guilt (sedulously nurtured) furthered the notion of subjugation and strengthened the Sisters' rule. Above all in these institu-tions, religious indoctrination was an effective form of power.[21]

Such practices surface over the course of the two films, as the leading nuns— Sister Bridget and Sister Bernadette, respectively—brutally batter the girls while

---

[20] Ailbhe Smyth, "Paying Our Disrespects to the Bloody States We're in: Women, Violence, Culture and the State," in *Stirring It: Challenges for Feminism*, eds. Gabrielle Griffin et al. (London: Taylor and Francis, 1994), 14.

[21] Frances Finnegan, *Do Penance or Perish: Magdalene Asylums in Ireland* (Piltown, Co. Kilkenny: Congrave Press, 2001), 69.

also using a perverse rhetorical religiosity aimed at legitimating their methods. In *The Magdalene Sisters*, the Mother Superior terrifies the girls by flogging the back of their legs with a stick and emphasizes their condition as "hopeless sinners," insisting on their need to purge their sins through the flesh. The first victims of such penalization are Bernadette, "a little temptress" who was sent to the laundry from a nearby orphanage simply because of her exceptional beauty and potential "fall" into temptation; and then Crispina, the girl with a slight mental disability whose bastard child was handed over to her sister shortly after birth. Their infringement of the rule of silence brings them to Sister Bridget's office, where they are also verbally abused and indoctrinated about avoiding temptation before being told that "disobedience will not be tolerated." The ritual is also featured in *Sinners* at several moments, although this merging of religious propaganda and Magdalene victimization becomes especially apparent through Kitty, the former primary school teacher confined to the laundry by her family for having refused to marry her illegitimate baby's father. After talking to the girls while washing the linen, she is reprimanded by Sister Bernadette, and by appealing to her presumed knowledge of discipline, the nun hits her on the palms with a strap. Not only does she point out that Kitty lost her rights the moment she "succumbed," but she also reasserts the Magdalene's lowliness and humiliation by making Kitty vow to her and say, "I'm so sorry, Mother." The scene closes with Sister Bernadette saying, "I forgive you, my child," while the bell ringing announces the praying of the Angelus, led afterwards by the nun in a solemn, unconcerned way. The conflation of power assertion and religious discourse is evident in the two scenes, and it coalesces with critic Paula Murphy's discussion about the nuns' abuse of power, as described in Mullan's film:

> Blaming patriarchy for crimes that the women who were in charge of these laundries committed is simply ignoring their culpability in the Magdalene Asylum system, while also positing the abuse of power as an inherently male fault. Defeating this myth [...] makes obvious that both men and women have a capacity for extreme violence [...]. But as Mullan suggests with the character of Sister Bridget, women who were empowered did not behave any better than men.[22]

---

[22] Murphy, "Wayward Girls and Fallen Women," 142.

As the stories in the films progress, the violence plot is further constructed through repeated schemes of terror. Central to the practices of penance imposed on the Magdalenes—and to the Irish religious consciousness in general—was self-negation for the sake of remission.[23] Consequently, the two films provide insights into the brutal punishment habits devised by the nuns and extensively used on different occasions of perceived sin and misconduct, as declared by former Magdalene survivors. Very illustrative in this respect is the scene in which Bernadette's hair is butchered after she has tried to escape from the laundry by conspiring with the delivery man. At Sister Bridget's office, she is held by several nuns and, putting up fierce resistance, ends up with her scalp and face covered with blood. This new strand of violence culminates with a close-up of Bernadette's bloody eye and the reflection of Sister Bridget in her eyeball. It appears as the manifestation, again, of the extreme manipulation of individuality that was widely performed in the laundries. Indeed, on the pretext of saving the women from the mortal sin of vanity, the nuns sometimes shaved off the women's hair, not only to dehumanize them but to take away their female identity.[24] The objective is clear when Sister Bridget tells Bernadette: "Now that your vanity is gone and your arrogance defeated, you're free. Free to choose between right and wrong, good and evil. So you must look deep into your soul, find that which is pure and decent, and offer it up to God. Then and only then you'll find salvation." This radical scheme of corporeal discipline and its inherent religiosity has been equated by Mullan with the Taliban regime: "The Catholic Church is not that different from the Taliban. It seems that every religion considers their enemy the young women, their sexuality, their vitality, maybe because they break the rules of patriarchal society."[25]

In *Sinners*, there is also the added insight that suffering and violence were forced on the Magdalenes during the delivery of their babies. The practice of withholding relief at labor has been confirmed by the testimonies of former nurses and midwives who worked in these institutions. In *The Light in the Window*, June Goulding attests to this cruel procedure by noting that analgesics were deliberately withheld and sutures were commonly avoided after childbirth. For her, the custom not only raises ethical questions about human suffering but also contra-

[23] Luddy, "Magdalen Asylums: 1765–1922."

[24] Murphy, "Wayward Girls and Fallen Women," 142.

[25] Mullan, "Magdalene Sisters: Women's Oppression," *Il Manifesto*, August 8, 2002.

venes medical maxims: "I was trained to make pregnant women as comfortable as possible during the delivery and afterwards and [...] apart from my horror at the cruelty I was witnessing, the rules in this place were making a mockery of my training."[26] Walsh's awareness of this mortifying scheme is evident in her visual narration of Kitty's labor. In the maternity ward, the medical expertise of the attending nurse and her complicity with the Magdalene are immediately replaced by the inflexible orders of Sister Bernadette. A shot of the nun moving around the ward while monitoring the delivery and verbally abusing Kitty illustrates the invasive handling of the pregnant deviant body, as inferred from her comments: "There will be no screaming. If you die, it would be no more than you deserve [...]. What do you reckon your pupils would make of all this, Kitty? Do you think they've learnt a thing or two?" Her reprimanding tone and perverse supervision of pain echo the forbidding practices told by Goulding, and again, underline the discourse of expiation and sinful embodiment mentioned above.

The degree of violence exerted over the women can also be grasped in the several cases of sexual molestation in the films. Both directors equally indicate the collision between the role of the clergy as moral instructors and their own depraved interpretations of such indoctrination. As Diarmaid Ferriter points out, "It was often the priests who were seen musing on relationships and offering advice, condemnations or solutions when it came to sexual frustration. What was not acknowledged until very recently was that they suffered from their fair share of that frustration."[27] Ferriter also notes that according to the clergy, "sexual abuse was seen more as 'a moral failure than a crime.'"[28] This distinction is problematized by Mullan and Walsh as they offer clear pictures of how the victims of priests' sexual assault were condemned while the perpetrators were simply scolded in private. The one-sided implications of these assaults are highlighted by Pat Bereton in his analysis of *The Magdalene Sisters*, noting that "all forms of sexual activity in this narrative are coded as deviant, but only the women in the end are punished." Mullan reproduces this controversy through the character of Crispina, who is seen performing oral sex on the convent chaplain, Father Fitzroy. The situation embodies the individual failures of the Catholic hegemony

---

[26] Goulding, *The Light in the Window*, 31.

[27] Diarmaid Ferriter, *Occasions of Sin: Sex and Society in Modern Ireland* (London: Profile Books, 2009), 325.

[28] Ibid., 356.

but also, and most poignantly, the re-victimization of the Magdalenes in cases of institutional clerical abuse. Again, the act is not filmed directly, but it is witnessed by Margaret, who sees them through the window and decides to expose the priest. Thus during the celebration of mass after the Corpus Christi procession, and in a rather surreal mode, the priest suddenly begins to disrobe, itching because of the poison ivy that Margaret used while washing his underwear. Horrified at his nakedness and impropriety, the nuns, the Magdalenes, and the community remain paralyzed. It is Crispina who elucidates the story rather dramatically, as she begins to scratch her legs, also inculpating herself in the sin. Her insistent screaming "You are not a man of God!" up to twenty-five times culminates the scene, but the impact of this revelation rests on the extended process of victimization by which she is immediately taken to Mount Vernon psychiatric hospital, where, as we later learn, she eventually died of anorexia. In *Sinners*, Walsh also brings to the fore the gender polarities that existed in cases of clerical abuse, as portrayed through Father Flannery's fixation on Angela, a pretty young girl. The sexual abuse is also juxtaposed with a discourse of female defilement that, again, is intended to elude male responsibility, as the priest constantly says she is the one to blame because she is "a filthy little slut." In line with Mullan's final treatment of Crispina, Walsh also portrays Angela's eventual institutionalization in a mental sanatorium, in an equally tragic scene where her frenetic screams merge with Theresa's devastation for the unforeseen consequences of having reported the inappropriate behavior of the priest.

Furthermore, the two films convey the persisting intrafamily violence that haunted the girls inside the laundries, although this is more explicitly described in *The Magdalene Sisters*. Mullan underlines the fact that because of their perceived shamefulness, the Magdalenes were usually expected to stay in the laundries forever, and he shows how their attempts to escape and get back to their families were usually punished with an even more severe form of violence. This repudiation is strikingly articulated through a dramatic and revolting scene in which the father of a Magdalene who had tried to escape from the convent (Una O'Connor) literally drags her back in the middle of the night. Mr. O'Connor— played by Mullan himself—harshly beats his daughter in front of the girls and the nuns, who watch the incident passively, while she asks in vain for his forgiveness and mercy. This character encapsulates the paternal response to sexual deviance and also a double-sided interpretation of violence by which the male right to female corporeal ownership is conflated with a complete rejection of the beaten, victimized body, as implied by his last words: "You got no home. You got no mother. You got no father. You killed us, you slut. You killed us both. You run away again, I'll cripple you. I swear to God." The episode constitutes the most direct expression of intergenerational gender violence in the film, and it sustains the deep-rootedness of the systems of beliefs and morality referred to above. At the core of such implications lies the widespread belief that sexual deviance, like any other form of family disruption, should remain private and covertly dealt with. In her study *Emerging Voices* the Irish sociologist Pat O'Connor deplores the intrinsically private notion of gender violence that has recurred in Ireland's collective consciousness as well as the consequences of its underrepresentation. To use her own words: "The depiction of male violence, rape, sexual harassment, child sexual abuse, marital violence or pornography as 'not that serious' erodes women's sense of their own bodily integrity and ultimately their sense of their own value."[29] Similarly, Ailbhe Smyth insists on the notion of ownership that is usually attached to patriarchal manipulations of the female body and which is epitomized in situations of gender violence:

> The right of The Family not to be interfered with by the State is *de facto* the right of the male family members not to have their rights of "ownership" of "their" women interfered with. [...] In conservative Catholic ideology and politics, The Family as an abstract ideal is of infinitely higher value than the rights, freedoms and survival of women and children.[30]

Thus Mullan is blurring this private-public delimitation by artistically rendering visible a private act of power assertion, while he offers an interesting outlook on the persisting denial of individual rights to the Magdalenes and the complete loss of their sense of belonging. Likewise, O'Connor and Smyth's comments are echoed in *Sinners*, whose protagonists bear witness to the family betrayal felt by the inmates, mostly represented by Theresa and her detachment from Eamon and the rest of her relatives. As in Margaret's case, the girl is only allowed to leave once

---

[29] Pat O'Connor, *Emerging Voices: Women in Contemporary Irish Society* (Dublin: Institute of Public Administration, 1998), 14.

[30] Ailbhe Smyth, "Seeing Red: Men's Violence against Women in Ireland," in *Women in a Violent World: Feminist Analyses and Resistance across Europe*, ed. Chris Corrin (Edinburgh: Edinburgh University Press, 1996), 67–68.

her brother signs her out, an act that in Walsh's film acquires a deeper significance, since the fact that he was also her rapist bears out the paradox underlying
the patriarchal notion of ownership mentioned above.

Conclusions

To a large extent, both films record the effects of the ongoing dialectics between
culture and the individual when it comes to violence, as introduced earlier in
this chapter through Glucklich's ideas of the social construction of pain. The
Irish attachment to cultural tradition and religious identity are equally highlighted in the two texts, which at the same time essentially constitute narratives
of resistance to the perpetuation of such a system of beliefs and actions. Like
the many other critical, artistic, and personal accounts of the Magdalene laundries mentioned throughout my analysis, they certainly stir Ireland's national
consciousness about social complicity in the processes of Magdalene victimization. Besides, with the "memory-enabling effect" of this type of historical film, as
Ruth Barton puts it, the practices of gender inequality, and specifically, violence
against women, are not only displayed but also interrogated for the many trou-
bling issues that they entail. For Barton, "the victims of historical injustice in
turn became the ghosts of the Celtic Tiger, in need of exorcism for modernity to
triumph. By becoming consumers of our own past, we were able to express our
control over it."[31] In transcending time, these two productions connect gender
violence to present-day Ireland as they posit uncomfortable questions about the
prevalence of those codes of behavior. By describing different forms of Magdalene violence, I believe, the films claim the need to find a social order in which
Irish women are the creators and guarantors of their own rights. In this light,
the directors arguably contribute to the current wave of social claims for state
intervention into the aftermath of the Magdalene laundries network, as far as
the victims are concerned. The creation of lobby groups and associations, like
Justice for Magdalenes or Magdalene Survivors Together,[32] with their ongoing
efforts to act on behalf of the survivors and their families, and their commit-

---

[31] Ruth Barton, "The Ghost of the Celtic Tiger," in *Glocal Ireland: Current Perspectives on Literature and the Visual Arts*,
eds. Marisol Morales Ladrón and Juan F. Elices Agudo (Cambridge: Cambridge Scholars Publishing, 2011), 32.

[32] For further information about their campaigns and agenda, visit the websites www.magdalenelaundries.com and www.
magdalenesurvivorstogether.net.

ment to achieve Magdalene redress, have meant a remarkable step forward in the recovery of this part of Ireland's recent history, or herstory. Similarly, the two directors seek to prevent further unawareness and confusion about the Magdalene reality, so that a new ethos about Irish women's reproductive and maternal rights may be brought in.

Implications for teaching

As an afterthought of my analysis, and in order to highlight the didactic possibilities of the Magdalene imaginary in Ireland and its different artistic representations, I would like to point out that the films as well as the present chapter could be used in class, either together or separately, and for purely informative purposes or to develop in-depth commentary. The main events and ideas discussed could raise a number of debates that could be adapted depending on the level of the students or the area of study. Thus teachers could pose questions like the ones listed below:

1. What effect did the socio-political context of Ireland throughout the twentieth century have upon the perpetuation of the Magdalene laundries network?
2. In Ireland, religious discourse has had an important social role in the process of female identity formation. How do these Catholic institutions contravene the Church's own dogmas?
3. What regular tools of violence intervention were disregarded during the period in which the laundries operated?
4. Why did families throughout Ireland comply with this system of female internment and its various forms of terrorization?
5. The films stress the fact that women can be perpetrators of violence upon other women. What further implications does this have for a feminist analysis of terrorization in the films?

Questions

Subsequently, the following assignments can be given so that students formulate further interrogations on the main ideas described in the films and the chapter:

1. Look for other artistic representations of Magdalene violence in Ireland and compare their portrayal of abuse.
2. Find similar cases of institutional abuse (upon women, men, or children) in other European contexts.
3. Search for the recent socio-political and legal developments in relation to Magdalene redress in Ireland and describe to what extent justice for the survivors has been achieved.

All in all, the ideas derived from the screening of the films, the readings, and the discussions would expediently contribute to the ultimate objectives of the directors that I mentioned above. In this way the films could reach their inner and outer coherence by virtue of not only informing and engaging the audience, but also playing an active role in the imperative social movement in favor of the achievement of Magdalene justice and compensation.

REFERENCES

Barton, Ruth. "The Ghost of the Celtic Tiger." In *Glocal Ireland: Current Perspectives on Literature and the Visual Arts*, eds. Marisol Morales Ladrón and Juan F. Elices Agudo, 26–38. Cambridge: Cambridge Scholars Publishing, 2011.

Brereton, Pat. "Religion and Irish Cinema: A Case Study." *An Irish Quarterly Review* 97 (2008): 321–332.

Burke Brogan, Patricia. *Eclipsed*. Galway: Salmon Publishing, 1994.

Burke Brogan, Patricia. *Stained Glass at Samhain*. Cliffs of Moher, Co. Clare: Salmon Publishing, 2003.

Conlon-McKenna, Marita. *The Magdalen*. London: Bantam Books, 1999.

Ferriter, Diarmaid. *Occasions of Sin: Sex and Society in Modern Ireland*. London: Profile Books, 2009.

Finnegan, Frances. *Do Penance or Perish: Magdalene Asylums in Ireland*. Piltown, Co. Kilkenny: Congrave Press, 2001.

Glucklich, Ariel. *Sacred Pain: Hurting the Body for the Sake of the Soul*. Oxford: Oxford University Press, 2003.

González Casademont, Rosa. "The Glocalisation of Contemporary Irish Cinema." In *In the Wake of the Tiger: Irish Studies in the Twentieth-First Century*, eds. David Clark and Rubén Jarazo Álvarez, 127–140. La Coruña: Netbiblio, 2010.

Goulding, June. *The Light in the Window*. Dublin: Poolbeg, 1998.

Herr, Cheryl. "The Erotics of Irishness." *Critical Inquiry* 17, no. 1 (1990): 1–34.

Jordison, Sam. "Irish Gulags for Women: The Catholic Church's Magdalene Asylums." In *Everything You Know about God Is Wrong,* ed. Russ Kick, 188–196. New York: The Disinformation Company, 2007.

Luddy, Maria. "Magdalen Asylums: 1765–1922." In *The Field Day Anthology of Irish Writing.* Vol. 5, *Irish Women's Writing and Traditions*, eds. Angela Bourke et al., 736–751. Cork: Cork University Press, 2002.

The Magdalene Sisters. Directed by Peter Mullan. PFP Production in association with Temple Films, 2002.

Mullan, P. "Magdalene Sisters: Women's Oppression." *Il Manifesto,* August 8, 2002.

Murphy, Paula. "'Wayward Girls and Fallen Women': Negotiating Fact and Fiction in the Magdalen Laundries." In *Single Motherhood in Twentieth-Century Ireland: Cultural, Historical, and Social Essays,* eds. Cinta Ramblado-Minero and Auxiliadora Pérez-Vides, 139–153. Lewiston, NY: Edwin Mellen Press, 2006.

O'Beirne, Kathy. *Kathy's Story: A Childhood Hell inside the Magdalen Laundries.* Edinburgh: Mainstream Publishing, 2005.

O'Connor, Pat. *Emerging Voices: Women in Contemporary Irish Society*. Dublin: Institute of Public Administration, 1998.

O'Malley, Kathleen. *Childhood Interrupted: Growing up under the Cruel Regime of the Sisters of Mercy*. London: Virago Press, 2005.

O'Toole, Fintan. "Attitudes That Led to Abuse Entrenched in System." *Irish Times*, May 15, 1999.

O'Toole, Fintan. "The Sisters of No Mercy." *Observer*, February 15, 2003.

Raftery, Mary, and Eoin O'Sullivan. *Suffer the Little Children: The Inside Story of Ireland's Industrial Schools*. Dublin: New Island Books, 1999.

Sex in a Cold Climate. Directed by Steve Humphries. Testimony Films for Channel Four, 1998.

Sinners. Directed by Aisling Walsh. Parallel Productions/ BBC Northern Ireland, 2002.

Smith, James M. *Ireland's Magdalen Laundries and the Nation's Architecture of Containment.* Notre Dame, IN: University of Notre Dame Press, 2007.

Smyth, Ailbhe. "Paying our Disrespects to the Bloody States We're in: Women, Violence, Culture and the State." In *Stirring It: Challenges for Feminism*, eds. Gabriele Griffin et al., 13–39. London: Taylor and Francis, 1994.

Smyth, Ailbhe. "Seeing Red: Men's Violence against Women in Ireland." In *Women in a Violent World: Feminist Analyses and Resistance across Europe*, ed. Chris Corrin, 53–76. Edinburgh: Edinburgh University Press, 1996.

Song for a Raggy Boy. Directed by Aisling Walsh. Subotica Entertainment, 2003.

GENDER AND DOMESTIC VIOLENCE IN PORTUGAL: INTERVENTION PRACTICES AND THEIR EFFECTS

Marlene Matos, Anita Santos, Rita Conde

Introduction

The current relevance of domestic violence is mainly due to the social construction of this type of victimization. The ongoing public recognition of violence as a serious problem can be attributed to several factors, namely the greater transparency of family relationships, the redefinition of women's role in the family, the greater possibility for women to exercise their individual rights, the public testimonies of victims, and emergent civic movements (e.g., non-governmental organizations). The growing public awareness goes together with the proliferation of information services easily accessible to the community (e.g., help lines) and media attention. Indeed, in Portugal the media have recently taken an important role in raising awareness of the problem,[1] increasing the opportunities for clarification, discussion, and reflection (e.g., in news reports, debates, and seminars). Similarly, those in politics and the judiciary have placed a special focus on the subject.[2] The recent adjustment in the legal taxonomy of domestic violence crimes[3] contributed to a differentiated approach toward this criminalized conduct. Nevertheless, as described in the Fourth National Plan Against Domestic Violence (PNCVD IV), domestic violence includes not only the criminal perspective but also "socio-cultural dynamics and civilization values that have been sustaining gender imbalances and inequalities, and that are in the base of its emergence and reproduction,"[4] despite the progressive social criminalization of the violent behavior. In fact, it is important to emphasize the contribution of the National Plans against Domestic Violence (each one with a duration of three

---

[1] Ana Rita Dias and Carla Machado, "Representações da mulher no discurso mediático, de 1965 até à actualidade," *Psicologia: Teoria, Investigação e Prática* 2 (2007): 193.

[2] Marlene Matos, "Violência nas relações de intimidade: estudo sobre a mudança psicoterapêutica na mulher" (PhD diss. Universidade do Minho, Braga, 2006), http://repositorium.sdum.uminho.pt/handle/1822/5735.

[3] Law 59/152/2007, September 4, 2007.

[4] Republic Diary, *Council of Ministers Resolution no. 100/2010*, chapter 1, preamble of the PNCVD IV (2010): 5765.

years), showing how the efforts against domestic violence in Portugal have been assumed as a core political goal to achieve a fairer and more egalitarian society. The purpose of these plans has been to outline a national strategy against domestic violence through the implementation of a resolute and structured policy: in order to protect victims, to condemn those who assault, to understand and to prevent the problem, to qualify professionals, and to create and develop support structures and services.[5]

In the scientific domain, there is now a considerable amount of knowledge about the prevalence, dynamics, and impact of domestic violence. In Portugal, several studies have contributed significantly to the knowledge of this problem.[6] Domestic violence became an object of study in Portugal mainly in the 1990s, when the first publications on the subject came out.[7] Since then, one of the scientific community's concerns has been documenting the prevalence of this social phenomenon. The first national survey, conducted in 1995,[8] looked at the Portuguese reality, describing the characteristics of the victims and the victimization. Simultaneously, studies on the social and economic costs involved in violence against women[9] and about the health care economic costs related to victims of domestic violence[10] have been developed.

As stated in the international literature, these studies confirm that women who are exposed to domestic violence report high levels of use of health care facilities and are at risk of reduced physical and mental health.[11] In addition,

---

[5] Ibid., 5763–5773.

[6] Manuel Lisboa et al., *Custos sociais e económicos da violência contra as mulheres. Síntese dos resultados do inquérito nacional de 2002* (Lisbon: CIDM, 2003); Nacional Lourenço, Manuel Lisboa, and E. Pais, *Violência contra as mulheres* (Lisbon: CIDM, 1997); Carla Machado et al., "Child and Partner Abuse: Self-Reported Prevalence and Attitudes in the North of Portugal," *Child Abuse and Neglect* 31, no. 6 (2007): 657; Marlene Matos, *Violência conjugal: O processo de construção de identidade da mulher* (PhD diss. Universidade do Minho, Braga, 2000); Al. Sani, "Avaliação de crianças expostas à violência interparental," in *Psicologia Forense,* eds. Abrunhosa R. Gonçalves and Carla Machado, 247–271 (Coimbra: Quarteto, 2005); Luísa Ferreira da Silva, *Entre marido e mulher alguém meta a colher* (Celorico de Basto: À Bolina, 1995).

[7] See Nelson Lourenço and Manuel Lisboa, *Representações da Violência. Percepção social do grau, da frequência, das causas e das medidas para diminuir a violência em Portugal* (Lisbon: Centro de Estudos Judiciários, 1992); Nelson Lourenço, Manuel Lisboa, and E. Pais, *Violência contra as mulheres* (Lisbon: CIDM, 1997).

[8] Lourenço, *Violência contra as mulheres.*

[9] Lisboa, *Custos sociais e económicos.*

[10] Comissão para a Igualdade e para os Direitos das Mulheres, Presidência do Conselho de Ministros, *II Plano Nacional Contra a Violência Doméstica: 2003–2006* (Lisbon: CIDM, 2003).

[11] Rose Constantino, Yookyung Kim, and Patrica A. Crane, "Effects of a Social Support Intervention on Health Outcomes in Residents of a Domestic Violence Shelter: A Pilot Study," *Issues in Mental Health Nursing* 26, no. 6 (2005):

behavioral, emotional, and relational difficulties are documented; so are the destructive (e.g., homicide and suicide) and the disabling nature of the maltreatment.[12] In 2007 a new national survey on gender violence was conducted, with the same objectives as the 1995 survey;[13] the comparison of both surveys provided an opportunity to evaluate the progression of the problem in Portugal.[14] It was found that "in 2007, the whole of victimization related to physical, sexual and psychological abuse against women (of 18 or more years of age, and in the past 12 months or in the last year) has a prevalence of 38.1% in Portugal, affecting, on average, approximately one in three women. Comparing the same types of violence with those detected in the 1995 survey, there is a decrease of 48% to 38.1% in the victimization prevalence."[15]

Given this data, the authors concluded that "the gender-based violent acts that occur within the home/family are a dramatized expression of the economic, social and cultural inequalities together with women's and men's power struggle in society. Domestic violence acts are already criminalized; however, a sustained solution for this social problem requires a more comprehensive approach, in time and space, laying down the boundaries of the invisible territories, hidden over the centuries."[16]

In a complementary way, the annual reports of internal security[17] focus on the statistical dimension of the phenomenon. In 2012 the police recorded 26,084

575; Catherine Itzin, Ann Taket, and Sarah Barter-Godfrey, *Domestic and Sexual Violence and Abuse: Tackling the Health and Mental Health Effects* (London and New York: Routledge, 2010); Therese Zink and Frank Putnam, "Intimate Partner Violence Research in the Health Care Setting: What Are Appropriate and Feasible Methodological Standards?" *Journal of Interpersonal Violence* 20, no. 4 (2005): 365.

[12] Carla Machado, "Intervenção psicológico com vítimas de crimes: Dilemas teóricos, técnicos, técnicos e emocionais," *International Journal of Clinical and Health Psychology* 4, no. 2 (2004): 399.

[13] Republic Diary, *Council of Ministers Resolution no. 100/2010*, 5763–5773.

[14] Ibid.

[15] Manuel Lisboa et al., *Violência e Género. Inquérito Nacional sobre a Violência exercida contra Mulheres e Homens* (Lisbon: Comissão para a Igualdade e para os Direitos da Mulheres, 2009), 3.

[16] Ibid., 118.

[17] Internal Security System, *Annual Report of Internal Security 2011* (Internal Administration Ministry, 2011), http://www.portugal.gov.pt/media/555724/2012-03-30_relat_rio_anual_seguran_a_interna.pdf (accessed April 12, 2012); Internal Security System, *Annual Report of Internal Security 2010* (Internal Administration Ministry, 2011), http://www.portugal.gov.pt/media/564302/rasi_2010.pdf (accessed March 2, 2012); Internal Security System, *Annual Report of Internal Security 2009* (Internal Administration Ministry, 2010), http://www.portugal.gov.pt/media/564305/rasi_2009.pdf (accessed March 2, 2012); Internal Security System, *Annual Report of Internal Security 2008* (Internal Administration Ministry, 2009), http://www.portugal.gov.pt/media/564308/rasi_2008.pdf (accessed March 2, 2012).

domestic violence crimes (against wife or equivalent).[18] So the actual numbers are still alarmingly high.

Within this universe, one of the most dramatic effects of domestic violence is wife homicide. According to the national Observatory of Women Murdered, in 2012, 40 women died as victims of gender violence in intimate relationships at the hands of their husbands, partners, boyfriends, ex-husbands, ex-partners, or ex-boyfriends.[19]

Furthermore, a pioneering national study[20] revealed that 15.5% of youth reported having been victims of at least one abusive act during the previous year, and 21.7% said they had adopted this type of behavior towards their partner. Like other international studies,[21] "what are commonly known as minor acts of violence are dominant: to insult, to denigrate, or to make statements to humiliate or to cause serious harm, to threat or to scream with the intention of causing fear, to break or to damage objects intentionally, and to slap."[22] Concerning gender differences, no significant differences were found, although with regard to minor acts of violence, women admit a higher rate of aggression.[23]

Finally, and also with regard to prevalence, it is important to say that the numbers found certainly do not reflect the totality of the acts committed. Shame, guilt, or fear still prevent disclosure and reporting of violence; additionally, some women may not even perceive some behavior as abuse or tend to minimize "minor" violence.[24]

In the context of advances in this field, intervention with female victims was established as a priority, because of the high costs that are usually associated with this problem (e.g., family, social, economic). The significant impact of domestic violence, in the short- and long-term, and the financial costs associated

---

[18] Ibid., 2008.

[19] União de Mulheres Alternativa Resposta, *Observatório de Mulheres Assassinadas – OMA 2011. Dados preliminares,* http://www.umarfeminismos.org/images/stories/oma/2011/Dados_Preliminares_Nov_2011.pdf (accessed April 19, 2012).

[20] Carla Machado, Marlene Matos, and Al I. Moreira, "Violência Nas Relações Amorosas: Comportamentos e Atitudes Na População Universitária," *Psychologica* 33 (2003): 69.

[21] Shelby A. Kaura and Allen M. Craig, "Dissatisfaction with Relationship Power and Dating Violence Perpetration by Men and Women," *Journal of Interpersonal Violence* 19 (2003): 576.

[22] Matos, "Violência nas relações de intimidade," 60

[23] Ibid.

[24] Marlene Matos et al., "Prevenção Da Violência Nas Relações De Namoro: Intervenção Com Jovens Em Contexto Escolar," *Revista Psicologia-Teoria e Prática* 8, no. 1 (2006).

with it indicate the need to develop an appropriate intervention and its respective evaluation.[25]

Still, there is no ideal intervention, a technical response perfectly suited to all situations, nor a type of help considered most effective from a single component. Regardless of the victim's condition, the complexity of problems associated with domestic violence often calls for the use of integrated models of professional help.[26] On the other hand, although there is a considerable effort to expand the answers that were intended to reduce the impact of domestic violence on women, the literature on intervention continues to emphasize the immediate protection of women (e.g., house shelter, crisis intervention) and acting towards the perpetrators.[27] Moreover, although the intervention in this area assumes an increasing relevance and expression, different modalities of clinical intervention with abused women have been poorly described in the scientific literature.[28] Simultaneously, in Portugal, the problem is that both victims and offenders need a larger and more diversified range of responses in terms of psychotherapy. The network of intervention with the victim and the offenders is still very scarce and mainly remedial in nature.[29] Furthermore, the efficacy of the main interventions currently used is unknown.[30]

Given that domestic violence is a social problem with a strong cultural trait, it should be treated as such: "It is important to deal with the many social issues that involve violence, instead of focusing only on the victim's personal difficulties. The group work helps the development of this social approach. It is a

---

[25] Constantino, "Effects of a Social Support Intervention."
   Robert Walker et al., "An Integrative Review of Separation in the Context of Victimization Consequences and Implications for Women," *Trauma, Violence, and Abuse* 5, no. 2 (2004): 143.

[26] Matos, "Violência nas relações de intimidade."

[27] Celina Manita, *A intervenção em agressores no contexto da violência doméstica em Portugal: Estudo preliminar de caracterização* (Lisbon: CIDM, 2005); D.L. McBride, "Groups for Abused Women: Treatment Outcome" (PhD diss. Department of Applied Psychology: University of Calgary, Alberta, 2001); Leslie M. Tutty, Bruce A. Bidgood, and Michael A. Rothery, "Support Groups for Battered Women: Research on Their Efficacy," *Journal of Family Violence* 8, no. 4 (1993): 325.

[28] Lesley Laing, *Research and Evaluation of Interventions with Women Affected by Domestic Violence*, Australian Domestic and Family Violence, 2003, http://www.adfvc.unsw.edu.au/PDF%20files/evaluation_of_interventions_with_women.pdf (accessed April 16, 2012); McBride, "Groups for Abused Women"; Jean Ramsey, Carol Rivas, and Gene Feder, *Interventions to Reduce Violence and Promote the Physical and Psychological Well-Being of Women who Experience Partner Violence: A Systematic Review of Controlled Evaluations; Final Report* (London: Department of Health, 2005); Tutty, "Support Groups for Battered Women."

[29] Manita, *A intervenção em agressores no contexto.*

[30] Matos, "Violência nas relações de intimidade."

safe space that allows creating bonds that let women talk about what is often seen as unspeakable."[31]

Although several works have helped establish the scientific and social relevance of the problem in Portugal, producing a set of knowledge that has clearly oriented public policies and technical interventions with women victims, the emphasis on the impact of violence and its consequences means that victims are usually portrayed as traumatized, powerless, and passive, with relatively little attention directed to their change processes.[32] The traditional approaches concerning victims' interventions have been criticized for that reductionism.[33]

With those limitations in mind, we have been conducting studies that identify the coping efforts through which women try to deal with domestic violence, recognizing the psychological processes involved in the construction of adaptive trajectories. Specifically, we have been studying the contribution of psychological interventions with female victims in a group setting.

Research developments in Portugal Group intervention: Pathways to change?

The group intervention philosophy with women victims of domestic violence relates to some extent to the feminist movements of the 1960s and 1970s.[34] It usually results from the intent, frequently expressed by victims, to share their experience with other women with similar life trajectories.[35]

According to Tutty, Bidgood, and Rothery,[36] support groups are the most common type of intervention among women who have experienced abuse. There are already several examples of group intervention described in the literature, showing how this type of intervention has been developed internationally. Doc-

---

[31] Margarida Martins et al., *Poder para Mudar: Como estabelecer grupos de suporte e de ajuda mutual para vítimas e sobreviventes de violência doméstica* (Budapest: Daphne, 2008), 12.

[32] Kim Anderson, *Enhancing Resilience in Survivors of Family Violence* (New York: Springer, 2009); Jo Goodey, *Victims and Victimology: Research, Policy and Practice* (London: Pearson Education, 2005); Basia Spalek, *Crime Victims: Theory, Policy and Practice* (New York: Palgrave Macmillan, 2006).

[33] Anderson, *Enhancing Resilience in Survivors of Family Violence.*

[34] K.J. Wilson, *When Violence Begins at Home* (Alameda, CA: Hunter House Publishers, 1997); Mollie Whalen, *Counseling to End Violence against Women: A Subversive Model*, vol. 18 (Thousand Oaks, CA: Sage, 1996).

[35] Judith Worell and Pamela Remer, *Feminist Perspectives in Therapy: Empowering Diverse Women* (New York: John Wiley and Sons, 2002).

[36] Tutty, "Support Groups for Battered Women."

umented studies have been carried out with women with PTSD[37] and among older abused women.[38]

One of the advantages of this type of intervention is that it breaks the isolation to which these women are often subjected. The group context also allows them to validate their experience, obtain information, give and receive support (e.g., emotional, instrumental), and allow them to realize that their problem is not unique and that there are alternative ways to deal with the abusive situation. The group can help a woman "to notice she is not alone and that their feelings of confusion, fear and despair are real and shared by other women."[39]

Furthermore, the group intervention is a pragmatic and cost-effective model for support, and it is relatively simple to implement. It has also the advantage of being a very practical approach to the problems brought by such women and has significant efficacy in the consolidation of the results produced at the individual level.[40] Although they are still few, some published studies support this idea,[41] indicating statistically significant improvements in several areas: self-esteem, anger, depression, and attitudes toward marriage and family. A study by McBride[42] indicates results in the same direction, as do others that also provide evidence about the benefits of the intervention group.[43] Thus these results allowed us to anticipate the effectiveness of this type of intervention, especially

---

[37] Karin A. Schlee, Richard E. Heyman, and K. Daniel O'Leary, "Group Treatment for Spouse Abuse: Are Women with PTSD Appropriate Participants?" *Journal of Family Violence* 13, no. 1 (1998): 1.

[38] Bonnie Brandl et al., "Feeling Safe, Feeling Strong," *Violence against Women* 9, no. 12 (2003): 1490.

[39] Wanda Webb, "Treatment Issues and Cognitive Behavior Techniques with Battered Women," *Journal of Family Violence* 7, no. 3 (1992): 209.

[40] Carla Machado and Marlene Matos, "A intervenção narrativa com um grupo de mulheres maltratadas: Da desconstrução da posição de vítima à reconstrução de identidades preferenciais," in *Psicoterapia, discurso e narrativa: A construção conversacional da mudança,* ed. Miguel M. Gonçalves, 207–234 (Coimbra: Quarteto Editora, 2001); Machado, "Intervenção psicológico com vítimas."

[41] Judy Woods Cox and Cal D. Stoltenberg, "Evaluation of a Treatment Program for Battered Wives," *Journal of Family Violence* 6, no. 4 (1991): 395; Marjorie Holiman and Rebecca Schilit, "Aftercare for Battered Women: How to Encourage the Maintenance of Change," *Psychotherapy* 28, no. 2 (1991): 345; Maryse Rinfret-Raynor and S. Cantin, "Feminist Therapy for Battered Women: An Assessment," in *Out of the Darkness: Contemporary Perspectives on Family Violence,* eds. Glenda Kaufman Kantor and Jana L. Jasinski, 219–234 (Thousand Oaks, CA: Sage, 1997); Holiman, "Aftercare for Battered Women"; Rinfret-Raynor, "Feminist Therapy for Battered Women"; Tutty, "Support Groups for Battered Women."

[42] McBride, "Groups for Abused Women."

[43] Constantino, "Effects of a Social Support Intervention"; Jonathan P. Schwartz et al., "Effects of a Group Preventive Intervention on Risk and Protective Factors Related to Dating Violence," *Group Dynamics: Theory, Research, and Practice* 8, no. 3 (2004): 221.

in decreasing tolerance towards abuse, reducing victimization, and increasing the participants' personal and social skills.

Establishing a group intervention program

From this point of departure, a group intervention with Portuguese women victims of domestic violence was implemented.

The main aims and the strategies adopted to reach them were to cease partner violence and to reduce tolerance towards interpersonal violence (IPV), through education concerning the violence cycle, cognitive restructuring, the planning of personal security, and new ways of coping with violence; to diminish clinical symptoms, through strategies such as stress management, assertiveness training and cognitive restructuring; to help women reduce social isolation, through the rehabilitation of relational networks and the promotion of relational and social abilities; to encourage new ways of communication with the partner, through the awareness of gendered performances in society, and assertiveness and empowerment training; to support skills of decision-making, through the promotion of adaptive decision-making; and to develop new life projects, through the increase of self-esteem and self-concept and also through projection into the future, namely in intimate relationships.

In order to fulfill its aims, we used some therapeutic approaches, namely the cognitive-behavioral, the feminist, and the psycho-educational.

To participate in the group intervention, one had to be a woman victim of IPV in a current situation of violence or who had recently (within the last 12 months) left an abusive relationship. Twenty-three women participated in the group intervention in a total of three groups (first group = eight women; second group = eight women; third group = seven women). Participants were recruited through victim support agencies and notices in newspapers. Thus a vast diversity of women's provenance was observed (referral and self-proposal) in recruitment. This also means that some of them already benefited from some type of help, namely crisis intervention, social support, and/or judicial support.

The women were between 26 and 58 years old (M = 39); they were mostly married or divorced; they were generally unemployed and had completed between six and 12 years of school. Regarding IPV, they were in an abusive relationship for between two and 35 years (M = 16) and had between one and four children (M = 2). They were mainly victims of physical and psychological violence (63.6%). Almost all of the women (82%) were, at intake and at the end of intervention, out of the abusive relationship. At intake, the majority of women had diagnosis criteria for dysthymic disorder (using SCID-I).

The research design laid on psychological evaluation to verify the inclusion criteria: pre-test, post-test and follow-up (after three months) with an assessment protocol. No control group was used, since this would imply some ethical questions concerning the waiting list that we did not comply with.

The group intervention program had three main phases:[44]

- The first phase included three sessions: presentation; comprehension of the dynamics of violence; "news" about violence.
- The second phase relied on developing skills: emotional coping; communication skills; self-esteem.
- The third phase completed the last two sessions: prevention of violence and promoting healthy relationships; conclusion.

A wide range of cognitive-behavioral oriented strategies were applied, such as integration/conclusion dynamics, debate, case-study, role-play, cognitive debate, relaxation training, video visualization, and positive reinforcements.

Each group lasted for two months (with weekly sessions of 90 minutes), with one follow-up session after three months. Two psychologists with wide experience on IPV intervention facilitated the groups.

Results and discussion

This section presents the assessment instruments used, giving a glimpse of the main findings and linking them to the main processes involved in group sessions. Assessment was completed before treatment started, or at intake (pre-test), when intervention ended (post-test), and six months after finalizing (follow-up).

One of the most important aims in the group intervention with women victims of IPV is to prevent revictimization. In this sense, the Partner Violence

---

[44] Marlene Matos and A. Machado, *Manual GAM para profissionais. Violência doméstica: Intervenção em grupo com mulheres vítimas* (Lisbon: CIG, Comissão para a Igualdade de Género, 2011).

Inventory[45] was used to identify violence behavior received or perpetrated by women. It has twenty-one items involving physical behavior (e.g., kicking), emotionally abusive behavior (e.g., insults) and coercive or intimidating behavior (e.g., breaking the woman's possessions). Women reported violent behavior received from their partner and also behavior they perpetrated in the context of the violent relationship. They scored this inventory at pre-test referring to the last six months and, at post-test and follow-up, to the period since the last evaluation was completed.

Before intervention started, participants in group intervention reported much more violent behavior received from their partners than perpetrated by them against their partners. These data seem to present a clearly gendered violence, with a high prevalence received by women and perpetrated by the male partner. Nevertheless, violent behavior presented by women at intake was understood in the group setting as responsive.

Taking these types of behavior as baseline, it was found, at post-test, that there was a clear (statistically significant) decrease of the received victimization, configuring a reduction of types of violent behavior received, frequency, and severity. Perpetration also dropped (statistically significantly) to near absence.

Thus group participants seem to have benefited from the sessions related to education about violence and its dynamics, as shown by the reduction of violent behavior not only received but also perpetrated. The session titled "News" about violence can be seen as pivotal in the sense that it provides an education about types of violent behavior and their criminal status under Portuguese law. On the other hand, this session aimed to deconstruct the socio-cultural discourses about women's role in society and in the maintenance of violent relations in present and future generations. At that first stage, the core aim was to deconstruct common and gendered beliefs about intimate violence, promoting new or alternative gender performances. This diminishing of violence is a clear achievement concerning the main goal, as stated, of preventing revictimization.

Another important goal of group intervention was to reduce tolerance towards interpersonal violence. The Scale on Marital Violence Beliefs[46] assessed tolerance towards violence through women's beliefs. Participants answered, in a five-point Likert scale, to twenty-five affirmations referring to ways of attributing

---

[45] Carla Machado, Miguel Gonçalves, and Marlene Matos, *Escala de Crenças sobre Violência Conjugal e Inventário de Violência Conjugal. Escalas de avaliação e Manual* (Braga: Psiquilíbrios, 2007; 2nd ed., 2008).

[46] Ibid.

legitimacy to violence in a relationship. High scores mean high tolerance towards violence, while low scores mean low tolerance.

When women were assessed at intake, data from the scale showed that women already had a global score showing low tolerance for violence in the context of a relationship. This seems to reveal a tendency to disagree with traditional beliefs about partner violence. It is possible that this group of women sought help because they had already put aside attitudes (personal, social) of tolerance towards domestic violence. Experiencing clinically significant symptoms as effects of a violent relationship probably helped them to understand that violence is not an adaptive way to relate to partners. On the other hand, it is possible that campaigns in Portugal against gender violence and promoting equality helped change minds about traditional gender roles and women's rights. Moreover, these women were recruited in several support agencies, where they did not have psychological help but had contact with other professionals (such as lawyers), whose intervention could have had some positive impact. Even so, these beliefs of "no tolerance" towards violence did not remain unchanged when the intervention ended. They actually decreased (with statistically significant differences) as the group evolved to the end and even at follow-up, showing even lower tolerant beliefs. As regards the questionnaire's subscales, factor 3 (Legitimization of violence by attribution to external causes) also reduced significantly from pre-test to post-test, and to follow-up. It is interesting to acknowledge that, even after the group ceased, women kept changing their causal attribution of violence, perhaps along with the idea that it was no longer acceptable to attribute it to external causes. At the same time, the attribution of responsibility to the offender was a transversal goal achievement in group intervention. Factor 4 (Legitimization of violence through preservation of the family intimacy) changed significantly from post-test to follow-up, as women did not use family preservation as a way to postpone decisions and to keep "holding on" to their marriage because they were not good wives or needed to "protect" their children from divorce or separation. Curiously, this last factor was the one with lower values since the beginning.

From a feminist point of view, intervention should help women to be aware of their socialization process and their gendered performances.[47] Data

---

[47] Sofia Neves and Conceição Nogueira, "Terapias feministas, intervenção psicológica e violências na intimidade: uma leitura feminista crítica," *Psychologica* 36 (2004): 15.

showed some level of awareness of these gendered discourses, indicating a low tolerance toward violence. Even so, intervention can help to facilitate specific changes towards beliefs about violence, like assigning a more accurate responsibility to the offender.

Factor 1 (Legitimization and trivialization of "minor" violence*)* and factor 2 (Legitimization of violence by attribution to women's behavior) did not undergo significant changes from the previous scale. In the same vein, the research by Tutty, Bidgood, and Rothery showed an increase of perceived emotional support, self-esteem, internal control locus, and decrease of stress at the end of group intervention, but traditional attitudes towards family and marriage also changed. Congruently, marital communication changed and violent behavior decreased.

At intake, women also revealed clinically significant symptoms, such as dysthymic disorder, although no trauma or anxiety-related disorders were found. These women were probably immersed in violent relations for so long, with children, that they found ways to cope with it. Thus they had no signs of acute disorder, but instead signs of prolonged depression resulting from a chronic situation. Others can see long-lasting depressive symptoms as not requiring intervention, as long as women stay functional (e.g., work, take care of the children). So these symptoms can easily be masked and not seen by others who can give social and emotional support.

Facing this tendency of dysthymic disorder, depressive symptoms were assessed by the BDI-II—Beck Depression Inventory,[48] which is one of the most-used instruments to evaluate depressive symptoms. In fact, before the group intervention, women seemed to show mild depression (almost moderate), which means that their depressive symptoms were clinically relevant and in need of intervention. However, these symptoms became minimal at post-test and follow-up, meaning that depressive symptoms decreased to a normal condition. It may be argued that group intervention provided for venting emotions and sharing experiences, leading to the diminishing of these symptoms. Indeed, even not focusing specifically on the change of clinical symptoms, the focus on violent

---

[48] Aaron T. Beck, Robert A. Steer, and Gregory K. Brown, *BDI-2, Beck Depression Inventory* (San Antonio, TX: Psychological Corporation, 1996); R. Coelho, A. Martins, and H. Barros, "Clinical Profiles Relating Gender and Depressive Symptoms among Adolescents Ascertained by the Beck Depression Inventory II," *European Psychiatry* 17, no. 4 (2002): 222.

relationships and ways of coping with them can be effective in reducing these symptoms, as they can be consequences of a violent relationship.

As a complementary view of clinical symptoms, the OQ45-Outcome Questionnaire[49] was used to assess clinical symptoms and their progress throughout the group intervention. As stated before, the impact of domestic violence on psychological well-being is well known, and findings corroborate that women started the group intervention with clinical relevant symptoms. Nevertheless, this psychological discomfort evolved to a condition of symptoms with no clinical relevance at post-test, and gains were maintained at follow-up assessment. Concerning subscales, it was interesting to find that there were significant differences from pre- to post-test on the subscale of subjective discomfort. This subscale reflects anxiety disorders, affective disorders, adjustment disorders, and stress-related illness. Although they did not have specific constellations of symptoms constituting a specific disorder, women had clinically relevant symptoms as consequence of domestic violence, which decreased at the end of group intervention, even though these were not a primary focus of intervention.

Several studies on group intervention efficacy have documented this kind of improvement in the psychological well-being of victimized women, depressive symptoms, and the reduction of violence.[50] The study of Rinfret-Raynor and Cantin[51] accessed three different group modalities. Results showed no differences in treatment orientation but did show significant differences in diminishing violence and psychological variables (e.g., self-esteem, assertiveness, social adjustment). It also showed that with proper treatment, women were able to rebuild their personal and social lives. In another study, McBride[52] conducted a group intervention highly structured with feminist and cognitive-behavioral techniques. The author studied self-esteem, depression, and intrusive symptoms as an effect of violence and also avoidance related to violence trauma memo-

---

[49] Michael Lambert et al., *Administration and Scoring Manual for the Outcome Questionnaire (OQ 45.2)* (Wilmington, DE: American Professional Credentialing Services); Paulo P. Machado and John M. Klein, "Outcome Questionnaire-45: Portuguese Psychometric Data with a Non-Clinical Sample" (paper presented at the 37th Annual Meeting of the Society for Psychotherapy Research. Edinburgh, Scotland, June 21–24, 2006).

[50] Cox, "Evaluation of a Treatment Program"; Rinfret-Raynor, "Feminist Therapy for Battered Women"; McBride, "Groups for Abused Women."

[51] Rinfret-Raynor, "Feminist Therapy for Battered Women."

[52] McBride, "Groups for Abused Women."

ries. All these variables had significant improvement. Cox and Stoltenberg[53] assessed a psycho-educational group intervention with several techniques: cognitive therapy, social abilities, problem resolution, vocational guidance, and self-image. Both control and experimental groups had changes in self-esteem, but the therapeutic group showed significant improvement in depressive and anxiety symptoms.

From these studies, self-esteem appeared to be an important goal in the group intervention. The Rosenberg Self-Esteem Scale (RSES)[54] was used to assess self-esteem. Total scores mean that the higher the scores related to higher self-esteem were, the more the participants evaluated see themselves worthy and self-respecting. At intake, before the group started, women showed a medium level of self-esteem, which increased at post-test and was sustained at follow-up. The differences from pre- to post-test and follow-up are statistically significant. The group intervention was intended to increase self-esteem, and it seemed to be successful in this matter. Specific strategies can be credited with prompting this increase, but the group context can also be considered important in increasing self-worth. The group program has a specific session with the goal of promoting self-esteem and self-worth in personal and social performances. Additionally, self-knowledge was promoted along the group program, as well as positive self-characteristics, resulting in an increase of self-esteem.

The literature has also pointed out the need to assess social support of women victims of domestic violence. This variable was measured with the Social Support Satisfaction Scale,[55] with a higher value indicating a higher social support perceived. The differences from pre- to post-test were statistically significant, and gains were maintained at follow-up. Concerning the subscales, curiously enough, the one related to *friendship* was the one with higher scores throughout the group intervention, meaning that the women seemed to perceive friends as social support. The least scored subscale was *social activities*. Some of the women were still with the violent offender, and others were in shelters, meaning that their engagement in social activities was probably still constrained. However, it

---

[53] Cox, "Evaluation of a Treatment Program."

[54] Morris Rosenberg, *Society and the Adolescent Self-Image* (Princeton: Princeton University Press, 1965); Paulo Jorge Santos, "Validação da Rosenberg Self-Esteem Scale numa amostra de estudantes do ensino superior" (Proceedings of the Thirteenth International Conference on Psychological Assessment: Methods and Contexts. Braga, Portugal, October 2–4, 2008).

[55] José Pais-Ribeiro, "Escala de Satisfação com o Suporte Social (ESSS)," *Análise Psicológica* 17, no. 3 (1999): 547.

increased at post-test and at follow-up. Besides, with a similar purpose, Constantino[56] developed a group intervention with the aim of giving information about social resources in the community. Overall findings showed that general health seemed to improve with the intervention, related to the perception of increased social support.

Additionally, we were interested in knowing more about coping skills. We used the Ways of Coping Questionnaire[57] to evaluate ways that women cope with their stressful experiences. The questionnaire was not designed specifically for victimized women, and the scope of usage is very broad. Higher scores meant increased frequency in using coping strategies. Subscales are defined by their contribution to the way women cope with violence. Thus it is interesting to look to the specific contribution of the subscales. At pre-test one found that *seeking social support* (instrumental and emotional) and *accepting responsibility* (recognizing one's role in the problem and efforts to change) were the ones with higher scores, followed by *positive re-evaluation* (positive meaning-making and personal development) and *self-control* (regulation of one's own emotions and actions). *Problem resolution, confrontation, avoidance,* and *distancing* were the ones with less contribution in the ways of coping with violent relationships. At post-test and at follow-up, *positive re-evaluation, seeking social support, accepting responsibility,* and *problem resolution* were the ones that characterize coping strategies used by these women.

We found that *confrontation, avoidance* and *distancing* were coping strategies less often used. *Confrontation* would probably be a non-secure way to cope with violence, as it utilizes aggressive means. *Distancing* could be seen as a way of minimizing the problem, which does not happen with these women who sought help. These could actually be maladaptive strategies to cope with violence.

Positive re-evaluation increased from pre- to post-test. This coping strategy seems to be adaptive, helping women to give a proper understanding of violence experience (instead of avoiding it) and integrate it in their life history. Avoidance (to avoid the problem) coping strategy saw a statistically significant decrease from pre- to post-test.

---

[56] Constantino, "Effects of a Social Support Intervention."

[57] Susan Folkman and Richard S. Lazarus, *Manual for the Ways of Coping Questionnaire* (Palo Alto, CA: Consulting Psychologists Press, 1988); José Pais-Ribeiro and Carla Santos, "Estudo conservador de adaptação do Ways of Coping Questionnaire a uma amostra e contexto portugueses," *Análise Psicológica* 19, no. 4 (2001): 491.

Some of these coping strategies were not directly addressed in our group program, such as problem resolution. In fact, some of the women were experiencing demanding tasks in their lives (e.g., deciding to leave the relationship; managing children's visits with the abusive partner), which might have been an obstacle to a higher development of this coping skill.

Lastly, one of the main gains was increasing the level of awareness of violent relationships and the basis for healthier ones. There was an increase of demand for social support and an increased sense of social support from friends. From the feminist point of view, a new sense of empowerment was promoted in these new social performances.

Implications for practice

These empirical results are fundamental for the victims' intervention; they provide an integrated understanding of domestic violence victimization and allow practitioners to reinforce their adaptive efforts to help women to cope with domestic violence. More specifically, we highlight the following results:

a. A clear dominance of received victimization by women (violence is less perpetrated by women), revealing a gendered nature of violence: intervention facilitates a significant reduction in violence received and perpetrated, so it prevents revictimization. As we said, providing education on violence and its dynamics is important to decreasing or ending it. As feminist perspectives suppose, when we offer education about the problem (violent behavior, dynamics, criminal status in Portuguese law, protection) and about its sociocultural roots (e.g., cultural issues in the socialization processes around gender and power imbalances), we help dismantle the sociocultural discourses/ideology about women's role in society and the maintenance of violent relations.[58] The traditional female's role promotes a system of beliefs and values that relegates women to a secondary status, thus contributing to their personal devaluation. This has to do with the responsibility of women in the

---

[58] Neves, "Terapias feministas, intervenção psicológica."

management of the relationship that made them remain in the abusive relationship and, ultimately, to hide and tolerate the abuse.[59]

b. A reduction in some beliefs that legitimated violence: although women demonstrated lower levels of tolerance towards violence, after intervention they reveal changes in some beliefs, namely (i) *legitimization of violence by attribution to external causes* and *(ii) legitimization of violence through preservation of family intimacy.* With regards to the "legitimization and trivialization of minor violence," which did not change significantly, we believe that this is an area that should continue to receive attention, with cultural beliefs that minimize and sustain this type of violence. Studies at the national level of both the juvenile population[60] and the adult population[61] reveal the persistence of attitudes and discourses that minimize it, and even conceptualize this kind of violence as acceptable, thus perpetuating it and making difficult its eradication. Thus the intervention should seek to identify the beliefs and attitudes internalized by women relating to gender roles and promote the rebuilding of gender roles and relations on an egalitarian footing.

c. A reduction in the clinically relevant symptoms and an increase of self-esteem: they presented clinically relevant symptoms, which showed a clear decrease as the intervention progressed. Additionally, there was an improvement in the psychological well-being of women and also on perception of their self-esteem.

These data reinforce the feminist idea of the "depathologization" of women, the idea that it is necessary to consider the external circumstances in which women live. Intervention with women victims should be cautious, avoiding blaming the woman for the symptoms. The purpose of intervention is not helping the woman adapt to the circumstances but supporting her in the transformation of the circumstances that contributed to the problem and are objectively part of the problem.[62]

---

[59] Matos, "Violência nas relações de intimidade."

[60] Sónia Caridade, *Vivências íntimas violentas: uma abordagem científica* (Coimbra: Almedina, 2011).

[61] Ana Rita Dias et al., "Repertórios interpretativos sobre o amor e as relações de intimidade de mulheres vítimas de violência: Amar e ser amando violentamente?" *Análise Psicológica* 30, nos. 1–2 (2012): 143.

[62] Rachel T. Hare-Mustin and Jeanne Marecek, "Abnormal and Clinical Psychology: The Politics of Madness," in *Critical Psychology: An Introduction*, eds. D. Fox and I. Prilleltensky (Thousand Oaks, CA: Sage Publications, 1997), 104–120, quoted in Neves, "Terapias feministas, intervenção psicológica."

Thus the intervention should support skills that promote change.

a. Some increase regarding social support: friends are seen as the main source of social support, in contrast with social activities, which are rare. However, both rise with intervention (although social activities continue to be limited). These outcomes inform us that the personal support strategies need to be complemented with social support strategies mobilization. This social support must be available for women victims. So community contexts may serve to support and enable the establishment of social activities.

b. Globally, there is no improvement in the coping skills, but results show some variations in the subscales, revealing subtle changes in this domain. Regarding the changes, we highlight an increase in positive re-evaluation (helping women to have a proper understanding of their violence experience) and a decline in the avoidance of the problem. However, some important adaptive coping skills showed no improvement.

The fact that there is no overall difference on this topic reveals the need for intervention to focus more on coping strategies. This called our attention to the need for further research and analysis on the processes of change and coping efforts of women victims, especially the most vulnerable ones. So at present, we are developing a longitudinal research project that seeks to identify the coping efforts through which women try to deal with and actively fight against violence in their lives, trying to understand the psychological processes involved in the construction of adaptive trajectories. Within this new research project, we try to differentiate socially vulnerable women who had no intervention, who were able to produce significant changes in their lives in a one-year period, from those that continue to cope with violence in their lives. The results of this ongoing project will also be fundamental for the intervention with women victims, providing an integrated understanding of resilience, coping strategies, and adaptive pathways.

Final remarks

The empirical results described are actually informative for victim intervention programs, providing an integrated understanding of domestic violence victimization and allowing practitioners to reinforce their adaptive efforts to help women to cope with domestic violence. Globally, results showed improvement in the psychological well-being of women, especially in reducing depressive symptoms and violence. This represents a significant input for intervention efforts with victims, showing the importance of considering intervention models that rely on their resources, strengthening and empowering women.[63] The results highlight the relevance of intervention models that analyze culture, gender roles, and power within relationships; work on demystifying gender stereotypes; and promote women's re-socialization in order to achieve changes in their lives.

It reinforces the idea that it is important to offer support groups, to establish equality relationships, to value competences and strengths, to support women in skills that promote change, to assist women to expand freely chosen behavior, and to help empower women.

Nevertheless, our experience also indicates that there is still much to do, particularly concerning extremely adverse structural and social difficulties (exclusion, poverty, lack of social support), coping efforts, and psychological processes involved in the construction of adaptive trajectories. Studying this intersection is our new challenge.

Implications for teaching

This chapter can be used in higher education, such as clinical psychology, forensic psychology, women's studies, gender studies, politics, law, and social and cultural studies, as well as in courses for practitioners working in the area of family violence, more specifically in intimate partner violence.

The introduction shows that domestic violence is a social problem with a strong cultural trait, alerting students and professionals that they can play an active role in the construction of contexts that fight domestic violence against women.

Social and psychological intervention may be one of these contexts where it is important to deal with the many issues that involve violence, instead of focusing only on the victim's personal difficulties. To deal with those issues, evidence shows that group work is a privileged setting, bringing positive effects. It is an advantage that the victim makes use of the support services and intervention.

---

[63] Neves, "Terapias feministas, intervenção psicológica."

Another important contribution of this chapter is to stress how important it is that intervention does not fall into the reductionist view of victims as "traumatized," "powerless," and "passive" and instead focuses on knowledge, skills, and resources that could empower them.

From the results of group intervention, it is also important to remember that:

- Education about violence, its criminal status, and its dynamics, as well as the deconstruction of socio-cultural discourses about the women's role in society, helps to reduce violence;
- Focusing beliefs concerning violence and revealing the gendered socialization process, gendered performances, and the gendered discourses helps to reduce violence tolerance and legitimization;
- Emphasizing the capacities and resources of women, as well as promoting social support and coping strategies, contribute to reducing symptoms, increasing self-esteem and self-worth, and dealing more effectively with the problems.

We hope that students, as future professionals, are inspired by these findings, and that they remember that information, deconstruction of gendered cultural discourses, and empowerment are essential elements to help prevent and cease violence.

Questions

- Which cultural traits are involved in domestic violence? Provide arguments in support of your answer.
- Various cultural beliefs play an important role in recognizing and combating violence. List some traditional themes and explain their importance in recognizing and fighting violence.
- Explain the advantages of group intervention over individual intervention.
- The findings of the Portuguese group intervention reinforce the feminist idea of the "depathologization" of women, the idea that it is necessary to consider the external circumstances in which women live. Explain this intersection.

Additional assignments for group/individual work

It is considered useful for students dealing with domestic violence from different starting points, as a social problem and as a gendered issue, to use case studies and debates to reflect on the gendered nature of violence. The following case can be presented for students to analyze and reflect upon, individually or in groups.

Mary is 26 years old. She has been married for five years, and she has suffered abuse from her partner ever since they married five years ago. When she asked for clinical help, she said:

Really, I... I feel very bad, I did not expect it to happen to me.... I have been married for five years... five years of beating! Yesterday was the same, he insulted me, broke everything at home. I must be really stupid, that must be it... this is what he always tells me, and he must be right, you know.... I really have difficulties in pleasing him and promoting a good environment at home.... I have no value and no one likes me, just him. I couldn't even finish my degree.... He was very jealous. He did not like that I had friends in college. If I were not so stupid and such a nothing, today I could have a degree, be employed and would not need to ask for help.... I'm so ashamed.

I'm really scared... I feel like a failure, a miserable wretch.... I'm 26 years old and never worked before. I feel completely alone in the world with my son.

Using Mary's story and the content covered in this chapter, critically reflect on the following points:

- What are the sociocultural discourses on the role and status of women revealed in her account?
- Identify gendered beliefs and attitudes that legitimate violence.
- Should intervention with Mary be focused mainly on the reduction of symptoms or on her empowerment? Or on both? Explain.
- Considering the gendered issues concerning violence, would group intervention be beneficial for Mary? Explain.

REFERENCES

Anderson, Kim. *Enhancing Resilience in Survivors of Family Violence.* New York: Springer, 2009.

Beck, Aaron T., Robert A. Steer, and Gregory K. Brown. *BDI-2, Beck Depression Inventory.* San Antonio, TX: Psychological Corporation, 1996.

Brandl, Bonnie, Michelle Hebert, Julie Rozwadowski, and Deb Spangler. "Feeling Safe, Feeling Strong." *Violence against Women* 9, no. 12 (2003): 1490–1503.

Caridade, Sónia. *Vivências íntimas violentas: uma abordagem científica.* Coimbra: Almedina, 2011.

Coelho, R., A. Martins, and H. Barros. "Clinical Profiles Relating Gender and Depressive Symptoms among Adolescents Ascertained by the Beck Depression Inventory II." *European Psychiatry* 17, no. 4 (2002): 222–226.

Comissão para a Igualdade e para os Direitos das Mulheres, Presidência do Conselho de Ministros. *II Plano Nacional Contra a Violência Doméstica: 2003–2006.* Lisbon: CIDM, 2003.

Constantino, Rose, Yookyung Kim, and Patrica A. Crane. "Effects of a Social Support Intervention on Health Outcomes in Residents of a Domestic Violence Shelter: A Pilot Study." *Issues in Mental Health Nursing* 26, no. 6 (2005): 575–590.

Cox, Judy Woods, and Cal D. Stoltenberg. "Evaluation of a Treatment Program for Battered Wives." *Journal of Family Violence* 6, no. 4 (1991): 395–413.

Dias, Ana Rita, and Carla Machado. "Representações da mulher no discurso mediático, de 1965 até à actualidade." *Psicologia: Teoria, Investigação e Prática* 2 (2007): 193–217.

Dias, Ana Rita, Carla Machado, Rui Abrunhosa Gonçalves, and Celina Manita. "Repertórios interpretativos sobre o amor e as relações de intimidade de mulheres vítimas de violência: Amar e ser amando violentamente?" *Análise Psicológica* 30, nos. 1–2 (2012): 143–160.

Folkman, Susan, and Richard S. Lazarus. *Manual for the Ways of Coping Questionnaire.* Palo Alto, CA: Consulting Psychologists Press, 1988.

Goodey, Jo. *Victims and Victimology: Research, Policy and Practice.* London: Pearson Education, 2005.

Holiman, Marjorie, and Rebecca Schilit. "Aftercare for Battered Women: How to Encourage the Maintenance of Change." *Psychotherapy* 28, no. 2 (1991): 345–353.

Internal Security System. *Annual Report of Internal Security 2008.* Internal Administration Ministry, 2009. http://www.portugal.gov.pt/media/564308/rasi_2008.pdf (accessed March 2, 2012).

Internal Security System. *Annual Report of Internal Security 2009.* Internal Administration Ministry, 2010. http://www.portugal.gov.pt/media/564305/rasi_2009.pdf (accessed March 2, 2012).

Internal Security System. *Annual Report of Internal Security 2010.* Internal Administration Ministry, 2011. http://www.portugal.gov.pt/media/564302/rasi_2010.pdf (accessed March 2, 2012).

Internal Security System. *Annual Report of Internal Security 2011.* Internal Administration Ministry, 2011. http://www.portugal.gov.pt/media/555724/2012-03-30_relat_rio_anual_seguran_a_interna.pdf (accessed April 12, 2012).

Itzin, Catherine, Ann Taket, and Sarah Barter-Godfrey. *Domestic and Sexual Violence and Abuse: Tackling the Health and Mental Health Effects.* London and New York: Routledge, 2010.

Kaura, Shelby A., and Allen M. Craig. "Dissatisfaction with Relationship Power and Dating Violence Perpetration by Men and Women." *Journal of Interpersonal Violence* 19 (2003): 576–588.

Laing, Lesley. *Research and Evaluation of Interventions with Women Affected by Domestic Violence.* Australian Domestic and Family Violence, 2003 http://www.adfvc.unsw.edu.au/PDF%20files/evaluation_of_interventions_with_women.pdf (accessed April 16, 2012).

Lambert, Michael J., Jared J. Morton, Derick Hatfield, Cory Harmon, Stacy Hamilton, Rory C. Reid, Kenichi Shimokawa, Cody Christopherson, and Gary M. Burlingame. *Administration and Scoring Manual for the Outcome Questionnaire (OQ 45.2).* Wilmington, DE: American Professional Credentialing Services, 2004.

Lisboa, Manuel, Isabel Carmo, Luisa Branco Vicente, and Antonio Nóvoa. *Custos sociais e económicos da violência contra as mulheres. Síntese dos resultados do inquérito nacional de 2002.* Lisbon: Comissão para a Igualdade e para os Direitos da Mulheres, 2003.

Lisboa, Manuel, Zelia Barroso, Joana Patrício, and Alexandra Leandro. *Violência e Género. Inquérito Nacional sobre a Violência exercida contra Mulheres e Homens.* Lisbon: Comissão para a Igualdade e para os Direitos da Mulheres, 2009.

Lourenço, Nelson, and Manuel Lisboa. *Representações da Violência. Percepção social do grau, da frequência, das causas e das medidas para diminuir a violência em Portugal.* Lisbon: Centro de Estudos Judiciários, 1992.

Lourenço, Nelson, Manuel Lisboa, and E. Pais. *Violência contra as mulheres.* Lisbon: CIDM, 1997.

Machado, Carla, and Marlene Matos. "A intervenção narrativa com um grupo de mulheres maltratadas: Da desconstrução da posição de vítima à reconstrução de identidades preferenciais." In *Psicoterapia, discurso e narrativa: A construção conversacional da mudança,* ed. Miguel M. Gonçalves, 207–234. Coimbra: Quarteto Editora, 2001.

Machado, Carla, Marlene Matos, and Al I. Moreira. "Violência Nas Relações Amorosas: Comportamentos e Atitudes Na População Universitária." *Psychologica* 33 (2003): 69–83.

Machado, Carla, Miguel Gonçalves, and Marlene Matos. *Escala de Crenças sobre Violência Conjugal e Inventário de Violência Conjugal. Escalas de avaliação e Manual.* Braga: Psiquilibrios, 2007; 2nd ed., 2008.

Machado, Carla, Miguel Gonçalves, Marlene Matos, and Ana Rita Dias. "Child and Partner Abuse: Self-Reported Prevalence and Attitudes in the North of Portugal." *Child Abuse and Neglect* 31, no. 6 (2007): 657–670.

Machado, Carla. "Intervenção psicológica com vítimas de crimes: Dilemas teóricos, técnicos, técnicos e emocionais." *International Journal of Clinical and Health Psychology* 4, no. 2 (2004): 399–411.

115

Machado, P.P.P., and John M. Klein. "Outcome Questionnaire-45: Portuguese Psychometric Data with a Non-Clinical Sample." Paper presented at 37th Annual Meeting of the Society for Psychotherapy Research. Edinburgh, Scotland, June 21–24, 2006.

Manita, Celina. *A intervenção em agressores no contexto da violência doméstica em Portugal: Estudo preliminar de caracterização.* Lisbon: CIDM, 2005.

Martins, Margarida, Petra Viegas, Alessandra Pauncz, Györgyi Tóth, Reet Hiiema, Nicola Harwin, and Sally Cosgrove. *Poder para Mudar: Como estabelecer grupos de suporte e de ajuda mutual para vítimas e sobreviventes de violência doméstica.* Budapest: Daphne, 2008.

Matos, Marlene, and A. Machado. *Manual GAM para profissionais. Violência doméstica: Intervenção em grupo com mulheres vítimas.* Lisbon: CIG, Comissão para a Igualdade de Género, 2011.

Matos, Marlene, Carla Machado, Sonia Caridade, and Maria Joao Silva. "Prevenção Da Violência Nas Relações De Namoro: Intervenção Com Jovens Em Contexto Escolar." *Revista Psicologia-Teoria e Prática* 8, no. 1 (2006).

Matos, Marlene. "Violência nas relações de intimidade: estudo sobre a mudança psicoterapêutica na mulher." PhD diss., Universidade do Minho, Braga, 2006. http://repositorium.sdum.uminho.pt/handle/1822/5735.

Matos, Marlene. *Violência conjugal: O processo de construção de identidade da mulher.* PhD diss., Universidade do Minho, Braga, 2000.

McBride, D.L. "Groups for Abused Women: Treatment Outcome." PhD diss., Department of Applied Psychology, University of Calgary, Alberta, 2001.

Neves, Sofia, and Conceição Nogueira. "Terapias feministas, intervenção psicológica e violências na intimidade: uma leitura feminista crítica." *Psychologica* 36 (2004): 15–32.

Pais-Ribeiro, José, and Carla Santos. "Estudo conservador de adaptação do Ways of Coping Questionnaire a uma amostra e contexto portugueses." *Análise Psicológica* 19, no. 4 (2001): 491–502.

Pais-Ribeiro, José. "Escala de Satisfação com o Suporte Social (ESSS)." *Análise Psicológica* 17, no. 3 (1999): 547–558.

Ramsey, Jean, Carol Rivas, and Gene Feder. *Interventions to Reduce Violence and Promote the Physical and Psychological Well-Being of Women who Experience Partner Violence: A Systematic Review of Controlled Evaluations. Final Report.* London: Department of Health, 2005.

Republic Diary. *Council of Ministers Resolution no. 100/2010, 1st series* 243 (2010): 5763–5773.

Rinfret-Raynor, Maryse, and S. Cantin. "Feminist Therapy for Battered Women: An Assessment." In *Out of the Darkness: Contemporary Perspectives on Family Violence,* eds. Glenda Kaufman Kantor and Jana L. Jasinski, 219–234. Thousand Oaks, CA: Sage, 1997.

Rosenberg, Morris. *Society and the Adolescent Self-Image.* Princeton: Princeton University Press, 1965.

Sani, Al. "Avaliação de crianças expostas à violência interparental." In *Psicologia Forense,* eds. Abrunhosa R. Gonçalves and Carla Machado, 247–271. Coimbra: Quarteto, 2005.

Santos, Paulo Jorge. "Validação da Rosenberg Self-esteem Scale numa amostra de estudantes do ensino superior." Proceedings of the Thirteenth International Conference on Psychological Assessment: Methods and Contexts. Braga, Portugal, October 2–4, 2008.

Schlee, Karin A., Richard E. Heyman, and K. Daniel O'Leary. "Group Treatment for Spouse Abuse: Are Women with PTSD Appropriate Participants?" *Journal of Family Violence* 13, no. 1 (1998): 1–20.

Schwartz, Jonathan P., Melani M. Magee, Linda D. Griffin, and Cynthia W. Dupuis. "Effects of a Group Preventive Intervention on Risk and Protective Factors Related to Dating Violence." *Group Dynamics: Theory, Research, and Practice* 8, no. 3 (2004): 221–231.

Silva, Luísa Ferreira da. *Entre marido e mulher alguém meta a colher.* Celorico de Basto: À Bolina, 1995.

Spalek, Basia. *Crime Victims: Theory, Policy and Practice.* New York: Palgrave Macmillan, 2006.

Tutty, Leslie M., Bruce A. Bidgood, and Michael A. Rothery. "Support Groups for Battered Women: Research on Their Efficacy." *Journal of Family Violence* 8, no. 4 (1993): 325–343.

União de Mulheres Alternativa Resposta. *Observatório de Mulheres Assassinadas – OMA 2011. Dados preliminares.* http://www.umarfeminismos.org/images/stories/oma/2011/Dados_Pre-liminares_Nov_2011.pdf (accessed April 19, 2012).

Walker, Robert, T.K. Logan, Carol E. Jordan, and Jacquelyn C. Campbell. "An Integrative Review of Separation in the Context of Victimization Consequences and Implications for Women." *Trauma, Violence, and Abuse* 5, no. 2 (2004): 143–193.

Webb, Wanda. "Treatment Issues and Cognitive Behavior Techniques with Battered Women." *Journal of Family Violence* 7, no. 3 (1992): 205–217.

Whalen, Mollie. *Counseling to End Violence against Women: A Subversive Model*, vol. 18. Thousand Oaks, CA: Sage Publications, 1996.

Wilson, K.J. *When Violence Begins at Home.* Alameda, CA: Hunter House Publishers, 1997.

Worell, Judith, and Pamela Remer. *Feminist Perspectives in Therapy: Empowering Diverse Women.* New York: John Wiley and Sons, 2002.

Zink, Therese, and Frank Putnam. "Intimate Partner Violence Research in the Health Care Setting: What Are Appropriate and Feasible Methodological Standards?" *Journal of Interpersonal Violence* 20, no. 4 (2005): 365–372.

THE EFFECTIVENESS OF THE EMPOWER PROJECT AND INTERVENTION: PSYCHODRAMA AND THE ELABORATION OF DOMESTIC VIOLENCE IN ITALY, AUSTRIA, BULGARIA, PORTUGAL, ROMANIA, AND ALBANIA

Ines Testoni, Alessandra Armenti, Michael Wieser, Alice Bertoldo, Mihaela Bucuta, Galabina Tarashoeva, Lucia Ronconi, Maria Silvia Guglielmin, Gabriela Dima, Gabriela Moita, Adriano Zamperini, Sibylla Verdi, Daniela Di Lucia Sposito

Introduction

Gender-based violence within families is a complex phenomenon that cuts across all social classes, geographical locations, and periods of human history.[1] Studies of this issue have only recently gained an important role in psychological and social thinking and have developed in parallel with an awareness by women of the existential disadvantage they have. The previous contribution of Marlene Matos, Anita Santos, and Rita Conde is positioned in this area of research, and it describes the discursive and cognitive approach in the intervention with victims of domestic violence. In the present chapter we discuss another kind of treatment, which integrates both the narrative approach of social service counseling, developed by Urie Bronfenbrenner's[2] ecological standpoint, and psychodrama

---

[1] CEDAW, *Convention on the Elimination of All Forms of Discrimination against Women* (United Nations Department of Public Information, 2000/2009). http://www.un.org/womenwatch/daw/cedaw/cedaw.htm; World Health Organization, *World Report on Violence and Health* (Geneva: World Health Organization, 2002).

[2] See Urie Bronfenbrenner, *Making Human Beings Human: Bioecological Perspectives on Human Development* (Thousand Oaks, CA: Sage, 2005). Bronfenbrenner's ecological perspective has been adopted by feminist psychological counseling in order to promote the psychosocial empowerment of women. The basis of this perspective is Carolyn Zerbe Enns and Elizabeth Nutt Williams, *The Oxford Handbook of Feminist Counseling Psychology* (Oxford University Press, 2012). The intersection of the "ecological systems theory" and feminist perspective considers that human development reflects the influence of several environmental systems. This model identifies five environmental systems with which an individual interacts: *microsystem, mesosystem, exosystem, macrosystem,* and *chronosystem*. Each system contains roles, norms, and rules that may shape psychological development. The counseling derived from this viewpoint, applied to the field of domestic violence, does not consider the woman victim of violence as mentally ill but as a victim of a multi-systemic pathology that she must become conscious of in order to defend herself.

activities supporting it. It is particularly important because with this perspective it is possible to achieve the goals promoted by Third Wave Feminism, which has highlighted the importance of involving the body in the promotion of female empowerment, subjectivity, and agency.[3] In fact, psychodrama is an action method, often used as a type of psychotherapy, that uses dramatization, role-playing, and dramatic self-presentation. This technique was invented by Jacob Moreno,[4] who incorporated theatrical properties in recreating real-life situations aimed at elaborating psychological problems and acting them out in the present. Thanks to the theatrical action, patients have the opportunity to evaluate their behavior and more deeply understand their situation. This type of intervention enables the body to play a fundamental role and in fact embodies a new perception of the individual's own subjectivity.

This model was utilized by EMPoWER (Empowerment of Women Environment Research), a European longitudinal research-intervention in the real world included in the EU Daphne III Program covering the years 2007 to 2013 and involving six countries: Italy, Austria, Albania, Bulgaria, Portugal, and Romania. The research used ecological and psychodramatic techniques in order to promote the empowerment of adult female victims of domestic violence. As the results demonstrate, psychodrama was an excellent starting-point strategy for promoting the reconstruction of agency and subjectivity of female victims of subjugation and violence. In fact, these two constructs are deeply intertwined with the roles played by women in their own life, underlying the need to ensure that they become aware that a change in their condition is necessary.[5] Agency is the ability of persons to act for themselves, and feminist and gender studies have structured a specific theory of women's agency, inherent to the female capacity for individualized choice and action. This key concept indicates that women's identities took shape in settings that were in some respects adverse to their interests and that they were unjustly subordinated, causing a diminishing of their selfhood

---

[3] See Daniela Gronold, Brigitte Hipfl, and Linda Lund Pedersen, eds., 2006, *Teaching with the Third Wave: New Feminists' Explorations of Teaching and Institutional Contexts*, ATHENA3, University of Utrecht and Centre for Gender Studies, Stockholm University.

[4] Jacob L. Moreno, *Who Shall Survive? Foundations of Sociometry, Group Psychotherapy and Sociodrama* (Beacon, NY: Beacon House, 1953) (student edition by American Society of Group Psychotherapy and Psychodrama, 1993).

[5] John Hamel and Tonia Nicholls, *Family Interventions in Domestic Violence: A Handbook of Gender-Inclusive Theory and Treatment* (New York: Springer, 2007); Murray Straus, "Physical Assaults by Wives: A Major Social Problem," in *Current Controversies on Family Violence,* eds. Richard J. Gelles and Donileen Loseky (Newbury Park, CA: Sage, 1993), 67–87.

and agency.[6] The concept is very similar to the construct of "spontaneity" introduced by Moreno with his psychodrama techniques. Individuals who regain their spontaneity have also conquered their subjectivity and agency, because they can be autonomous in learning social and coping skills that rationally develop personal self-direction in a world populated by impinging judgments and entangling commitments that orient their behavior towards maintaining their subjugation.

The second key concept of EMPoWER is the mother-daughter relationship. Feminist family studies have shown how primary socialization is responsible for the perpetuation of the females' lack of agency.[7] Indeed, they have broadened the idea of what counts as context and have revealed the dialectical relationship between what happens within families and what happens in the communities and society, pointing out the psychosocial dimensions present in a male-dominated society and how these are related to a cultural framework that helps explain and document female victimization.[8] More rare and difficult are the investigations that study the responsibilities that women themselves have in regards to the social conditioning that preps them to become potential victims of violence. EMPoWER intervened in the mother-daughter relationship and developed as a research/intervention that increases the chances of victims' emancipation through their liberation from a specific traditional maternal mandate that has been unconsciously taken on. Our research[9] carried out with female victims of trafficking (in Italy, Albania, and some former Soviet republics) illustrated how the maternal figure plays a potentially crucial role in the adoption of subjugated roles by some women involved in certain types of mother-daughter relationships. EMPoWER project's hypothesis was that, throughout the course

---

[6] Peggy Antrobus, *The Global Women's Movement: Issues and Strategies for the New Century* (London: Zed Books, 2004).

[7] Nancy Chodorow, *The Reproduction of Mothering: Psychoanalysis and the Sociology of Gender* (Berkeley: University of California Press, 1978; 2nd ed., 1999); Nancy Chodorow, *Feminism and Psychoanalytic Theory* (New Haven: Yale University Press, 1989); Julia Kristeva, *Powers of Horror: An Essay on Abjection* (New York: Columbia University Press, 1982); Sally A. Lloyd, April L. Few, and Katherine R. Allen, eds. *Handbook of Feminist Family Studies* (Thousand Oaks, CA: Sage, 2009).

[8] Ellen P. Cook, *Women, Relationships, and Power: Implications for Counseling* (Alexandria, VA: American Counseling Association, 1993); Michael Flood and Bob Pease, "Factors Influencing Attitudes to Violence against Women," *Trauma, Violence, and Abuse* 10, no. 2 (2009): 125.

[9] Ines Testoni, Paolo Cottone, and Alessandra Armenti, "Psychodrama Research in the Field of Women Suffering from Violence: A Daphne Project" (Proceedings of the Fourth Regional Mediterranean Congress IAGP SPP "Other Seas," September 7–10, 2011, Porto, Portugal), 162–169; Ines Testoni, Lucia Ronconi, and Daniela Boccher, "The Question of the Mafia-Style Sub-Culture Role in Female Subordination: Traditional Culture, Religion and Gender Role Representation in Both Emigrated and Non-Emigrated Albanian Women," *World Cultural Psychiatry Research Review* 2, no. 1 (2006): 164.

of human history, where culturally defined reference values accept the supremacy and power of men, the attitudes leading to the subordination and victimization of women are potentially transmitted down the generations through the mother-daughter relationship.[10] In fact, the results of the research that preceded EMPoWER enabled us to speculate that the traditional and religious values promoting female subordination are passed down by some mothers as a social script that has been internalized.[11]

The third key concept of this chapter is Empirical Research in the Real World (ERRW). Following feminist and Morenian theories, the aim of this paper is to show how psychodramatic techniques can be considered an elective intervention for helping support victims of intimate partner violence. The importance of this work lies in the fact that we have used a structured and rigorous design methodology that enabled us to analyze the effectiveness of psychodrama in its entirety, trying to consider all the intervening psychosocial variables. EMPoWER is not laboratory research but considers society like a large laboratory, where it is not possible to control all the variables, but it is nevertheless feasible to measure some critical factors that define changes made by a planned intervention. This is what ERRW demonstrates as scientifically practicable. As Colin Robson defines it,[12] ERRW focuses on the lives and experiences of diverse groups (e.g., women, minorities, and persons with disabilities) that have traditionally been marginalized; analyzes how and why resulting inequities are reflected in asymmetrical power relationships; examines how results of social inquiry on inequities are linked to political and social action; and uses an emancipatory theory to develop a research approach. From a methodological point of view, it adopts an exploratory strategy to find out what is happening, to seek new insights, to ask questions, to assess phenomena in a new light, and to generate ideas and hypotheses for future research. Adopting this scientific perspective, this chapter utilizes a specific language, which is very methodologically rigorous, but we believe it can provide one good alternative for gender social intervention.

---

[10] Ravneet Kaur and Suneela Garg, "Domestic Violence against Women: A Qualitative Study in a Rural Community," *Asia-Pacific Journal of Public Health* 22, no. 2 (2010): 242.

[11] Lisa Y. Zaidi, John F. Knutson, and John G. Mehm, "Transgenerational Patterns of Abusive Parenting: Analog and Clinical Tests," *Aggressive Behavior* 15, no. 2 (1989): 137.

[12] Colin Robson, *Real World Research: A Resource for Social Scientists and Practitioner-Researchers* (Oxford: Blackwell, 1993).

Lack of female agency as a sociatry problem in domestic violence

One of our findings concluded that the female response is the product of a social dynamic within a particular family type in which social relationships are focused on emotional ties, starting from the relationship with the mother. This social dynamic produces a substantial critical incapacity in women and young girls to trust in men. Trained by their mothers to become subordinate to men, young women/daughters are not able to make conscious choices that promote their autonomous will. Therefore, since our goal is to end the transmission of subordination implicitly handed down from certain types of mothers, EMPoWER initiated its research action from the women themselves. For women who have been victims of violence, it has made them aware of their responsibility in taking on the role of victim and unwittingly transmitting this way of thinking to their daughters.[13] The main difficulty with respect to this problem is managing cognitive dissonance,[14] determined by the trust in male power and the trust placed in maternal teaching, from which learned helplessness derives:[15] the mother teaches her daughter to obey in the name of love, and the result is that men use and abuse women without finding any obstacle, because for centuries, female agency has been castrated. As this is primarily a cultural problem that feminist and gender studies consider a result of socialization, women who are victims of family violence are not mentally ill, but are expressing a severe social pathology. The recent worldwide concern about violence against women in general and domestic violence in particular[16] requires new strategies to tackle this phenomenon. EMPoWER may offer an important alternative through the use of psychodrama, which has proven to be an effective technique in these situations. EMPoWER has linked the concept of social pathology to a similar idea of "sociatry" utilized by Moreno,[17] and as a play off the word "psychiatry" translated from the indi-

---

[13] Marta Codato et al., "Overcoming Female Subordination: An Educational Experiment Changes the Levels of Non-Attachment and Objectification in a Group of Female Undergraduates," *Interdisciplinary Journal of Family Studies* 17, no. 1 (2012): 235; Ines Testoni, "The State of the Art in Research and Intervention against Gender Based Violence," *Interdisciplinary Journal of Family Studies* 17, no. 1 (2012): 4.

[14] Leon Festinger, *A Theory of Cognitive Dissonance* (Stanford, CA: Stanford University Press, 1957).

[15] Martin E.P. Seligman, *Helplessness: On Depression, Development, and Death* (San Francisco: Freeman, 1975).

[16] CEDAW, *Convention on the Elimination of all Forms of Discrimination against Women*.

[17] Jacob L. Moreno, *Who Shall Survive? Foundations of Sociometry, Group Psychotherapy and Sociodrama* (Beacon, NY: Beacon House, 1953) (student edition by American Society of Group Psychotherapy and Psychodrama, 1993).

vidual into the collective dimension. In Moreno's[18] opinion, sociatry tries to bring the best insights of clinical and social psychology, psychiatry, and sociology to the general population in order to heal social problems, race relations, gender violence, discrimination, and educational challenges. Gender violence may be an elective area of sociatrical intervention. This is the reason for using Morenian psychodrama in order to promote female agency in women who have been victims of domestic violence. In Gillian Rose's[19] opinion, both feminism and psychodrama offer new ways of being that can help women transform inadequate systems and behavior, since the former offers the latter strategies for the promotion of women's emancipation, where dramatization is the key concept. It is important to note that Moreno went further than simply using drama. Indeed, he considered the activity of improvised personal drama as a kind of liminal field in which people could experience psychological and social elements of transformation. He called "surplus reality" the ontological validity of actions that are performed "as if" in play or in drama. Such events are not actually real, but they are also not unreal, because they express the reality of the psyche and show "psychological truths," and in this sense, they are concrete. "What if..." is the basis of the psychotherapeutic tool of the Morenian method, which promotes awareness through "role-taking." This technique is different from "role-playing," as it uses a powerful way to develop the capacity for understanding the difference between self-identity and others' identity, through the "reversal role," which is the operational method for distinguishing the perimeters of personal identity.[20]

Through the EMPoWER project we have been able to help a particular population of women achieve resilience and effective self-determination by rising above the limits imposed by certain types of intergenerational relationships. The goal of empowering and improving coping strategies towards greater resilience has been accomplished through psychodramatic techniques that teach women how the dynamics of their role and position in society have determined their own lives, and by offering counseling that adopts the ecological model.[21]

---

[18] Jacob L. Moreno, *Psychodrama*, 4th ed., vol. 1 (Beacon, NY: Beacon House, 1972).

[19] Gillian Rose, "J.L. Meets the Warrior Princess: Exploring Psychodrama and Feminism," *Australian and New Zealand Psychodrama Association Journal* 15 (2006): 22.

[20] Moreno, *Who Shall Survive? Foundations of Sociometry*; Moreno, *Psychodrama*.

[21] Urie Bronfenbrenner, *The Ecology of Human Development: Experiments by Nature and Design* (Cambridge, MA: Harvard University Press. 1979).

According to Bronfenbrenner,[22] an individual's development reflects the influence of five environmental systems in which individuals interact: *microsystem* (family, peer groups, etc.); *mesosystem* (social realities to which microsystems are connected and in which individuals are active participants: school, work, school, religious institutions, neighborhood); *exosystem* (social realities to which microsystems are connected and in which individuals are not active participants); *macrosystem* (culture and social structure/organizations in which individuals live); and *chronosystem* (patterning of environmental events and transitions over the life course, as well as sociohistorical circumstances). This model is utilized in counseling for dealing with family issues and family violence.[23] From this perspective, the Feminist Ecological Model (FEM) arose; it suggests that gender and culture will influence how individuals interact with their family and immediate environment. This model was developed in order to understand and intervene in the context of intimate partner violence; it takes into account interactions between the different system levels and social, historical, institutional, *and* individual factors.[24] Generally speaking, the Ecological Model is used in many forms of counseling and treatment aimed at helping female victims of violence reintegrate themselves into each systemic level. In summary, for project EMPoWER, psychodrama provided victims with an environment for psychological development, offering special attention to the roles and scripts they have internalized, and through the ecological matrix counseling, the relational space in which women interact was also taken care of.

---

[22] Ibid.; Bronfenbrenner, *Making Human Beings Human: Bioecological Perspectives on Human Development* (Thousand Oaks, CA: Sage, 2005).

[23] Kevin J. Swick and Reginald D. Williams, "An Analysis of Bronfenbrenner's Bio-Ecological Perspective for Early Childhood Educators: Implications for Working with Families Experiencing Stress," *Early Childhood Education Journal* 33, no. 5 (2006): 371; Mary Pipher, *The Shelter of Each Other: Rebuilding Our Families* (New York: Ballantine Books, 1996).

[24] Mary B. Ballou, Atsushi Matsumoto, and Michael Wagner, "Toward a Feminist Ecological Theory of Human Nature: Theory Building in Response to Real-World Dynamics," in *Rethinking Mental Health and Disorder: Feminist Perspectives*, eds. Mary B. Ballou and Laura S. Brown (New York: Guilford Press, 2002), 99–141; Colette Browne and Crystal Mills, "Theoretical Frameworks: Ecological Model, Strengths Perspective, and Empowerment Theory," in *Culturally Competent Practice: Skills, Interventions, and Evaluations*, eds. Rowena Fong and Sharlene M. Furuto (Boston: Allyn and Bacon, 2001), 10–32; Shamita D. Dasgupta, "A Framework for Understanding Women's Use of Nonlethal Violence in Intimate Heterosexual Relationships," *Violence against Women* 8 (2002): 1364; Lorie L. Heise, "Violence against Women: An Integrated, Ecological Framework," *Violence against Women* 4 (1998): 262.

EMPoWER research design

This research-intervention adopts methods focused on determining the biographies of women by examining the dynamics at play according to role and status in society and culture. We adopted the integration of two kinds of interventions: counseling, through the use of the Ecological Systemic Approach, which supports the social network of victims in order to permit them to re-integrate into everyday social life, and Psychodramatic Techniques (of groups and/or individuals), which, like the sociatrical intervention, is aimed at enhancing relational resources.

This longitudinal study involving the treatment of abused women is organized into three stages: taking the victim into care and conducting the initial battery tests (T1, at the beginning of the program); creating psychodrama intervention groups; final testing (T2, at the end of the program) and return, exchange, and discharge.

The project planned for all six participating countries (Italy, Albania, Austria, Bulgaria, Portugal, and Romania) to have two groups: one group led only by social workers providing ecological counseling support (Ecological Groups—EG) and another group that, in addition to this support, offered psychodrama (Psychodrama Groups—PG). This methodology involved participation in a psychodrama group for six months for a total of twenty-five sessions lasting two hours each. The only exception was Albania, where the groups taking part in the psychodrama participated in four marathon sessions lasting three days.

The basic premise is that psychodramatic techniques may represent a useful methodology of intervention in domestic violence cases. To measure this effect, EMPoWER compared this form of intervention with more traditional forms of counseling that are widely used in anti-violence centers. We consider both methods useful because they promote women's changing role: the first through group work that builds the experience of overcoming internalized roles and scripts, and the second through the support provided to get out of the relationship and reintegrate into society.

Hypothesis and aim

The hypothesis is that there is a positive relationship between indices of spontaneity and psychological well-being. High levels of spontaneity are associated with well-being, while low or nonexistent levels are associated with psychopathology. Spontaneity also acts on personal well-being through its close relationship with the intrinsic motivation of the person and their internal voluntary drive to reach a goal. Moreover, high levels of spontaneity are related to a sense of personal self-efficacy, whereas low levels of spontaneity lead to low self-esteem, depression, and thoughts of a negative and denigrating nature towards oneself and external situations.

The verification of the theoretical model presented here enables us to set the underlying assumptions for the six countries studied and make cross-cultural comparisons. The first aim enabled us to verify whether the two methods were effective. The second aim investigated whether there was a difference between these positive measures and to what degree, thus highlighting the differences between the results of the groups of women in the Eastern European countries studied (Albania, Bulgaria, and Romania) and the results of the groups of women in the Western and Central European countries studied (Italy, Austria, and Portugal).

Our interest in comparing the two halves of Europe (East and West) arose from the fact that the historical U.S.-Soviet bipolarism has determined a specific difference in the two parts of Europe. In Eastern Europe the trafficking[25] of women developed, and Western and Central Europe became the destination of choice for the sex market. In fact, the EMPoWER project is the continuation of a previous project involving trafficked women from Albania and Romania, and in this phase of our research, we wanted to verify whether we could find any differences between these two different geographical areas.[26]

---

[25] Edna Erez, Peter R. Ibarra, and William F. McDonald, "Transnational Sex Trafficking: Issues and Prospects," *International Review of Victimology* 11, no. 1 (2004): 1; Natalia Ollus, *Protocol to Prevent, Suppress and Punish Trafficking in Persons, Especially Women and Children* (Helsinki: HEUNI, 2002); United Nations General Assembly Resolution 55/25 of November 15, 2000; UNESCO, "Data Comparison Sheet, Worldwide Trafficking Estimates by Organizations" (data compiled in September 2004), http://www.unescobkk.org/fileadmin/user_upload/culture/Trafficking/project/Graph_Worldwide_Sept_2004.pdf; UNIFEM, "Facts and Figures on Violence against Women," http://www.unifem.org/attachments/gender_issues/violence_against_women/facts_figures_violence_against_women_2007.pdf (accessed November 6, 2012); World Bank, "Human Trafficking: A Brief Overview," *Social Development Notes–Conflict, Crime, and Violence* no. 122 (2009), http://siteresources.worldbank.org/EXTSOCIALDEVELOPMENT/.

[26] This hypothesis is important because, as noted by the Council of Europe Convention on Action against Trafficking in Human Beings, the awareness of women in Eastern Europe concerning the risk of being trafficked is increasing, and therefore the way they handle social and intimate relationships with men who are their potential exploiters (fathers, husbands, brothers, friends, and acquaintances) is also changing. We hypothesize that in such a specific sociocultural area, victims of gender violence may present some specific differences with respect to victims in Western Europe that should be investigated. See Council of Europe, *Council of Europe Convention on Action against Trafficking in Human Beings and its Explanatory Report*, Council of Europe Treaty Series no. 197 (Warsaw, May 16, 2005).

A previous phase of the model validation on a non-clinical sample in each EMPoWER country[27] revealed high levels of internal consistency for the individual instruments, and they were therefore considered valid to measure the constructs investigated.

Furthermore, the results that emerged from the comparison of the instruments in each country and on the total sample provided valuable support to the theories underpinning the research project, namely the importance of spontaneity in determining personal well-being. The relationship between the two constructs has already been verified in the literature[28] and was further confirmed by the validation of the cross-cultural model assumed[29] through the correlation analysis between SAI-R and CORE-OM. The results of this first phase show and confirm the positive correlation between the two constructs, highlighting that as the aspects related to spontaneity grow, levels of well-being also increase.

Assessment

The Assessment involved the administration of a battery test at the beginning (T1) and at the end of the program (T2), in order to evaluate the efficacy of the EMPoWER program intervention.

The battery tests consist of three scales:

- SAI-R (Spontaneity Assessment Inventory-Revised)[30]: will be adopted to measure the change in spontaneity. We will use the proper translation for each country;
- CORE-OM (Clinical Outcomes in Routine Evaluation Outcome Measure)[31]: to evaluate the clinical efficiency of the interventions. We will administer the proper translation for each country;

---

27 Ines Testoni et al., "Psychodrama and Management of Sufferance from Domestic Violence: CORE-OM and SAI-R to Assess Empower Project Efficacy," *Gender Research* (forthcoming).

28 David A. Kipper and Jasdeep Hundal, "The Spontaneity Assessment Inventory: The Relationship between Spontaneity and Nonspontaneity," *Journal of Group Psychotherapy, Psychodrama and Sociometry* 58, no. 3 (2005): 119; David A. Kipper and Eva Buras, "Measurement of Spontaneity: The Relationship between the Intensity and Frequency of the Spontaneous Experience," *Perceptual and Motor Skills* 108, no. 2 (2009): 362–366.

29 Testoni, "Psychodrama Research: A Daphne Project."

30 David A. Kipper and Haim Shemer, "The Spontaneity Assessment Inventory-Revised (SAI-R): Spontaneity, Well-Being and Stress," *Journal of Group Psychotherapy, Psychodrama and Sociometry* 59, no. 3 (2006): 127.

31 Chris Evans et al., "Towards a Standardised Brief Outcome Measure: Psychometric Properties and Utility of the CORE-OM," *British Journal of Psychiatry* 180 (2002): 51.

- BDI-II (Beck Depression Inventory-II version)[32] is a self-reported analysis of depressive symptoms. The second version reflects revisions made in the fourth edition of the Diagnostic and Statistical Manual of Mental Disorders (DSM-IV). We will utilize the translated version for each country.

Participants

The total sample was composed of $N=136$ women victims of domestic violence, between the ages of 15 and 68 ($M=36.6$, $SD=12.95$), with an average of 11 years of education. All participants took part in the study voluntarily, and they did not receive any type of compensation for their participation. Of the total sample, 88.1% had at least one child, and 11.9% had no children. The following figures (1 and 2) illustrate the distribution (in percentages) of the socio-demographic characteristics of the total sample ($N=136$).

The marital status was classified into six clusters (single, married, separated, divorced, widows, and concubines). Figure 1 highlights that the majority of the sample was made up of either married (40%) or single (30%) women.

The occupations were also classified into five clusters (student, employed, housewives, pensioners, and unemployed). One participant from the original sample was missing. Figure 2 demonstrates that the majority of the sample was made up of employed women (60%).

Figure 1. Percentages "Marital status" variable (N= 136).

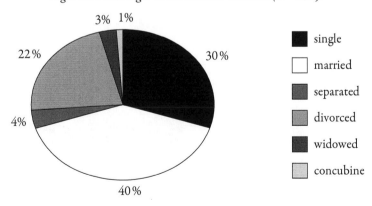

---

32 Aaron T. Beck, Robert A. Steer, and Gregory K. Brown, *Manual for the Beck Depression Inventory: (BDI-II)*, 2nd ed. (San Antonio, TX: Psychological Corporation, 1996).

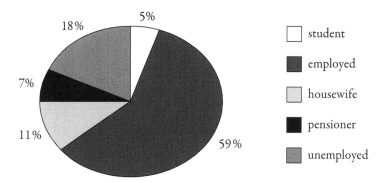

Figure 2. Percentages "Occupation" variable (N= 136).

- student
- employed
- housewife
- pensioner
- unemployed

As we mentioned in the previous paragraph, the experimental design used was longitudinal (T1, at the beginning of the program, and T2, at the end of the program), and this provided the data collected for two different groups: the group that participated in the ecological intervention (EG) and the group that participated in the psychodramatic techniques (PG).

Figure 3 highlights the composition of the sample for each country; 66 participants belong to the EG group, and 70 make up the PG group.

Figure 3. Sample distribution per country and per type of intervention.

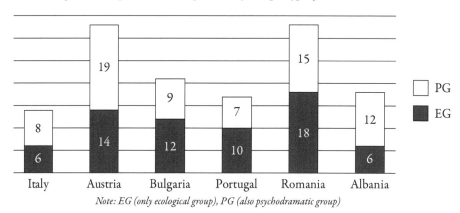

Note: EG (only ecological group), PG (also psychodramatic group)

Table 1 highlights how the Italian, Austrian, Bulgarian, and Romanian samples attained a higher level of education and were older than the Albanian group.

130

Table 1. Socio-demographic data sample for each country.

	Average age	Years of education
Italy	39	13
Austria	41	12
Bulgaria	40	14
Portugal	46	8
Romania	33	11
Albania	20	7

Most of the women who belong to the Italian group stated that they are separated (42.9%), while women who belong to the Portuguese and Romanian group reported that they are mostly married (58.8% and 60.6%, respectively). Women in the Albanian group are for the most part single (83.3%), while in the Austrian and Bulgarian samples there are more married women (33.3% and 38.1%, respectively), single (33.3%) or divorced (38.1%). These variables are quite heterogeneous. It is important to note the heterogeneity of these socio-demographic variables in light of subsequent interpretations of the results that we present in the following section.

In the Romanian and Albanian samples, all the women have at least one child (100%), in contrast to the other groups, which appear to be more heterogeneous, though for the most part concordant. 90% of Italian, Bulgarian and Portuguese women and 63% of Austrian women have at least one child.

Results

Below the key results are reported. First, an analysis of the reliability of the measurement scales used was carried out: we verified the internal consistency of the scales of spontaneity (SAI-R) and psychological well-being (CORE-OM) by calculating Cronbach's Alpha coefficient to verify the existence of internal consistency. Next we calculated the mean scores and performed comparisons between the means through an analysis of variance (ANOVA), and then we calculated the bivariate correlations between the composite scores using Pearson's correlation coefficient. The software used for this analysis was statistical package SPSS (version 19).

Internal consistency

The internal consistency of the SAI-R in the total sample in T1 was .95 (Cronbach's Alpha), and in T2 it was .96.[33] Table 1 illustrates the internal consistency index in each country in T1 and T2.

The internal consistency of the CORE-OM in the total sample in T1 was .89 (Cronbach's Alpha), and in T2 it was .91.[34] Table 2 illustrates the internal consistency index in each country in T1 and T2.

Table 2. Cronbach's Alpha, SAI-R. CORE-OM.

Country	T1	T2
Italy	.93	.97
Austria	.96	.97
Bulgaria	.78	.93
Portugal	.93	.95
Romania	.94	.93
Albania	.77	.83

Table 3. Cronbach's Alpha,

Country	T1	T2
Italy	.93	.93
Austria	.92	.96
Bulgaria	.83	.78
Portugal	.75	.81
Romania	.78	.80
Albania	.90	.94

The results indicate that all Cronbach's alpha coefficients calculated for both scales and for each dimension of the CORE-OM (spontaneity and psychological well-being) in each country and at two different time points indicated good internal consistency, so that the scales used in the EMPoWER Daphne project actually measured the two constructs of spontaneity and psychological well-being in all six countries considered.

Once we ascertained the reliability of the measuring instruments, we calculated the average scores in each country at two points in time (before and after the intervention) in order to perform an analysis on the measurement of the effectiveness of change.

---

[33] In the literature, the internal consistency of the SAI-R is .79. The average score on the SAI-R was 66.41, $SD=10.16$.

[34] Evans et al., 2002; the internal consistency of the CORE-OM was .94, and for each domain the Alpha values were: Well-being $\alpha= .68$, Problems $\alpha= .85$, Functioning $\alpha= .72$, Risk $\alpha= .62$, and Non-risk items $\alpha= .90$. The average score was .76 (SD=.59), and for each of the CORE-OM domains: Well-being (W) $M= .91$ ($SD= .59$), Problems (P) $M= .90$ ($SD= .72$), Functioning (F) $M= .85$ (SD= .65), Risk (R) $M= .20$ ($SD= .45$), and Non-risk items (-R) $M= .88$ ($SD= .66$).

The average score and the differences between the means and cut-offs

SAI-R

The average score of the total sample on the SAI-R in T1 was 49.75 (*SD*=16.48), and in T2 it was 54.71 (*SD*=14.74). The average score of the total sample on the SAI-R in PGT1 was 51.95 (*SD*=15.66), and in EGT1 it was 47.42 (*SD*=17.11). The average score of the total sample on the SAI-R in PGT2 was 56.47 (*SD*=15.37), and in EGT2 it was 52.94 (*SD*=13.19).

These results would seem to indicate that levels of spontaneity are lower in T1 and that there is an improvement in the level of spontaneity in T2, both in the total sample as well as in the two groups (EG and PG). Table 4 illustrates the average scores in each country at T1 and T2.

Table 4. Average score, SAI-R.

Country	T1		T2	
	M	*SD*	*M*	*SD*
Italy	58.84	16.66	58.13	18.34
Austria	42.47	15.84	49.18	16.22
Bulgaria	45.48	7.80	49.90	11.79
Portugal	47.45	15.48	54.73	12.91
Romania	46.35	15.23	53.93	11.84
Albania	69.42	10.31	69.20	8.22

The average score on the SAI-R in total sample $PG_{(T1)}$ (*n*=70) was 51.95 (*SD*=15.66). Figure 4 illustrates the average PG score, in each country and at T1 and T2.[35]

---

[35] 66.89 (*SD*=11.32) in Albania, 40.40 (*SD*=15.49) in Austria, 46.89 (*SD*=5.18) in Bulgaria, 54.38 (*SD*=16.92) in Italy, 52.97 (*SD*=14.63) in Portugal, and 55.89 (*SD*=11.83) in Romania. The average score on the SAI-R in total sample $PG_{(T2)}$ (*n*=70) was 56.47 (*SD*=15.37). The average score in each country was 70.14 (*SD*=9.61) in Albania, 44.79 (*SD*=16.21) in Austria, 59.89 (*SD*=16.21) in Bulgaria, 54.22 (*SD*=18.21) in Italy, 56.57 (*SD*=12.86) in Portugal, and 59.45 (*SD*=10.38) in Romania.

Figure 4. The average PG score in each country and at T1 –T2, SAI-R.

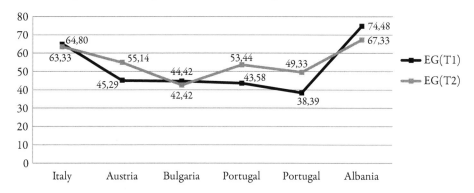

The average score on the SAI-R in total sample $EG_{(T1)}$ (n=66) was 47.42 (SD=17.11). Figure 5 illustrates the average EG score in each country and at T1 and T2.[36]

Figure 5. The average EG score in each country and at T1 –T2, SAI-R.

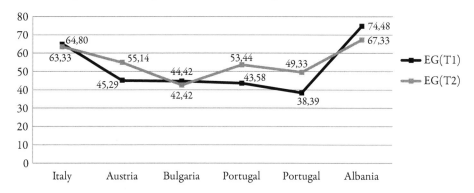

---

[36] The average score in each country was 74.48 (SD=5.73) in Albania, 45.29 (SD=16.43) in Austria, 44.42 (SD=9.39) in Bulgaria, 64.80 (SD=15.70) in Italy, 43.58 (SD=15.57) in Portugal, and 38.39 (SD=13.19) in Romania.

The average score on the SAI-R in total sample $EG_{(T2)}$ (n=66) was 47.42 (SD=17.11). The average score in each country was 67.33 (SD=4.50) in Albania, 55.14 (SD=14.75) in Austria, 42.42 (SD=7.28) in Bulgaria, 63.33 (SD=18.78) in Italy, 53.44 (SD=13.47) in Portugal, and 49.33 (SD=11.21) in Romania. In order to consider the differences between Western and Eastern Europe, the results are as follows: the average score in the Eastern European sample at T1 in the PG group (Albania, Bulgaria, and Romania) was 57.31 (SD=12.76), and in the Western and Central European countries (Austria, Italy, Portugal) the score was 46.28 (SD=16.61). The average score in the East European countries at T2 in the PG group (Albania, Bulgaria, and Romania) was 63.12 (SD=10.75), and in the Western and Central European

CORE-OM

Figures 6 and 7 illustrate the average score of PG[37] and EG,[38] in each country and in T1 and T2.[39]

Figure 6. The average PG score in each country and at T1 –T2, CORE-OM.

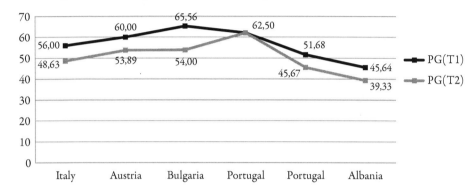

sample (Austria, Italy and Portugal) it was 49.43 (SD=16.51). The average score of the East European sample at T1 in the EG group (Albania, Bulgaria, and Romania) was 46.41 (SD=16.92), and in the Western and Central European sample (Austria, Italy and Portugal) it was 48.62 (SD=17.53). The average score in the East European sample at T2 in the EG group (Albania, Bulgaria, and Romania) was 50.03 (SD=12.33), and in the Western and Central European sample (Austria, Italy, and Portugal) it was 56.21 (SD=15.11).

[37] 45.64 (SD=24.64) in Albania, 60.00 (SD=21.17) in Austria, 65.56 (SD=16.47) in Bulgaria, 56.00 (SD=32.88) in Italy, 62.50 (SD=13.11) in Portugal, and 51.68 (SD=13.03) in Romania. The average score on the CORE-OM in total sample PG$_{(T2)}$ (n=70) was 50.00 (SD=23.04). The average score in each country was 39.99 (SD=27.92) in Albania, 53.89 (SD=28.17) in Austria, 54.00 (SD=19.23) in Bulgaria, 48.63 (SD=25.10) in Italy, 62.29 (SD=12.88) in Portugal, and 45.67 (SD=13.15) in Romania.

[38] The average score in each country was 29.83 (SD=13.11) in Albania, 55.29 (SD=16.4) in Austria, 54.00 (SD=13.62) in Bulgaria, 59.46 (SD=19.69) in Italy, 62.15 (SD=11.75) in Portugal, and 61.22 (SD=13.10) in Romania. The average score on the CORE-OM in total sample EG$_{(T2)}$ (n=66) was 45.71 (SD=15.89). The average score in each country was 32.17 (SD=10.85) in Albania, 38.64 (SD=17.59) in Austria, 51.08 (SD=5.65) in Bulgaria, 29.33 (SD=20.42) in Italy, 54.49 (SD=13.82) in Portugal, and 52.71 (SD=11.49) in Romania.

[39] To consider the differences between Western and Eastern Europe, the results are as follows: the average score in the Eastern European sample at T1 in the PG group (Albania, Bulgaria, and Romania) was 53.14 (SD=19.51), and in the Western and Central European sample (Austria, Italy, Portugal) it was 59.57 (SD=22.58). The average score for the East European sample at T2 in the PG group (Albania, Bulgaria, and Romania) was 45.86 (SD=20.68), and for the Western and Central European sample (Austria, Italy, Portugal) it was 54.38 (SD=24.86). The average score in the East European countries at T1 in the EG group (Albania, Bulgaria, Romania) was 53.58 (SD=17.12), and in the Western and Central European countries (Austria, Italy, Portugal) it was 58.41 (SD=15.50). The average score for the Eastern European countries at T2 in the EG group (Albania, Bulgaria, Romania) was 48.74 (SD=12.17), and in the Western and Central European countries (Austria, Italy, Portugal) it was 42.06 (SD=19.03).

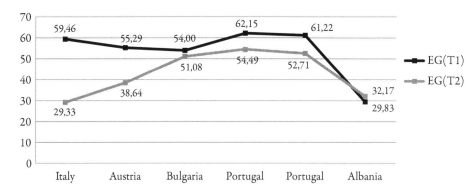

Figure 7. The average EG score in each country and at T1 –T2, CORE-OM.

Differences between the means

The ANOVA showed that there is a significant effect of time (factor "within") [F *(1,132)* = 19.73, *p* <0.01] but also that there are no significant interactions between time, group, and region. However, among the factors "between" (group and geographical area), there is a significant interaction among groups by geographical area [F *(1, 132)* = 12.96, *p*<0.01]. The post-hoc analysis was performed using the Bonferroni method, which revealed a trend similar to that established through the CORE-OM measurement: SAI-R scores at T2 increased significantly only in Eastern Europe PG ($\bar{d}$ = -5.82, *p*<0.05) and Western countries EG ($\bar{d}$ = -7.59, *p*<0.05).

The ANOVA showed that there is both a significant time effect [F *(1, 132)*= 27.12; *p*<0.01] and an effect of interaction time for group by geographical area [F *(1, 132)*= 4.426; *p*<0.05]. The post-hoc analysis performed with the Bonferroni method showed that scores on the CORE-OM at T2 significantly decreased only in the PG of Eastern Europe ($\bar{d}$= -7,276, *p*<0.05) and in the EG of Western and Central European countries ($\bar{d}$ = -16.34, *p*<0.05).

In order to assess any possible changes of the Intervention Group scores from above the clinically significant threshold scores (cutoff) in the pre-stage to below the threshold in the post-measurement analysis, we conducted an analysis that took into account the clinical cutoffs of each of the CORE-OM domains in the literature (Evans et al., 2002) and compared them with the results obtained by the Intervention Group for each of the partner countries in all the CORE-OM domains in the initial stage (T1) and final stage (T2) of the project. Subsequently

136

the analysis between these two comparisons was conducted with the McNemar non-parametric test for paired samples with dichotomous variables of interest; the value of alpha was set to 0.05 for each of the tests carried out. This enabled us to see any statistically significant changes in the total sample.

Subjective well-being

With regards to the comparison made for the domain of subjective well-being, the McNemar test was significant (p<0.05). The percentage of women who went from being above the clinically significant threshold score in the pre-stage to below the threshold score in the post-stage was 22.8%, while the percentage of women whose scores increased from under the threshold in the pre-stage to above the threshold in the post-stage was 8.8%. The percentage of women who instead remained stable below the cutoff in both the first and the second administration of the test was 25.7%, while the percentage of women who remained above the clinically significant threshold was 42.6% (Figure 8).

Figure 8. Percentage comparison between Intervention Group T1 *and* cut-off *with* Intervention Group T2 *and* cut-off, *for Subjective well-being.*

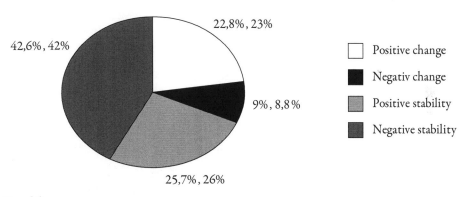

Problems

The McNemar test result carried out to compare the domain *problems* of the CORE-OM was significant (p<0.05). The percentage of women who went from being above the clinically significant threshold score in the pre-stage to below the threshold score in the post-stage was 26.5%, while the percentage of women who went in the opposite direction was 5.1%. The percentage of women who instead remained stable below the cutoff in both the first and the second administration of the test was 27.9%, while the percentage of women who remained stable above the clinically significant threshold score was 40.4% (Figure 9).

Figure 9. Percentage comparison between Intervention Group T1 *and* cut-off *with* Intervention Group T2 *and* cut-off, *for Problems domain.*

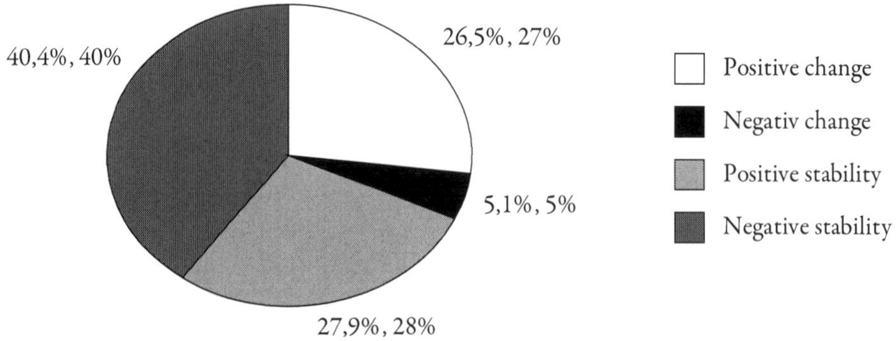

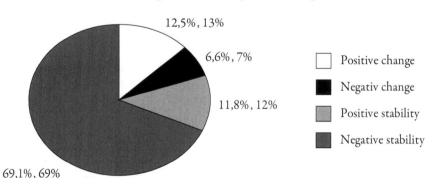

Functioning

With regard to the functioning domain of the CORE-OM, the McNemar test results were not statistically significant (p = 0.16). In all, 12.5% of women went from being above the clinically significant threshold score in the pre stage to below the threshold score in the post stage, while the percentage of women who went in the opposite direction was equal to 6.6%. The percentage of women who instead remained stable below the cutoff after the intervention was 11.8%, while 69.1% of women remained stable above the clinically significant threshold (Figure 10).

Figure 10. Percentage comparison between Intervention Group T1 *and* cut-off *with* Intervention Group T2 *and* cut-off, *for Functioning domain.*

Risk

The McNemar test results carried out on the *risk* items of the CORE-OM of all the countries involved in the project were statistically significant ($p< 0.05$). The percentage of women who went from being above the clinically significant threshold score to below the threshold score was 24.3%, while the opposite results (from under to above the threshold) were measured in 8.8% of cases; 37.5% of women remained stable below the cutoff in both the first and the second administration of the test, while the percentage of women who remained stable above the clinically significant threshold was 29.4% (Figure 11).

Figure 11. Percentage comparison between Intervention Group T1 and cut-off with Intervention Group T2 and cut-off, for Risk factors.

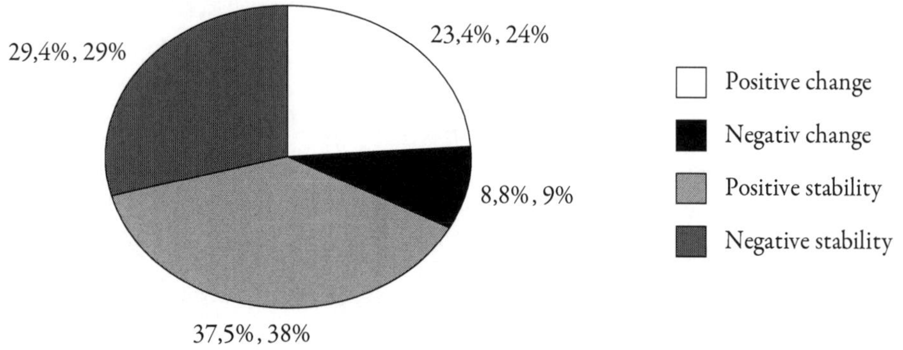

Items without risk

As for the comparisons carried out for all items except for risk items, the McNemar test results were statistically significant ($p<0.05$). The percentage of women who went from being above the clinically significant threshold score to below the threshold score was 23.5%, while 3.7% of women rose from under the threshold to above the threshold after the intervention. Score stability below the threshold was sustained in 17.6% of cases, while the percentage of women who remained stable above the clinically significant threshold after the intervention was 55.1% (Figure 12).

Figure 12. Percentage comparison between Intervention Group T1 *and* cut-off *with* Intervention Group T2 *and* cut-off, *for Without Risk items.*

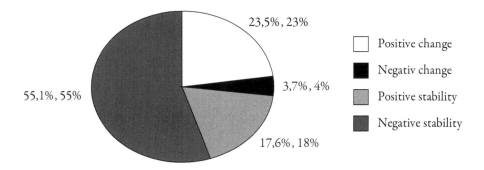

23,5%, 23%

□ Positive change

3,7%, 4%

■ Negativ change

55,1%, 55%

▨ Positive stability

17,6%, 18%

■ Negative stability

Totals

The McNemar test performed to compare all the CORE-OM items was significant (p< 0.05). In all, 24.3% of women went from being above the clinically significant threshold scores in the pre-stage to below the threshold scores in the post-stage, while 5.9% of women obtained the opposite results. The percentage of women who remained stable below the clinically significant threshold score both in the first and the second test administration was 17.16%, while the percentage of women who remained stable above the clinically significant scores was 52.20% (Figure 13).

Figure 13. Percentage comparison between Intervention Group T1 *and* cut-off *with* Intervention Group T2 *and* cut-off, *for all CORE-OM domains.*

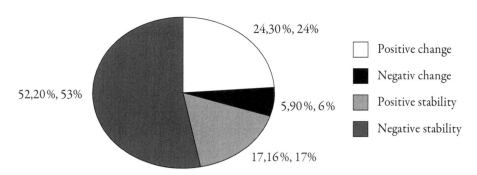

24,30%, 24%

□ Positive change

5,90%, 6%

■ Negativ change

52,20%, 53%

▨ Positive stability

17,16%, 17%

■ Negative stability

Correlations between spontaneity and well-being

The analysis carried out to verify the correlation between the instruments on the total sample ($N=136$) illustrates that the expected negative correlation between instruments is significant, both between the SAI-R and CORE-OM in T1 ($r= -0.58, p<0.001$) and between SAI-R and CORE-OM in T2 ($r= -0.58, p<0.001$). In all the countries investigated, there was a negative correlation between SAI-R and CORE-OM both at the first and the second test administration, with the exception of Bulgaria (both in T1 and T2), and in T2 in Portugal and Romania (see Table 5).

Table 5. Correlations between SAI-R and CORE-OM.

Country	T1	T2
Italy	-.66**	-.80**
Austria	-.63**	-.80**
Bulgaria	-.28	-.13
Portugal	-.67**	-.33
Romania	-.41**	-.23
Albania	-.62**	-.62**

*p<.05 **p<.01

Additional analysis was conducted to highlight any modulation effects of sociodemographic variables on test scores (SAI-R and CORE-OM) in T2.[40] Therefore, the repeated measure of ANOVA (in which time is the factor "within" subjects) was carried out at two levels (T1 and T2), while marital status (three levels: single, married, and divorced-separated-widowed), the location (two levels: Eastern Europe, and Western and Central Europe), and the groups (EG and PG) were considered factors "between" subjects. From this analysis, significant interactions between time and marital status and the SAI-R ($F(2,124)= 9.28, p<0.001$) and the CORE-OM ($F(2,124)= 4.93, p<0.001$) emerged. The direction of improvement is the same: married women score lower at T1 on the SAI-R ($M=45.17$, $SD=1.95$), begin with lower levels of spontaneity, and have higher CORE-OM scores ($M=1.85, SD=0.07$), thus resulting in greater levels of discomfort, followed by "separated-divorced-widowed" (SAI-R: $M=46.13$; $SD=2.3$; CORE-OM:

---

[40] The marital status distribution was not the same in the two groups. The PG was composed of 35.7% single individuals, 30% who were married, and 34.3% who were separated, divorced, or widowed. The EG was composed of 24.25% single individuals, 51.5% who were married, and 24.25% who were separated, divorced, or widowed.

M=1.32; SD=0.09) and finally by single women (SAI-R: M=60.02; SD=2.28; CORE-OM: M=1.67; SD=0.09), which is the group that has higher levels of spontaneity and lower levels of discomfort. At T2, married women report higher SAI-R scores (M=54.55; SD=1.86) and lower CORE-OM scores (M=1.42; SD=0.08) with respect to the women in the group that are "separated-divorced-widowed" (SAI-R: M=51.78; SD=2.2; CORE-OM: M=1.47; SD=0.09). At T2, single women score the highest in spontaneity (SAI-R: M=58.17; SD=2.18) and have lower levels of distress (CORE-OM: M=1.24; SD=0.09), but in relation to the variation in their scores between T1 and T2, their test scores show a slight deterioration in the measure of spontaneity and a slight improvement over discomfort, which is still lower when compared to the other two groups. Another significant result emerged for age: it is positively correlated (r=0.27, p<0.05) with the CORE-OM and negatively correlated with SAI-R scores (r= -0.40, p<0.001). This indicates that the older the individual is, the greater is the discomfort experienced and the further well-being scores decline.

Discussion

The results of the present research demonstrate a high validity of the research instruments used in the study. Moreover, the results obtained from the various samples of the different tests are positioned below the thresholds established by previous clinical studies of validation. The results confirm the hypothesized model, showing positive correlations between indices of spontaneity and psychological well-being. The research supports the idea that both models (psychodramatic and ecological) contribute to strengthening the empowerment of women who have been victims of violence. However, psychodramatic techniques seem to be most effective in Eastern European countries.

Comparing scores on the total sample in T1 and T2, we note that the SAI-R scores increased and those reported by the CORE-OM decreased. This means that both counseling and psychodrama led, on the one hand, to increased levels of spontaneity and thus psychological well-being, and on the other hand, to a decrease in the levels of discomfort. The analysis of variance carried out on average differences shows that in PG and EG, the size of this improvement is significant. The interaction effect between improvement at T2 and groups (EG and PG) does not emerge because both methods produce significant improvements.

On this basis, we can say that the first hypothesis was confirmed: both interventions (counseling and psychodrama) improved the women's well-being significantly at T2: the SAI-R scores increased, indicating the presence of greater spontaneity, and the CORE-OM scores decreased, indicating less discomfort.

The achievement of the second objective has several implications that we discuss below. The results show that all groups in both geographical areas received a benefit from the interventions, but in a different way. In fact, a difference with respect to the relationship intervention/region emerges. In Eastern Europe, psychodrama is the intervention of choice, as it produces significantly greater improvements, while in Western and Central European countries, ecological counseling produces the most significant change. The CORE-OM scores at T2 significantly decreased in the PG of Eastern Europe and in the EG of Western and Central European countries. However, the SAI-R scores at T2 increased significantly in the PG of Eastern Europe and in the EG of Western and Central European countries.

This result could be due to two factors mentioned above. First, women from Eastern Europe are increasingly aware of the phenomenon of abuse linked to trafficking; and since ecological counseling is a psychosocial intervention, based on activities aimed at integrating the victims into society, it might be that they do not trust society to "save" them from their condition. Second, in Eastern Europe, women's social integration is still lacking and needs to be improved. In this sense, the psychodramatic intervention, which takes place entirely in a protected setting, might provide an elaboration experience that is more reassuring.

The results obtained from comparing the intervention group in the pre-treatment (T1) and post-treatment (T2) phase with clinically significant threshold (cut-off) scores has enabled us to quantify the percentage of women with a critical discomfort score above the clinically significant threshold decreases after the intervention. In fact, for both the total and for all the CORE-OM domains except for the items related to functioning, nearly one out of four women measured a significant improvement. The significance of this change is that, compared to the percentage of women whose scores worsened beginning from below to ending above the clinically significant threshold, the percentage of women whose scores improved is statistically greater. The percentage of women who experienced a positive change[41] is significantly higher than the percentage of women

---

[41] Subjective well-being = 22.8%, problems = 26.5%, risk = 24.3%, no risk items = 23.5%, total of = 24.3%.

who experienced a negative[42] change except for items related to functioning that, however, was improved in 12.5% of women and is greater than the percentage of women who experienced a negative change (8.8%).

In any case, the results highlight that both psychodrama and ecological counseling are successful techniques that address the needs of individuals, since they increase levels of well-being. If we also consider spontaneity as an indicator of change that enables the women to break free from internalized relational scripts that give rise to a victim mentality, we can add that both interventions offer the opportunity to begin a process of change towards autonomy.

For the aforementioned reasons, we believe that the results obtained by this project are highly positive and that this model of intervention should be extended, possibly prolonging the intervention and also measuring the follow-up after one year.

Implications for teaching

This chapter focuses on psychodrama techniques and Empirical Research in the Real World (ERRW) methodology.

Psychodrama techniques enable women who are involved in certain types of mother-daughter relationships to become aware that they are in a subordinate position within the family structure and that the family structure is maintained by asymmetrical power relationships that sustain hierarchical family positions. In particular, these techniques are used with women who are victims of domestic violence. The importance of Morenian techniques lies in the fact that through dramatization, women victims of violence are able to develop coping strategies and resilience. The aim is to strengthen women's agency in order to break the cycle of violence within the family.

ERRW focuses on the lives and experiences of diverse groups that traditionally have been marginalized and analyzes how and why resulting inequities are reflected in asymmetric power relationships, examining how results of social inquiry on inequities are linked to political and social action. It adopts an exploratory strategy of research, but also classical research design methods, to measure events and to generate ideas and hypotheses for future research. In

---

[42] Subjective well-being = 8.8%, problems = 5.1%, risk = 8.8% and items without risk = 3.7%, total of = 5.9%.

this chapter we developed three fundamental sections: first, we touched on the theoretical basis upon which the problem of VAW rests and the methodology of intervention; then we discussed the participants and the instruments used with an accompanying statistical analysis; and lastly, we discussed the results.

The research highlights the efficacy of applying psychodramatic methods in different European countries. Nevertheless, the results also stress the complexity of the problem and the specificity of the issues for each European country. Many factors are involved in the definition of family ties and family roles, which is why each European state must be examined with a tailored approach. For instance, the historical perspective on the development of women's roles within the family and society needs to be taken into account when we work on VAW research, support, and interventions.

Questions

Our research gives rise to questions concerning the relationship between the embodiment of patriarchal discourses and practices that affect women's lives:

1. From a feminist viewpoint, why are psychodramatic techniques and ecological systemic approaches considered potentially optimal for VAW interventions?
2. Why is ERRW a potentially excellent research methodology for VAW research?

Assignments

1. Describe how VAW prevention strategies (in one specific country) are used to support women who are victims of domestic violence.
2. Focus on a specific European country and try to trace social work's development within the intersections comprising the concept of "gender" and how this has been used to build asymmetrical power relationships that relegate women to a subordinate position, attributing to them the characteristics of being "naturally dedicated to the care of others"; "emotional," "passive," and so on.

3. Try to create an ERRW project in the area of VAW, following the structure of this chapter but adopting different intervention strategies.

REFERENCES

Antrobus, Peggy. *The Global Women's Movement: Issues and Strategies for the New Century*. London: Zed Books, 2004.

Ballou, Mary B., Atsushi Matsumoto, and Michael Wagner. "Toward a Feminist Ecological Theory of Human Nature: Theory Building in Response to Real-World Dynamics." In *Rethinking Mental Health and Disorder: Feminist Perspectives*, eds. Mary B. Ballou and Laura S. Brown, 99–141. New York: Guilford Press, 2002.

Beck, Aaron T., Robert A. Steer, and Gregory K. Brown. *Manual for the Beck Depression Inventory — (BDI-II)*, 2nd ed. San Antonio, TX: Psychological Corporation, 1996.

Bronfenbrenner, Urie. *The Ecology of Human Development: Experiments by Nature and Design*. Cambridge, MA: Harvard University Press. 1979.

Bronfenbrenner, Urie. *Making Human Beings Human: Bioecological Perspectives on Human Development*. Thousand Oaks, CA: Sage, 2005.

Browne, Colette, and Crystal Mills. "Theoretical Frameworks: Ecological Model, Strengths Perspective, and Empowerment Theory." In *Culturally Competent Practice: Skills, Interventions, and Evaluations*, eds. Rowena Fong and Sharlene M. Furuto, 10–32. Boston: Allyn and Bacon, 2001.

Council of Europe. *Council of Europe Convention on Action against Trafficking in Human Beings and its Explanatory Report*. Council of Europe Treaty Series no. 197. Warsaw, May 16, 2005.

CEDAW. *Convention on the Elimination of all Forms of Discrimination against Women*. United Nations Department of Public Information, 2000/2009. http://www.un.org/womenwatch/daw/cedaw/cedaw.htm.

Chodorow, Nancy. *The Reproduction of Mothering: Psychoanalysis and the Sociology of Gender*. Berkeley: University of California Press, 1978 (2nd ed., 1999).

Chodorow, Nancy. *Feminism and Psychoanalytic Theory*. New Haven: Yale University Press, 1989.

Codato, Marta, Ines Testoni, Maria Silvia Guglielmin, and Alessandra Armenti. "Overcoming Female Subordination: An Educational Experiment Changes the Levels of Non-Attachment and Objectification in a Group of Female Undergraduates." *Interdisciplinary Journal of Family Studies* 17, no. 1 (2012): 235–249.

Cook, Ellen P. *Women, Relationships, and Power: Implications for Counseling*. Alexandria, VA: American Counseling Association, 1993.

Dasgupta, Shamita D. "A Framework for Understanding Women's Use of Nonlethal Violence in Intimate Heterosexual Relationships." *Violence against Women* 8 (2002): 1364–1389.

Erez, Edna, Peter R. Ibarra, and William F. McDonald. "Transnational Sex Trafficking: Issues and Prospects." *International Review of Victimology* 11, no. 1 (2004): 1–9.

Evans, Chris, Janice Connell, Michael Barkham, Frank Margison, Graeme McGrath, John Mellor-Clark, and Kerry Audin. "Towards a Standardised Brief Outcome Measure: Psychometric Properties and Utility of the CORE-OM." *British Journal of Psychiatry* 180: (2002): 51–60.

Festinger, Leon. *A Theory of Cognitive Dissonance*. Stanford, CA: Stanford University Press, 1957.

Flood, Michael, and Bob Pease. "Factors Influencing Attitudes to Violence against Women." *Trauma, Violence, and Abuse* 10, no. 2 (2009): 125–142.

Gronold, Daniela, Brigitte Hipfl, and Linda Lund Pedersen, eds. *Teaching with the Third Wave: New Feminists' Explorations of Teaching and Institutional Contexts*. ATHENA3, University of Utrecht and Centre for Gender Studies, Stockholm University, 2006.

Hamel, John, and Tonia Nicholls. *Family Interventions in Domestic Violence: A Handbook of Gender-Inclusive Theory and Treatment*. New York: Springer, 2007.

Heise, Lorie L. "Violence against Women: An Integrated, Ecological Framework." *Violence against Women* 4 (1998): 262–290.

Kaur, Ravneet, and Suneela Garg. "Domestic Violence against Women: A Qualitative Study in a Rural Community." *Asia-Pacific Journal of Public Health* 22, no. 2 (2010): 242–251.

Kipper, David A., and Jasdeep Hundal. "The Spontaneity Assessment Inventory: The Relationship between Spontaneity and Nonspontaneity." *Journal of Group Psychotherapy, Psychodrama and Sociometry* 58, no. 3 (2005): 119–129.

Kipper, David A., and Haim Shemer. "The Spontaneity Assessment Inventory-Revised (SAI-R): Spontaneity, Well-Being and Stress." *Journal of Group Psychotherapy, Psychodrama and Sociometry* 59, no. 3 (2006): 127–136.

Kipper, David A., and Eva Buras. "Measurement of Spontaneity: The Relationship between the Intensity and Frequency of the Spontaneous Experience." *Perceptual and Motor Skills* 108, no. 2 (2009): 362–366.

Kristeva, Julia. *Powers of Horror: An Essay on Abjection*. New York: Columbia University Press, 1982.

Lloyd, Sally A., April L. Few, and Katherine R. Allen, eds. *Handbook of Feminist Family Studies*. Thousand Oaks, CA: Sage, 2009.

Maslow, Abraham H. *Motivation and Personality*, 2nd ed. New York: Harper and Row, 1970.

Moreno, Jacob L. *The Theatre of Spontaneity*. New York: Beacon House, 1947.

Moreno, Jacob L. *Who Shall Survive? Foundations of Sociometry, Group Psychotherapy and Sociodrama*. Beacon, NY: Beacon House, 1953 (student edition by American Society of Group Psychotherapy and Psychodrama, 1993).

Moreno, Jacob L. *Psychodrama*, 4th ed., vol. 1. Beacon, NY: Beacon House, 1972.

Ollus, Natalia. *Protocol to Prevent, Suppress and Punish Trafficking in Persons, Especially Women and Children*. Helsinki: HEUNI, 2002.

Pipher, Mary. *The Shelter of Each Other: Rebuilding Our Families*. New York: Ballantine Books, 1996.

Rose, Gillian. "J.L. Meets the Warrior Princess: Exploring Psychodrama and Feminism." *Australian and New Zealand Psychodrama Association Journal* 15 (2006): 22–29.

Seligman, Martin E.P. *Helplessness: On Depression, Development, and Death.* San Francisco: Freeman, 1975.

Straus, Murray. "Physical Assaults by Wives: A Major Social Problem." In *Current Controversies on Family Violence,* eds. Richard J. Gelles and Donileen Loseky, 67–87. Newbury Park, CA: Sage, 1993.

Swick, Kevin J., and Reginald D. Williams. "An Analysis of Bronfenbrenner's Bio-Ecological Perspective for Early Childhood Educators: Implications for Working with Families Experiencing Stress." *Early Childhood Education Journal* 33, no. 5 (2006): 371–378.

Testoni, Ines, Alessandra Armenti, Lucia Ronconi, Michael Wieser, Adriano Zamperini, Sibylla Verdi, and Chris Evans. "Violência de gênero. Testando um modelo: espontaneidade, bem-estar psicológico e depressão." [Gender violence. Testing a model of assumptions: spontaneity, psychological well-being, and depression]. *Rev Bras Psicodrama* [Brazilian Journal of Psychodrama] 21, no. 1 (2013): 95–110.

Testoni, Ines, Alessandra Armenti, Lucia Ronconi, Paolo Cottone, Michael Wieser, and Sibylla Verdi. "Daphne European Research Project: Italian Validation of Hypothesis Model (SAI-R, CORE-OM and BDI-II)," *Interdisciplinary Journal of Family Studies* 17, no. 1 (2012), Padova University Press, Padua.

Testoni, Ines. "The State of the Art in Research and Intervention against Gender Based Violence." *Interdisciplinary Journal of Family Studies* 17, no. 1 (2012): 4–14.

Testoni, Ines, Paolo Cottone, and Alessandra Armenti. "Psychodrama Research in the Field of Women Suffering from Violence: A Daphne Project." Proceedings of the Fourth Regional Mediterranean Congress IAGP SPP "Other Seas," September 7–10, 2011, Porto, Portugal.

Testoni, Ines, Lucia Ronconi, and Daniela Boccher. "The Question of the Mafia-Style Sub-Culture Role in Female Subordination: Traditional Culture, Religion and Gender Role Representation in Both Emigrated and Non-Emigrated Albanian Women." *World Cultural Psychiatry Research Review* 2, no. 1 (2006): 164–181.

Testoni, Ines, Alessandra Armenti, Chris Evans, Daniela Di Lucia Sposito, Michael Wieser, Gabriela Moita, Galabina Tarashoeva, Lucia Ronconi, and Paolo Cottone. "Psychodrama and Management of Sufferance from Domestic Violence: CORE-OM and SAI-R to Assess Empower Project Efficacy." *Gender Research.* At Gender (forthcoming).

United Nations General Assembly Resolution 55/25 of November 15, 2000.

UNESCO. "Data Comparison Sheet, Worldwide Trafficking Estimates by Organizations" (data compiled September 2004). http://www.unescobkk.org/fileadmin/user_upload/culture/Trafficking/project/Graph_Wrldwide_Sept_2004.pdf.

UNIFEM. "Facts and Figures on Violence against Women." http://www.unifem.org/attachments/gender_issues/violence_against_women/facts_figures_violence_against_women_2007.pdf (accessed November 6, 2012).

World Bank. "Human Trafficking: A Brief Overview." *Social Development Notes–Conflict, Crime, and Violence*, no. 122 (2009). http://siteresources.worldbank.org/EXTSOCIALDEVELOP-MENT/ (accessed December 30, 2012).

World Health Organization. *World Report on Violence and Health*. Geneva: World Health Organization, 2002.

Zaidi, Lisa Y., John F. Knutson, and John G. Mehm. "Transgenerational Patterns of Abusive Parenting: Analog and Clinical Tests." *Aggressive Behavior* 15, no. 2 (1989): 137–152.

"OVERCOMING FEMALE SUBORDINATION": AN EXPERIMENTAL PROCESS OF EMPOWERMENT— THROUGH SOCIODRAMA AND DIGITAL STORYTELLING—DIRECTED TOWARD A GROUP OF ITALIAN FEMALE UNDERGRADUATES

Vincenzo Calvo, Marta Codato, Ines Testoni, Alice Bertoldo

Introduction

Following the theory of Third Wave Feminism,[1] this research aims at highlighting new pedagogical strategies to transgress cultural practices that perpetuate female subordination.

In particular, this research aims at analyzing gender stereotypes internalized by young Italian women through the representational system proposed by the mass media. The innovative strategy proposed in this chapter concerns sociodrama techniques that are particularly relevant to investigate the internalization of female cultural representations.

Through sociodrama techniques the importance of the body is placed at the intersection of cultural/social/ethnic/national/transnational knowledge production. In particular the aim of the research is to open up a space to empower the variety of feminist "waves" as claimed by the third feminist wave, with alternative academic practices.

This, the last contribution of the volume, shares with the previous one, "The Effectiveness of the EMPoWER Project and Intervention" (Testoni et al.), the purpose of promoting integrated strategies that aim at deconstructing negative female stereotypes that work as a chain of symbolization keeping women in a subordinate position.

In this volume the concept of "empowerment" is central. It works both at the individual level and in a more general and transnational perspective. It broadened its own spectrum of analysis because it embraces the issues that deal with social

---

[1] Iris Van der Tuin, ed. *On Third-Wave Feminism's Generational Logic and Practices of Teaching Gender Studies*. Utrecht: Athena, 2009.

justice and human rights. From this perspective is highlighted the multidimensional characterization of the concept that takes into account theplurality of experiences of the actors involved. The claim that female subordination is universal is not an attempt to reduce the subjectivity of women's experiences to one model. Rather, it is the awareness that the tracks of academic knowledge and feminist practices need to run in the same direction, highlighting the specificity of each situation.

The volume *Teaching Gender in Social Work* (2009)[2] suggests a new approach that can promote "integrative learning," implying new and creative connections among different concepts, values, and skills. This kind of teaching should involve the use of active methods such as sociodrama and digital storytelling to promote in female students an acting of the submissive roles and simultaneously a process of awareness and a deconstruction of them. Digital storytelling is a short form of digital media production that allows people to share aspects of their life story, reflecting on them. Sociodrama is a dramatic play in which individuals act out assigned roles for the purpose of studying and solving problems in group or collective relationships. A reflection on the body's objectification—through digital storytelling and sociodrama—can stimulate a greater understanding of the dynamics that help to strengthen agency in young women. The undergraduates who participated in the course represented, both in short films and in sociodrama sessions, likely/everyday situations connected to female body objectification. The symbolic representations elicited strong emotions from the students, which they verbalized during the sociodrama's debriefing phase and with the professor in class. For the future professional social workers, the verbalization meant starting from themselves, from their feelings, from their gaze on themselves and on the external world instead of starting from the other's gaze on themselves (by "other" we refer to males, to parents, and to society in general). Promoting a new reflection on the relationship between mother and daughter—through active methods—can activate an exit from the symbiotic relationship that often connects Italian young women to their mothers. In this way it is possible to stimulate a greater flexibility of attachment style (an increased flexibility of the subjective relationship with the internal working models built during childhood thanks to the relationship with the significant figures) and to promote

---

[2] Vesna Leskošek, ed. *Teaching Gender in Social Work; Teaching with Gender; European Women's Studies in International and Interdisciplinary Classrooms.* Utrecht: Athena, 2009.

a stronger and more constructive investment (through the development of non-attachment) on peer relationships (with people external to the family).

Theoretical background

This research concerns the issue of "female subordination," which Ortner[3] claims is universal and present in every type of society.

This kind of subordination is expressed in the various forms of subjugation of women to the will and desire of men. Examples include objectification, relegation to secondary status, and violence. According to Fredrickson and Roberts,[4] objectification is the internalization of the observer's perspective as a primary vision of one's self and is evidenced by the constant monitoring of one's body and by the commitment to comply with aesthetic norms. The absolute relegation of women to family and intimate relationships effectively limits their completeness as people by delegating to men the protection of their rights and the management of systemic relationships.[5] Subjugation is also imposed through forms of violence,[6] such as domestic violence.[7]

The subordination of women in Italy, in particular, is considered to be greatly influenced by the cultural background of the Mediterranean area, informed by customary codes of social regulation, such as the code of honor, according to which women, through their segregation, preserve the honor of families against possible attacks from outside the family.[8]

The Daphne project

This research is closely connected to the activities of the European project Daphne Empower, which promotes awareness of co-responsibility regarding the

---

[3] Sherry B. Ortner, "Is Female to Male as Nature Is to Culture?" *Feminist Studies* 1, no. 2 (1974): 5.

[4] Barbara L. Fredrickson and Tomi-Ann Roberts, "Objectification Theory," *Psychology of Women Quarterly* 21, no. 2 (1997): 173.

[5] Ines Testoni, *La frattura originaria. Psicologia della mafia tra nichilismo e omnicrazia* (Napoli: Liguori, 2008).

[6] Lori Heise, Mary Ellsberg, and Megan Gottemoeller, "Ending Violence Against Women" (1999), http://www.isis.cl/jspui/handle/123456789/35904.

[7] Michael P. Johnson and Kathleen J. Ferraro, "Research on Domestic Violence in the 1990s: Making Distinctions," *Journal of Marriage and Family* 62, no. 4 (2000): 948.

[8] Testoni, *La frattura originaria*.

perpetuation of women's subordination passed down from mothers. The project has enabled a process of empowerment through Morenian psychodrama, a technique that allows people to redefine the roles they have unconsciously internalized, through awareness of their own way of relating to significant figures.[9] In particular, the Daphne IPRASE project "Overcoming Female Subordination" is a collaboration between the provincial institute for research and educational experimentation IPRASE (Trentino) and Prof. Ines Testoni of the Department of Philosophy, Sociology, Education and Applied Psychology at the University of Padua. It promotes awareness and transformation of patterns of subordination of female students and fosters women's solidarity and empowerment, by involving a mutual stimulus for the spontaneous emergence of female subjective features. It was a university course aimed at understanding the issues related to the exploitation of the female body. The course provided a theoretical reflection on the practical dimension of attachment[10] in order to promote in female students:[11]

1. the achievement of greater autonomy and freedom from past relationships;
2. a freedom from traditions and external pressures (nonattachment);[12]
3. a partial divestment from symbiotic attachment to the family of origin and a greater investment in relationships with people outside the family;
4. a transfer of attention from the judgment of others to one's own internal states;
5. the maturation of an awareness with respect to one's own ability to affect civic and political development and to influence others by one's own actions.

---

[9] Giovanni Boria, *Psicoterapia psicodrammatica. Sviluppi del modello moreniano nel lavoro terapeutico con gruppi di adulti* (Milan: Franco Angeli, 2005).

[10] John Bowlby, *Attachment and Loss: Attachment* (New York: Basic Books, 1969); John Bowlby, *Attachment and Loss: Sadness and Depression* (New York: Basic Books, 1980); John Bowlby, *Attachment and Loss: Separation, Anxiety and Anger* (New York: Basic Books, 1973).

[11] Cindy Hazan and Phillip Shaver, "Romantic Love Conceptualized as an Attachment Process," *Journal of Personality and Social Psychology* 52, no. 3 (1987): 511.

[12] Baljinder Kaur Sahdra, Phillip R. Shaver, and Kirk Warren Brown, "A Scale to Measure Nonattachment: A Buddhist Complement to Western Research on Attachment and Adaptive Functioning," *Journal of Personality Assessment* 92, no. 2 (2010): 116.

Research objectives and hypothesis

The main aim of this research project was to study the effects of an experimental process of empowerment on young adult female participants' attachment network, on their level of socio-political control and nonattachment.

The assumptions of this study were in accordance with the results of Testoni[13] and Druetta.[14] Specifically, we assumed that the condition of women during the young-adult developmental phase is generally characterized by a network of attachment whose core is the mother. Furthermore, we assumed that students with a stable romantic relationship had greater autonomy from the mother, compared to single students and to those who were in an uncommitted relationship with another person. We hypothesized that it was possible to modify the women's network of attachment, the level of nonattachment and of socio-political control through techniques such as sociodrama and digital storytelling, along with lectures on the causes of the "gender gap." These hypotheses were connected to the literature on the educational function of digital storytelling[15] and the associations between sociodrama and increased socio-political participation[16] and between psychodrama and attachment.[17] To test the above-mentioned hypotheses, we used an experimental group, who participated in the experimental process of empowerment consisting of students in the second year at the University of Padua, and a control group of students in the second year at the University of Trento, who attended the university courses without any empowerment intervention. The purpose of this study was to test the predictions, based on our hypotheses, that only the experimental group would show a significant change in the level of the variables taken into account. In particular, we tested four main predictions. First, we predicted an increase in the level of nonattachment and the

---

[13] Ines Testoni, *La frattura originaria.*

[14] Vanda Druetta, *Il sogno del femminile, il femminile del sogno* (Milan: FrancoAngeli, 2001).

[15] Monica Nilsson, "Digital Storytelling: A Multidimensional Tool in Education," in *Handbook of Research on Digital Information Technologies: Innovations, Methods, and Ethical Issues,* ed. Thomas Hansson (Hershey, PA: Information Science Reference, 2008), 131–145.

[16] Jacob Levi Moreno, *Sociometry, Experimental Method and the Science of Society: An Approach to a New Political Orientation* (New York: Beacon House, 1951).

[17] Turkan Dogan, "The Effects of Psychodrama on Young Adults' Attachment Styles," *The Arts in Psychotherapy* 37, no. 2 (2010): 112.

level of social and political control. Second, we predicted a modification in the attachment network, and in particular a decrease of the strength of attachment to the members of the family of origin, especially to the mother, and an increase in attachment to people outside the family. Third, we predicted an interaction between the composition of the attachment network and two other variables: the housing conditions and the relational status of the participants. Specifically, for the students who were living independently, we predicted that, following the experimental process of empowerment, they would create more relationships with people outside the family. For students who still lived with their parents, we predicted that after the trial even they would become more independent from the family and would create more relationships outside the family. Fourth, we predicted that after the experimental process of empowerment, even female students without a stable romantic relationship would become more independent from their mother.

Research design and variables

Independent variables. In order to verify the hypothesis, we identified the relational status and the housing conditions as independent variables. The relational status refers to the romantic relational status of respondents, which we characterized as "single," "dating with no commitment," or "in a stable romantic relationship." We expected data to be consistent with the studies conducted by Feeney[18] according to which there is a gradual reduction in the level of attachment to the family of origin at the formation of romantic relationships. It was also expected that after the experimental process of empowerment, students with a "single" or "dating with no commitment" status would be more independent from the family of origin and particularly from the mother.

The association between housing conditions and the attachment of Italian students was studied by Codato, Shaver, Testoni, and Ronconi.[19] That study showed how college students who reside with their parents tend to have an anxious, insecure attachment style, which is connected to a strong fear of explo-

---

[18] Judith A. Feeney, "Transfer of Attachment from Parents to Romantic Partners: Effects of Individual and Relationship Variables," *Journal of Family Studies* 10, no. 2 (2004): 220.

[19] Marta Codato et al., "Civic and Moral Disengagement, Weak Personal Beliefs and Unhappiness: A Survey Study of the 'Famiglia Lunga' Phenomenon in Italy," *Testing, Psychometrics, Methodology in Applied Psychology* 18, no. 2 (2011): 87.

ration, according to the literature.[20] Therefore we expected that people who still lived with the family of origin would show a greater attachment to parents and a lower attachment to people outside the family than those who lived on their own. We predicted, however, that the experimental process of empowerment would result in a change toward a higher relational investment outside the family, even from those still living at the family residence.

The intervening variables. We used "sociodrama" and "digital storytelling" as intervening variables to test the predicted effects on the dependent variables, which we will describe below. "Sociodrama" is an action method that refers to relations between groups and collective ideologies.[21] "Digital storytelling" combines the tradition of "storytelling" with innovative "multimedia communication." It involves "permanent narratives" that can be disseminated widely, making them available for reflection and critique.[22]

The dependent variables. We predicted that the dependent variables of "attachment network" and "socio-political control" would change under the influence of the intervening variables. "Attachment network" in adulthood implies the presence of several figures who fulfill the functions of attachment in different contexts and situations.[23] These attachment functions are *proximity seeking, secure haven, separation protest,* and *secure base.* Not all the figures in the attachment network are treated in the same way. On the contrary, it is likely that individuals differ in the extent to which they are directed towards specific figures for comfort and reassurance. It is known that many attachments are organized hierarchically, with the primary figure of attachment at the top.[24] The average

---

[20] Jeffrey D. Green and W. Keith Campbell, "Attachment and Exploration in Adults: Chronic and Contextual Accessibility," *Personality and Social Psychology Bulletin* 26, no. 4 (2000): 452.

[21] Giovanni Boria, *Psicoterapia psicodrammatica.*

[22] Alan Davis, "Co-Authoring Identity: Digital Storytelling in an Urban Middle School." *THEN: Technology, Humanities, Education, and Narrative* 1 no. 1 (2004): 1; Joe Lambert, *Digital Storytelling Cookbook* (Berkeley, CA: Digital Diner Press, 2010).

[23] Carollee Howes, Carol Rodning, Darlene C. Galluzzo, and Lisabeth Myers, "Attachment and Child Care: Relationships with Mother and Caregiver," *Early Childhood Research Quarterly* 3, no. 4 (1988): 403; Nicole A. Doherty and Judith A. Feeney, "The Composition of Attachment Networks throughout the Adult Years," *Personal Relationships* 11, no. 4 (2004): 469.

[24] Inge Bretherton, "Attachment Theory: Retrospect and Prospect," in *Growing Points of Attachment: Theory and Research,* eds. Inge Bretherton and Everett Waters (Chicago: University of Chicago Press for the Society for Research in Child Development, 1985), 3–35.

hierarchy during adulthood is identified (in descending order) with a woman's mother, partner, best friend, father, and brothers/sisters.[25]

With this study we wanted to verify if there was an enlargement of the attachment network after the experimental process of empowerment and whether the students would establish significant relationships outside of the family. Instead of the known attachment styles (secure, insecure, anxious, insecure avoidant), we considered the psychological construct of "nonattachment," which has been identified with the Buddhist concept of nonattachment.[26] Nonattachment is characterized by a fluidity of subjective working models (with respect to itself, the other, the reality) based on the responses of the attachment figures to proximity-seeking attempts.[27] This construct is crucial for psychological well-being, as it is positively related to subjective well-being (life satisfaction and emotional traits) and to eudemonic well-being (self-acceptance, personal growth, positive relations with others, and purpose in life). It is inversely correlated with depression, anxiety, stress, and difficulties with regulating one's emotions.

The construct of nonattachment was chosen in the knowledge that, through education, we cannot expect to modify the attachment styles developed in childhood relationships. Nonattachment, however, can be achieved regardless of one's relationships with primary attachment figures.

"Socio-political control" is a construct that implies "political control," that is, the subjective confidence in one's ability to influence policy decisions, as well as "leadership skills," meaning the confidence in one's ability to lead a group of people or to organize neighbors or others. This construct implies psychological well-being.[28] We expected an increase in the level of socio-political control of the students after experimentation.

---

[25] Vincenzo Calvo, A. de Romano, and M. Battistella, "The Structure of Attachment Networks in Italian Young Adults" (paper presented at the International Congress "Attaccamento: metodi a confronto," Padua, Italy, January 11–12, 2008); Doherty, "The Composition of Attachment," 469.

[26] Sahdra, "A Scale to Measure Nonattachment," 116.

[27] Bowlby, *Attachment and Loss: Attachment*; Bowlby, *Attachment and Loss: Sadness and Depression*; Bowlby, *Attachment and Loss: Separation, Anxiety and Anger*.

[28] Marc A. Zimmerman and James H. Zahniser, "Refinements of Sphere-Specific Measures of Perceived Control: Development of a Sociopolitical Control Scale." *Journal of Community Psychology* 19, no. 2 (1991): 189.

Methodology

Participants

The total sample ($N = 104$) is composed of female students of mean age 21 years ($SD = 1.45$). Of this entire group, 53 were studying at the University of Padua (the experimental group), and 51 were studying at the University of Trento (the control group). The experimental group attended the course "Psychology of Intergroup and Intra-group Relationships" (the total of those attending was 60 females and two males), within the degree program of Social Service. The control group did not participate in any similar course.

Instruments and measures

Participants anonymously completed questionnaires twice (at the beginning and at the end of the course, time of administration 1 and time of administration 2). They had access to the questionnaire through a personal identification code they set that was not known by the researchers. The questionnaire included several sections and took an average of 20 minutes to be completed.

One set of questions focused on *demographic variables* such as gender, age, educational level, current employment, university affiliation, residential status, and relational status.

To investigate individuals' attachment networks and the strength of attachment to various figures, participants completed an adaptation of the Italian version of the *Attachment Network Questionnaire-Revised* (ANQ-R).[29] The purpose of the scale is to investigate the strength of the participants' attachment toward various attachment figures. Participants were asked to make a list of all persons with whom they felt a strong emotional bond and note the type of relationship. Then participants had to complete eight items that assess the four attachment functions (proximity seeking, secure haven, separation protest and secure base): for each item, participants were asked to name people who fulfill that function and to list these people in order of importance (from 3 to 1). The ratings for each attachment function were averaged to produce the strength of attachment scores for each attachment figure. If participants wrote more than one

---

[29] Doherty, "The Composition of Attachment," 469; Calvo, "The Structure of Attachment Networks."

reference person for the same attachment function, the scores were totaled and divided by the total number of people. Following the methodology proposed by Doherty and Feeney,[30] we investigated for attachment strength only the five most frequently occurring figures: partner, mother, father, sibling, and best friend. We also calculated two overall measures of attachment strength: the total strength of attachment to family members (summing the scores referring to all the family members) and the total strength of attachment to non-family members.

The *Nonattachment Scale* (NAS)[31] is a seven-point Likert scale and consists of 30 items that measure the subjective level of nonattachment.

The *Sociopolitical Control Scale* (SPCS)[32] allowed for the evaluation of the subjective level of socio-political control and, in particular, the competence of leadership and political control. It is a six-point Likert scale and consists of 17 items that investigate the cognitive and motivational components of perceived control. The scale has two subscales: "leadership skills" and "political control." The first factor refers to the subjective sense of confidence in leadership skills. The second refers to the expectations that come from active participation, that is, the sense of competence in influencing policy decisions. Both measure the sense of self-efficacy in the social and political sphere.

Experimental process of empowerment

The experimental group participated in a series of experiments designed to promote their empowerment (for the total duration of 40 hours), which involved three distinct parts. First, a theoretical course introduced issues such as male and female psychology and the interactions between genders. Second, three socio-drama meetings focused on the representation of women. Third, the learners themselves created works of digital storytelling containing the following elements: a significant event in a woman's life that marks the beginning of a physical-emotional-intellectual or spiritual journey, the solution of the initial problem, the personal transformation of the protagonist, and the closure of history.

---

[30] Feeney, "Transfer of Attachment from Parents to Romantic Partners," 220.

[31] Sahdra, "A Scale to Measure Nonattachment," 116.

[32] Zimmerman, "Refinements of Sphere-Specific Measures of Perceived Control," 189.

Statistical analysis

Analyses were performed using SPSS statistical software. The Pearson's correlation coefficients were used for an initial analysis of the relationship between the average of NAS, SPCS, and the totals of ANQ-R. To analyze the effect of variables relevant to the research, such as participation in the empowerment process, housing conditions and relational status, we used the *t*-test on the totals of scale ANQ-R (strength of attachment to each relevant figure). To evaluate the results, we used the mean (*M*) values for significant *t*-test, the standard deviation (or ± SD), and the difference between the means (*dM*).

In order to verify the hypothesis that the experimental process of empowerment would significantly modify the above variables, we computed a series of analysis of variance (ANOVA) for repeated measures. The significance of all relationships was set at $p < .05$.

Results

Description of participants. Sixty-four students lived at home with their parents; 25 lived in a separate apartment, but they went to their parents' home on weekends; nine lived alone; four students lived in a dormitory; just one student lived with her husband and children; 56 had a stable romantic relationship; 10 were "dating" a person without commitment.

The contingency tables that analyze the relationship between the "housing conditions" and "relational situation" show that: within the experimental group, there is a higher number of people living with their parents: 79% of subjects in the first administration of the test (42 of 53) and 44% in the second one (22 of 50); within the experimental group there are fewer people in stable romantic relationships, 41.5% (22 of 53), compared to the control group, 48% (24 of 51). Moreover, the average age of the two groups (experimental and control group) was not statistically different (*M* experimental group = 20.92 years, *M* control group = 20.45 years, *tM = 4.33, SD = 0.79* (102) = 1.67, *ns*).

The overall situation before the experimental process of empowerment

Attachment figures and attachment strength. The most frequently occurring figures who were reported to serve as attachment figures were investigated in terms of attachment strength and primary attachment figures. The strength of attachment to each of the five main figures (partner, mother, father, sibling, and friend) was calculated by averaging scores across the four functions and could range from 0 to 6. Then we analyzed the attachment strength according to the relational status of participants. For the 57 women who had a stable romantic relationship, mean scores revealed that participants reported strongest attachment to partners (M = 4.40), then mothers (M = 2.25), followed by best friends (M = 1.23), fathers (M = 1.00), and siblings (M = 0.92). For the remaining 46 participants, single or without a stable romantic relationship, the strongest attachment was reported to mothers (M = 2.66), then to best friends (M = 1.92), fathers (M = 1.45), and siblings (M = 0.91).

Afterward, we classified the primary attachment figure of each participant, identifying the person with the highest composite score across the four functions (Doherty and Feeney, 2004). In other words, the primary attachment figure was the figure on whom a participant relied most for attachment needs according to the ANQ-R. Only for seven participants (6.7%) was the highest composite score the same for two or more attachment figures. Following Doherty and Feeney (2004), these women were judged not to have a primary attachment figure. Among the remaining 97 participants, there were several types of primary attachment figures (see Table 1). In descending order of frequency, primary attachment figures were partners, mothers, friends, fathers, and siblings.

Table 1. Percentages of different targets as primary attachment figures

	Percentage reporting target as primary attachment figure (% of total sample)	Participants with a partner N = 55 (% of subsample)	Participants without a partner N = 42 (% of subsample)
Partner	43.3	70.9	n/a
Mother	23.7	16.4	33.3
Best friend	19.6	9.1	33.3

162

	Percentage reporting target as primary attachment figure (% of total sample)	Participants with a partner $N = 55$ (% of subsample)	Participants without a partner $N = 42$ (% of subsample)
Father	6.2	0	14.3
Sibling	3.1	0	7.1
Other family members	2.1	0	4.8
Other non-family members	2.1	3.6	7.1

n/a = not applicable

We found significant mean differences in attachment network composition when considering the "emotional status" of participants. Women who were not in a stable romantic relationship tended to have a greater number of significant people in their lives ($M = 10.87 \pm 6.26$, $dM = 2.17$; $t(101) = 2.21$, $p = .030$), particularly outside the family ($M = 5.91 \pm 4.15$, $dM = 1.56$; $t(101) = 2.45$, $p = .016$), and a higher strength of attachment to family members ($M = 23.38 \pm 10.66$, $dM = 5.47$; $t(101) = 2.49$, $p = .014$). On the other hand, participants in a stable romantic relationship were strongly attached to non-family members ($M = 26.40 \pm 7.45$, $dM = -9.52$; $t(101) = -6.00$, $p < .001$).

Lastly, the t-test for independent samples showed that if we divide the sample according to the variable group membership (empowerment group and control group) and housing conditions, there were no significant differences in the ANQ-R measures.

Nonattachment. The NAS scale has 30 items with a Cronbach's Alpha equal to .88 (the scale is very reliable). The mean score of the scale is 3.83, with a standard deviation of .66; the distribution is normal. The mean is low in comparison to the one that characterized both the meditators' group ($M = 4.64$, $SD = 0.82$) and the randomly selected control group ($M = 4.33$, $SD = 0.79$) considered by Sahdra et al.[33]

Sociopolitical control. The subscale "leadership skills" has a Cronbach's Alfa of .79, a mean of 3.88 with standard deviation of .88. The subscale "political control" has a Cronbach's Alfa of .76. It has a mean of 3.71 with a standard deviation of .85. For both, the distributions of the test are normal.

---

[33] Sahdra, "A Scale to Measure Nonattachment," 116.

Correlations. The Pearson's *r* correlations were calculated between ANQ-R measures, NAS, and Sociopolitical SPCS. The ANQ-R measures did not correlate with the SPCS scales, and only the number of significant people ($r = .24, p = .016$) and the number of significant people outside the family ($r = .21, p = .029$) correlated with the NAS. These two significant correlations indicate that participants with larger attachment networks, and with more non-familial members in those networks, tend to have a higher subjective level of nonattachment.

In addition, the NAS correlates positively with both subscales of the SPCS ("leadership skills" $r = .38, p < .001$; "political control" $r = .41, p < .001$). This correlation shows how nonattachment is psychologically and socially adaptive, leading to a subjective perception of a high capability to organize a group of people and to influence political decisions.

Effects of the experimental process of empowerment on the participants' attachment networks, nonattachment sociopolitical control: Comparison between the first and second administration

Attachment network. In order to verify if the participation to the experimental process of empowerment yielded a significant modification of the individual's attachment network, we computed several ANOVA analyses for repeated measures, with three ANQ-R scores as dependent variables (attachment strength to mothers, to family members, and to non-family members) and the participation to the empowerment process as an independent variable. The analyses did not show any significant interaction between the participation in the empowerment process and the main measures of ANQ-R over time. In particular, the empowerment process did not modify the participant's strength of attachment to mothers ($F(1, 102) = .190$, *ns*), to family members ($F(1, 102) = .005$, *ns*), and to non-family members ($F(1, 102) = .167$, *ns*).

To further investigate the effect of the empowerment process on the attachment networks of participants, we also took into account their housing condition, with a set of three-way ANOVA analyses for repeated measures (empowerment participation X housing conditions with attachment network measures as dependent variables within subjects).

These analyses did not show a significant effect of the interaction between empowerment participation and housing condition on the attachment strength

164

to mothers ($F(1, 99) = .001$, *ns*) and to family members ($F(1, 99) = 2.682$, *ns*). Conversely, the interaction effect was significant on attachment strength to non-family members ($F(1, 99) = 7.398$, $p = .008$).

After the empowerment process, the participants who lived with their parents increased the attachment strength to non-family members. Participants of the experimental group who were living independently did the opposite: they decreased the attachment strength to non-family members. In other words, the empowerment process contributed to equilibrate the attachment balance between the outside and the inside of the family. The control group showed an opposite trend: attachment strength to non-family members tended to increase slightly over time in participants who lived independently, and it decreased in women living with their parents.

Similarly, we tested whether the empowerment process had an interaction effect with the relational status on the attachment networks of participants. Again, several ANOVA analyses for repeated measures were computed, with two fixed factors (group membership and relational status) and the measures of the strength of attachment derived from the ANQ-R (strength of attachment to mothers, to family people, and to non-family people) as dependent variables.

The results showed a significant interaction effect between participation in the empowerment process and relational status on the strength of attachment to mothers ($F(1, 99) = 4.141$, $p = .045$), family members ($F(1, 99) = 4.230$, $p = .042$), and non-family members ($F(1, 99) = 7.570$, $p = .007$).

Participants in a stable romantic relationship, after the empowerment process, augmented their attachment to mothers, and to family members, whereas they decreased the strength to those not in their family. Interestingly, participants not in romantic relationships showed an opposite trend after the empowerment process: the strength of their attachment to non-family members increased, and the attachment to mothers and to family members diminished. Again, the effect in the control group was the reverse.

Nonattachment. Two ANOVAs for repeated measures were computed to verify the effect of the experimental process of empowerment on the participants' subjective level of nonattachment. The results were statistically significant ($F(1, 102) = 3.717$, $p = .057$). More specifically, women who participated in the experimental process of empowerment showed a stable subjective level of nonattachment over time, whereas it was lowered in participants in the control group. This result is different from what we expected. Our hypothesis implied that the empowerment project would promote an increased level of nonattachment among the young women of the experimental group. We did not expect to find a decreased level of nonattachment among the students of the control group at the second administration. We had not considered the possible intervention of the variable of "stress due to the university exams," which may have affected the lowering of the level of nonattachment within the control group and whose effect has been countered within the experimental group by the experimental process of empowerment. Consequently we could imagine that the level of nonattachment within the control group could be lowered because of the stress due to the exams. At the same time the level remains steady and does not decrease within the experimental group, probably because of the empowerment experimental process.

Sociopolitical control. Lastly, we performed two ANOVAs to verify if the participation in the experimental process of empowerment would change the level of sociopolitical control. The participation in the empowerment process had significant effects both on the participants' leadership skills ($F(1, 102) = 4.851$, $p = .030$) and on their political control ($F(1, 102) = 6.160$, $p = .015$). As expected, the experimental group significantly increased the political control after the empowerment process (M time 1 = 3.77 ± .88, M time 2 = 3.82 ± .87, dM = .18; Bonferroni post-hoc test, $p = .010$), and the control group remained stable. On the other hand, contrary to our expectations, the subjective sense of confidence in leadership skills did not increase within the experimental group but decreased significantly within the control group over time.

We could say that the empowerment experimental process stimulated an increase of the "political control" in spite of the students' likely stress due to the exams. The hypothetical role of stress was more relevant in affecting the association between the empowerment experimental process and the "subjective sense of confidence in leadership skills," the level of which remained stable.

Discussion

The results do not confirm the hypotheses but are still encouraging for the purposes of this research project. The subjects who took part in the experimental work "Overcoming Female Subordination," consisting of a theoretical course, three meetings for sociodrama, and the realization of a digital storytelling, show some changes with regard to the constructs under investigation, namely the composition of network attachment, the level of nonattachment, leadership skills, and political control.

In summary, the students who participated in the experimental activities of the project "Overcoming Female Subordination" have had the opportunity to raise awareness of self-representation of subordination and begin a journey of self-determination and "de-objectification." This journey implies a greater capacity to listen to oneself and a higher subjective belief in one's ability to develop skills and contribute to civic development. The experiment has fostered greater independence from the mother, a greater investment in relationships with people outside the family, and increased levels of nonattachment and sociopolitical control.

These results are also a test of the validity of sociodrama and digital storytelling as a means of producing changes in the perspective of empowerment and prevention of gender violence.

Based on these limited but positive results, we propose the opening of centers for gender counseling and courses in gender pedagogy, beginning with the University of Padua. These centers would use digital storytelling workshops and sociodrama to promote critical thinking on gender stereotypes and to change the unconsciously-assumed mental and behavioral patterns.

Implications for teaching

The formation of female representations has been marked by the establishment of subordinate positions that involve women's roles within and outside the family. Nowadays female stereotypical representations are mediated by patriarchal discourses also created through the mass media.

In the case of Italy, mass media systems portray images of women that derive from the subconscious and idealization of male imaginary. Patriarchal discourses are directed to the female body, which has been used to construct stereotypical representations of women in Western society. The body is also a place of intersection among race/ethnicity/gender/class/nations, and it serves as a tool to perform subjectivity.

The present research can have implications for teaching related to inspiring female undergraduates to be aware of their own internalized subordination's schemas in order to help other females to become conscious too. In particular the research's participants were enrolled in a university course in social work. For people who are going to be social workers, it is fundamental to understand the mechanisms that produce and reproduce social inequalities, and in our case the inequalities between the genders. It is essential to consider that the ideal context for this kind of lecture is the Italian one. In fact, the phenomenon of female subordination connected to overattachment to the mother is characteristically Italian.

The results of this research can be linked to VAW interventions in terms of prevention strategies. For instance, one of the most dangerous representations depicts women as being "passive and submissive," thus impeding the development of a full agency. It is possible to fight violence against women by making students stage/act different female roles in order to reflect on their own inner schemas. The students will be more aware of themselves and less inclined to fit in victim/perpetrator relationships (in the role of victim). They will also become more able to recognize violence situations in which they are not directly involved. Once a critical awareness is achieved at this level, they will be able to discover in themselves a greater potential to engage critically with the broader complex forces in the organizations where they will work and in society more generally.

Questions

1. In what ways have patriarchal discourses on women's body affected women's body self-image? You could start by referring to the Objectification Theory (B.L. Fredrickson and T.A. Roberts, 1997).
2. What kind of differences are perceived among people of different races but living in the same cultural environment (for example, in Italy many school classes consist of mixed groups of peers who do not have the same experience of the self-body image)?
3. What are the connections between representations of women's bodies and the phenomenon of violence against women?
4. In what way can active methods promote the overcoming of female subordination?

Assignments

The goal is to outline a school project addressed to raise awareness within a group of young students (future social workers) on the limitations of the discourses implying women's body stereotypes.

The assignments involved are the following:

- Assignment 1: Outline a part of the project taking into account the socio-historical conditions of the country in which you are going to operate
- Assignment 2: Outline a part of the project particularly focusing on the sample (age, environment, sex, race, social class)
- Assignment 3: Outline a part of the project taking into account the theoretical part (the theories you will use to explain the internalization of patriarchal discourses on women's bodies)
- Assignment 4: Outline a part of the project by focusing on the operative setting (i.e., the methodology that you want to work with)

REFERENCES

Boria, Giovanni. *Psicoterapia psicodrammatica. Sviluppi del modello moreniano nel lavoro terapeutico con gruppi di adulti.* Milan: Franco Angeli, 2005.

Bowlby, John. *Attachment and Loss: Attachment.* New York: Basic Books, 1969.

Bowlby, John. *Attachment and Loss: Sadness and Depression.* New York: Basic Books, 1980.

Bowlby, John. *Attachment and Loss: Separation, Anxiety and Anger.* New York: Basic Books, 1973.

Bretherton, Inge. "Attachment Theory: Retrospect and Prospect." In *Growing Points of Attachment Theory and Research*, eds. Inge Bretherton and Everett Waters, 3–35. Chicago: University of Chicago Press for the Society for Research in Child Development, 1985.

Calvo, Vincenzo, A. de Romano, and M. Battistella. "The Structure of Attachment Networks in Italian Young Adults." Paper presented at the International Congress "Attaccamento: metodi a confronto," Padua, Italy, January 11–12, 2008.

Codato, Marta, Phillip R. Shaver, Ines Testoni, and Lucia Ronconi. "Civic and Moral Disengagement, Weak Personal Beliefs and Unhappiness: A Survey Study of the 'Famiglia Lunga' Phenomenon in Italy." *Testing, Psychometrics, Methodology in Applied Psychology* 18, no. 2 (2011): 87–97.

Davis, Alan. "Co-Authoring Identity: Digital Storytelling in an Urban Middle School." *THEN: Technology, Humanities, Education, and Narrative* 1, no. 1 (2004): 1.

Dogan, Turkan. "The Effects of Psychodrama on Young Adults' Attachment Styles." *The Arts in Psychotherapy* 37, no. 2 (2010): 112–119.

Doherty, Nicole A., and Judith A. Feeney. "The Composition of Attachment Networks Throughout the Adult Years." *Personal Relationships* 11, no. 4 (2004): 469–488.

Druetta, Vanda. *Il sogno del femminile, il femminile del sogno.* Milan: FrancoAngeli, 2001.

Feeney, Judith A. "Transfer of Attachment from Parents to Romantic Partners: Effects of Individual and Relationship Variables." *Journal of Family Studies* 10, no. 2 (2004): 220–238.

Fredrickson, Barbara L., and Tomi-Ann Roberts. "Objectification Theory." *Psychology of Women Quarterly* 21, no. 2 (1997): 173–206.

Green, Jeffrey D., and W. Keith Campbell. "Attachment and Exploration in Adults: Chronic and Contextual Accessibility." *Personality and Social Psychology Bulletin* 26, no. 4 (2000): 452–461.

Hazan, Cindy, and Phillip Shaver. "Romantic Love Conceptualized as an Attachment Process." *Journal of Personality and Social Psychology* 52, no. 3 (1987): 511–524.

Heise, Lori, Mary Ellsberg, and Megan Gottemoeller. "Ending Violence against Women" (1999). http://www.isis.cl/jspui/handle/123456789/35904.

Howes, Carollee, Carol Rodning, Darlene C. Galluzzo, and Lisabeth Myers. "Attachment and Child Care: Relationships with Mother and Caregiver." *Early Childhood Research Quarterly* 3, no. 4 (1988): 403–416.

Johnson, Michael P., and Kathleen J. Ferraro. "Research on Domestic Violence in the 1990s: Making Distinctions." *Journal of Marriage and Family* 62, no. 4 (2000): 948–963.

Lambert, Joe. *Digital Storytelling Cookbook.* Berkeley, CA: Digital Diner Press, 2010.

Leskošek, V., ed. *Teaching Gender in Social Work: Teaching with Gender; European Women's Studies in International and Interdisciplinary Classrooms.* Utrecht: Athena, 2009.

Moreno, Jacob Levi. *Sociometry, Experimental Method and the Science of Society: An Approach to a New Political Orientation.* New York: Beacon House, 1951.

Nilsson, Monica. "Digital Storytelling: A Multidimensional Tool in Education." In *Handbook of Research on Digital Information Technologies: Innovations, Methods, and Ethical Issues,* ed. Thomas Hansson, 131–145. Hershey, PA: Information Science Reference, 2008.

Ortner, Sherry B. "Is Female to Male as Nature Is to Culture?" *Feminist Studies* 1, no. 2 (1974): 5–31.

Sahdra, Baljinder Kaur, Phillip R. Shaver, and Kirk Warren Brown. "A Scale to Measure Nonattachment: A Buddhist Complement to Western Research on Attachment and Adaptive Functioning." *Journal of Personality Assessment* 92, no. 2 (2010): 116–127.

Testoni, Ines. *La frattura originaria. Psicologia della mafia tra nichilismo e omnicrazia.* Naples: Liguori, 2008.

Van der Tuin, Iris, ed. *On Third-Wave Feminism's Generational Logic and Practices of Teaching Gender Studies*. Utrecht: Athena, 2009.

Zimmerman, Marc A., and James H. Zahniser. "Refinements of Sphere-Specific Measures of Perceived Control: Development of a Sociopolitical Control Scale." *Journal of Community Psychology* 19, no. 2 (1991): 189–204.

CONCLUSION

This volume has considered various aspects of gender-based violence. It has traced a path that began with a discussion about policies created to protect women against domestic violence and the emancipation of women and ended with a description of concrete interventions that support victims and provide education for preventing women's dependence on men.

Following the reflections of Third Wave Feminist Teaching (TWFT) and respecting the commitment to acknowledge and respect the spaces within which education develops that makes equality possible between genders, the volume has followed a path along which various elements have been suggested that can now be defined as critical for empowerment. We want to focus our concluding remarks on those points.

From the perspective of human rights and the initiatives of the United Nations, international policies are promoting a historical change with respect to women's condition that is important to make evident to the new generations. The book started off with a discourse about the size of the problem, and it finished by entering into the merits of subjective micro-social experiences involved in psychological education. The choice of this logical structure arose from the conviction that the political dimension plays a part in every step towards the liberation of women from individual and social oppression. As illustrated by black feminism, discussed in the first part of the volume, the politicization of the personal dimension requires a constant exercise of memory, as well as the need to contextualize educational practices that involve new generations. In fact, young women can personally enjoy an improvement in their conditions of autonomy and self-determination without having to know either the broader social factors that currently allow such freedom nor the historical trajectory that has led to this change.

As *Teaching with Gender* series clarifies, the new frontier of women's education requires a continuous search for new methods of teaching and intervention, because society is also changing rapidly as a result of technological and scientific development worldwide. TWFT has already been able to respond to many of these demands by reflecting on these issues and introducing pedagogical approaches that have garnered considerable support in all areas of knowledge, such as the first-person narrative, situated perspective, and the involvement of the body in the construction of shared knowledge.

Making use of these resources, this volume was produced, taking into account some crucial aspects that should be developed in future educational practices for implementing TWFT. The first concerns the need to involve men in order to activate their capacity to respect women. The second is related to what we know about the traditional ways in which women were brought up in the past. Two main contributions of the volume—one at the end of the first part, the other at the beginning of the second part—sought to highlight these key concepts. One contribution discussed the experience of a project in South Africa that involved men in a campaign of "(de/re) construction of masculinities," and the other discussion involved the experience of the Irish Magdalene institute. In the first instance, we wanted to highlight the need to focus education on a systemic level so that the social space itself transforms in order to overcome female subordination and prevent the creation of the perpetrator/oppressor male. In the latter case, we wanted to highlight how much education from the past, which resulted from traditional absolutism, which provided the background against which patriarchal violence produced the subordination of women, is also involved in pitting women against women. This aspect was considered in the final part of this volume in relation to the mother-daughter relationship, where mothers linked to the traditions of the past do not enable their daughters to free themselves from their victimhood. Since feminism proceeds in tandem with the historical evolution in relationships of parity, even today one can still find in the West, the region that has promoted a culture of inalienable human rights, situations in which mothers still teach their daughters to subject themselves to the will of men.

An additional area that we wanted to consider in the volume was the enhancement of educational aspects through support activities that can return to the woman an awareness of her condition. To this end, we presented different types of interventions, including the initiatives in Portugal that have enhanced cognitive and discursive practices for activating processes that can be defined as "consciousness-raising." These are methods that enjoy a broad and growing consensus in women's social identity construction research in addition to the women's "personal possible roles" that increasingly draw the interest of clinical and social psychology. Interventions with victims of violence cannot be considered simply as a form of psychotherapy that needs to be carried out to treat psychological pathologies and mental dysfunctions. Instead it is necessary that classical psychological methods let themselves be pollinated by other fileds of social intervention and counseling, such as the feminist narrative methodology, and share their strategies, while not distorting their own specific methodology.

We have illustrated the use of psychodramatic techniques that involve the entire experience of awareness. This additional method presents a possible development with respect to its predecessor, as it enables one to dramatize the narrative that is being proposed by the victims, offering them the opportunity to put into play the entirety of their experience through action and the body. In the "stage" representation of the experiences of oppression led by the psychodramatists, it is possible for the woman to start thinking about new roles to take on, and to put these into action in a protected environment. The flow in a semi-reality in which the body can act, defining its presence as a feeling and action, makes it possible for memory, feeling, and words to take on the "new" role and change patterns that until now seemed to be unchangeable. By working with the body, the woman regains consciousness of herself and removes the representation of the self from the subordination of the imagined male. Along with this, however, we wanted to introduce a further aspect, concerning the definition of targeted intervention projects that measure change. Still taking on a psychosocial perspective, we took the work we carried out using a semi-experimental action-research design and presented it in the real world. Thanks to our work's methodological definition, it can provide additional opportunities for the exchange between various areas of research involved in this front of social change.

Still respecting this psychosocial strategy based on semi-experimental research-intervention, we concluded the volume by integrating the main themes of the text (the narrative method and psychodrama, the new generations' need to free itself from the traditional teachings of mothers) into an educational project with university students. This project used the narrative method to construct stories (storytelling) together with psychodramatic techniques for the elaboration of traditional and stereotypical models taught in the family by the mother with respect to the subordination of women to the desires of men. Even in this case, it was possible to show the ways in which the evaluation was carried out in order to detect change.

In view of the increasingly alarming reports concerning femicide, trafficking, domestic violence, and all forms of violence against women, we believe that the long road already traversed through *Teaching with Gender* has produced some good results, but we also think that we are faced with new challenges. In fact, while it is indeed certain that the increase in crime rates against women not only point to an increase in cases of violence but also to the emergence of the problem, it is equally certain that the phenomenon is starting to appear more objectively in all its severity and multiplicity. Indeed, it seems obvious now that it requires the preparation of research designs that are both complex and timely and that integrate multi-form techniques.

We believe that this book has been able to shed some light on these areas of intervention that will need to be developed even further in the future.

CONTRIBUTORS

ALESSANDRA ARMENTI is a postdoctoral researcher at IClab (Interaction and Culture Lab) at the Department of Philosophy, Sociology, Education, and Applied Psychology (FISPPA), University of Padua, Italy.

ALICE BERTOLDO is a researcher and editorial research associate in gender and women's studies (with a focus on VAW) for EMPoWER-Daphne III, Department of Philosophy, Sociology, Education, and Applied Psychology (FISPPA), Section of Applied Psychology, University of Padua, Italy.

VINCENZO CALVO is a research fellow at the Department of Philosophy, Sociology, Education, and Applied Psychology (FISPPA), Section of Applied Psychology, University of Padua, Italy. His research focuses on the field of psychodynamic psychology.

MARTA CODATO is a postdoctoral researcher at the Department of Literature and Philosophy, University of Trento. Her research focuses on European citizenship education and on national identity development. She is also an editorial associate for Elsevier Publishing Company.

RITA CONDE has a PhD in the psychology of justice. She works as a researcher in the fields of domestic violence and gender violence. Currently she is a researcher in the project "Multiple Victimization of Poor Women" at the Psychology Research Center (CIPsi), University of Minho, Portugal.

MIHAELA DANA BUCUȚĂ is professor at the Faculty of Social and Human Sciences, Department of Journalism, Public Relations, Sociology and Psychology, Lucian Blaga University, Sibiu, Romania. She is also a member of the Romanian Association of Classical Psychodrama.

ALISA DEL RE is associate professor at the Faculty of Political Science, University of Padua, Italy. She is director of CIRSPG, the Interdepartmental Center on Gender Studies, University of Padua, Italy.

DANIELA DI LUCIA SPOSITO is a researcher and editorial research associate in gender and women's studies (with a focus on death and violence) for EMPoWER-Daphne III at the Department of Philosophy, Sociology, Education, and Applied Psychology (FISPPA), Section of Applied Psychology, University of Padua, Italy.

GABRIELA DIMA is professor at the Faculty of Sociology and Communication at the Department of Social Sciences and Communication, Transylvania University of Brasov, Romania. She is a psychotherapist at the Romanian Association of Classical Psychodrama.

ANGELIKA GROTERATH is professor of social psychology and social pedagogy at the University of Darmstadt. Her expertise focuses on peacekeeping processes. She is also director of Moreno's Institute Stuttgart, DAGG.

MARIA SILVIA GUGLIELMIN is a psychotherapist and research coordinator for EMPoWER-Daphne III; Department of Philosophy, Sociology, Education, and Applied Psychology (FISPPA), Section of Applied Psychology, University of Padua, Italy. She is director of Psychodrama Theater in Treviso, Italy.

PHOEBE KISUBI MBASALAKI is a PhD candidate in gender studies at Utrecht University. Her research focus is on the construction of women's sexuality in South African townships.

MARLENE MATOS is professor at the University of Minho, Portugal. She works in the field of victimology, criminal psychology, and forensic psychology. She is responsible for coordinating various researches funded in the areas of intervention with victims, intimate violence, and stalking. Currently she coordinates the project "Multiple Victimization of Poor Women."

GABRIELA MOITA is professor at the Higher Institute of Social Services (ISSSP), Department of Social Service, Section of Research and Intervention Methodology, University of Porto, Portugal—Portuguese Society of Psychodrama.

SURYIA NAYAK is a senior lecturer in social work at the University of Salford, Greater Manchester, UK. Dr. Nayak has over 30 years of experience working with issues of women and sexual violence, trauma, and feminist strategies to confront violations of human rights. She has developed specific services for black, Asian, and minoritized ethnic women.

Auxiliadora Pérez-Vides is lecturer in the Department of English, University of Huelva, Spain. She is currently engaged in the project "Sexualities and New Gender Identities in Anglophone Cultures," funded by the Spanish Ministry of Economy and Competitiveness, through which she is conducting research on Ireland's Magdalene laundries.

Lucia Ronconi is a statistical consultant and analyst, FISSPA Department, Section of Applied Psychology, University of Padua, Italy. She is statistical consultant for the European Project EMPoWER-Daphne 2011–2013 as part of the Italian research group.

Anita Santos has a PhD in clinical psychology from the University of Minho (Braga, Portugal). She is currently assistant professor at Instituto Superior da Maia (ISMAI) (Maia, Portugal), and also a psychotherapist. She has been developing outcome and research processes on narrative and cognitive-behavioral therapy with victims of domestic violence.

Galabina Tarashoeva is a psychiatrist, psychodrama-psychotherapist, and manager of Mental Health Center, Prof. N. Shipkovensk. She is director of Psychodrama Center Orpheus, Sofia, Bulgaria. She is also Member of Board of Directors of IAGP (International Association of Group Psychotherapy).

Ines Testoni is professor of social psychology and director of the master "Death Studies and the End of Life" at the Department of Philosophy, Sociology, Education, and Applied Psychology (FISPPA), Section of Applied Psychology, University of Padua, Italy, and scientific director of EMPoWER Daphne III.

Sibylla Verdi is editorial associate at the Department of Philosophy, Sociology, Education and Applied Psychology (FISPPA), Section of Applied Psychology, University of Padua, Italy, for EMPoWER Daphne III.

Michael Wieser is professor of psychology at Alpen-Adria-Universitaet (Klagenfurt, Vienna, Graz), Department of Psychology, Austria. He is a psychotherapist (psychodrama) and a professor in the psychodrama training program of the Austrian Association of Group Therapy and Group Dynamics.

Adriano Zamperini is professor of social psychology, Department of Philosophy, Sociology, Education, and Applied Psychology (FISPPA), Section of Applied Psychology, University of Padua, Italy.